THE FATEFUL YEARS

THE FATEFUL YEARS

Memoirs of a French Ambassador in Berlin, 1931-1938

by ANDRÉ FRANÇOIS-PONCET

Translated from the French
by JACQUES LeCLERCQ

HOWARD FERTIG

NEW YORK · 1972

First published in French in 1946
under the title *Souvenirs d'une Ambassade à Berlin*

Copyright Flammarion 1946

Copyright 1949 by Reynal & Hitchcock, Inc.

HOWARD FERTIG, INC. EDITION 1972
Published by arrangement with Librairie Ernest Flammarion
and Harcourt Brace Jovanovich

Library of Congress Cataloging in Publication Data

François-Poncet, André, 1887–
The fateful years.

Translation of Souvenirs d'une ambassade à Berlin, septembre
1931–octobre 1938.
1. Germany—Politics and government—1933–1945. 2. National
socialism. 3. Hitler, Adolf, 1889–1945. I. Title.
DD256.5.F71513   1972   943.086   76–80549

PRINTED IN THE UNITED STATES OF AMERICA
BY NOBLE OFFSET PRINTERS, INC.

CONTENTS

PREFACE   ix

I.   CHANCELLOR BRÜNING   3

II.   PAPEN AND SCHLEICHER   23

III.   HITLER IN POWER   49

IV.   1934—THE CRUCIAL YEAR   109

V.   THE REBIRTH OF GERMANY'S ARMED FORCES   163

VI.   THE END OF LOCARNO   179

VII.   GAMES, FESTIVALS, VISITS AND VIGIL OF ARMS   203

VIII.   THE FALL OF VON FRITSCH   225

IX.   HITLER AND MUSSOLINI   236

X.   THE MUNICH CONFERENCE   253

XI.   THE EAGLE'S NEST:
MY LAST INTERVIEW WITH HITLER   278

XII.   HITLER, A MAN "POSSESSED"   289

FOREWORD TO THE
HOWARD FERTIG, INC. EDITION

THE present work was written a little more than twenty years ago. Since then the history of Nazism has given rise to the publication of innumerable accounts, memoirs, documents of every sort. They have brought forth nothing new that does not confirm the accounts, impressions and judgments contained in my *Souvenirs* (*The Fateful Years*). That is why I have not changed anything in this book.

Under favorable circumstances and in the face of the Soviet peril, Germany—which has become West Germany—has, as I had hoped, but more quickly than I had anticipated, reentered the circle of the great Western powers. To this rapid evolution, in my capacity as High Commissioner of France between 1949 and 1955, I contributed as best I could.

ANDRE FRANCOIS-PONCET
of the Academie Francaise

November 23, 1967

PREFACE

THE FOLLOWING memoirs are essentially based on the correspondence I addressed to Paris from September 1931 to October 1938. It was a very copious correspondence, I must confess, and one whose bulk dismayed its recipients.

It included, daily, a detailed analysis of the German press, telephoned to Paris at about 11:00 A.M. Every day a number of telegrams in code followed. Every week and often twice a week the "pouch" from Berlin delivered further numerous letters. Officials at the Quai d'Orsay discovered, not without consternation, that these "dispatches," contrary to usage, were twenty or thirty pages long. My excuse was that Nazism, its leader, the Third Reich, and its government, were not to be reduced within the scope of routine affairs. From every standpoint they were exorbitant and extraordinary.

After seven years, my dispatches comprised forty volumes. They were to suffer a singular fate. One batch of them perished on May 16, 1940, when the Ministry of Foreign Affairs destroyed its dossiers as the enemy moved in upon Paris. Another batch disappeared in the boiler of a ship whose skipper feared he could not commit them to safekeeping in time. A third, stored at the French Embassy in Berlin, was supposedly reduced to ashes in the fire following the bombing of the embassy; recently, however, it was discovered that the ruins had protected a small annex which I had built to house official records, and these papers, exhumed, were sent back to Paris more or less intact. Still another set of files was deposited in the cellars of the Château de Rochecotte when Paris was evacuated. It fell into the hands of the Germans, with results subsequently unfortunate for me.

Officials at the Wilhelmstrasse were appointed to examine and to pass judgment on these reports. Trained to identify their country with Nazism, they came to the conclusion that I should be considered an enemy of Germany. By a singular reversal of roles, they judged that I had deceived them by not allowing them to deceive me.

In fact Hitler had believed he had won me over. Naïve in their cynicism, the Nazis could not conceive of a man speaking German and familiar with Germany who was not captivated by them.

National Socialism I had always found revolting, for I was brought up as a liberal and a humanist. The spectacle of tyranny trampling human values, exalting brutality and glorying in savagery, I found odious. The earliest manifestations of Nazi rule filled me with an enduring aversion, and, step by step, I was alarmed by the burning of the Reichstag by government plot, by the indiscriminate persecution of Jews, Socialists, Communists, and Roman Catholics, by the founding of concentration camps, by the massacre of June 1934, and by the murder of Dollfuss. I did not display my feelings, but I did not seek to conceal them. Usually I gave vent to them in the ironic mode, in a form that would not offend. Most of the epigrams circulating in Berlin about the Nazis were attributed to me; but since I also showed my interest in Nazi ideology and in the reforms the Nazis introduced in every field, instead of holding these sallies against me, they found them amusing. My relations with the Nazis were not bad, or, to be more exact, I ended by being on fairly good terms with some of them.

Before 1933, during the period preceding their assumption of power, I had had no personal contact with them whatsoever, in spite of what has been said on the subject. Filled with contempt for diplomats but not free from a certain timidity toward them, Hitler treated me at the outset no differently from my colleagues. Moreover at this period he was, like the whole movement, fundamentally Anti-French. After the executions of June 1934, when Hitler imagined I had known and encouraged the maneuvers of Röhm and General von Schleicher, our relations became strained and my position critical. Later, convinced of his error and wishing to make me forget his suspicions, he paid me some marked attention in public. I was one of the rare diplomats able to converse directly with him without recourse to Schmidt, his interpreter. The dealings I was charged to have with him and the many ceremonies to which the diplomatic corps was regularly invited afforded us an opportunity to meet frequently. Thus, little by little, he grew accustomed to my presence. Besides I spoke to him very openly with a freedom which did not displease him.

Be that as it may, after the discovery of the files at the Château de Rochecotte the leaders of the Third Reich vented their spite upon me. They insisted that I be detached from government service and they forbade me to live in Paris. In June 1943 they forced the Italians to confine me to the house I was living in near Grenoble. On August 27, 1943, they arrested me together with Albert Lebrun, President of the French Republic. They kept me captive in the Austrian Tyrol until I was freed on March 2, 1945, by a detachment of the French Second Armored Division.

Thus I was privileged to be the only ambassador and, I believe, the only French diplomat whom the Nazis interned and deported. One-half of the reports which caused me so much hardship was later recovered in Germany, heavily penciled in many colors and lavishly margined with exclamation marks. Today all these scripts lie snugly in the archives of the Quai d'Orsay.

Throughout the years of my service in Berlin (as later in Rome), I gave advice of my own accord. I was never asked for it. Only once in those nine years was I summoned to Paris to confer with the minister and my fellow envoys from some other European capitals. The Quai d'Orsay was jealous of the prerogative enabling it to establish French foreign policy. I was chiefly a purveyor of information and a letter carrier; I had no hand whatever in drawing up the notes I delivered at the Wilhelmstrasse.

Under conditions prevailing in the Third Reich it was very difficult for the foreign observer to know exactly what was what. The French Embassy did not have funds to employ paid informers; its "secret appropriation" amounted to an annual sum of 54,000 francs. Nor could this money be used freely; the embassy was directed to pay it all to an old Parisian journalist who had been long established in the German capital. Nevertheless the embassy learned a great deal. Numerous visitors kept furnishing information free of cost. What is called "society" is a valuable source of news for diplomats. The discontented, the anxious, the persecuted, gladly confided their troubles. And then the German is talkative. Danger excites him. Despite censorship, police, and denouncement Berlin society could not help but gossip. The problem was not so much how to obtain information as to how sift the true from the false.

Since those days the Nuremberg trials have shed a brilliant light on the actions of Hitler and his gang. However, those trials revealed nothing which was not already suspected; they simply specified and aggravated what had been sensed and supposed from the beginning. This book was written before the opening of the War Crimes trials. I prefer to let it speak for itself without altering it in the light of testimony produced at Nuremberg.

THE FATEFUL YEARS

I. CHANCELLOR BRÜNING

IT WAS Brüning's visit to Paris in July 1931 that determined my mission to Germany as French Ambassador for the next seven difficult, eventful and fateful years.

Brüning was a pallid, scrupulously clean-shaven man with finely chiseled features. He might have passed for a Roman Catholic prelate or an Anglican bishop. His speech was timid in tone but clear and precise; he never raised his voice. As a man he inspired confidence and sympathy. True, his bushy brows, his narrow forehead, his tenuous lips, and the wavering glance behind his spectacles argued less favorably on his behalf. But an air of modesty and integrity, of intelligence and kindliness, stamped his appearance with its dominant, most impressive character. Since there was nothing about him to suggest the awkwardness or brutality of the Teuton, he came as an agreeable surprise. Far from indulging in recrimination or protest he dared on occasion to confess, with a wistful smile, the errors and faults of his countrymen. When he exposed the complexity of his task and the plight of his native land, his plea in favor of Germany proved so simple, so forthright, and of such dignity as to inspire his hearers with a lively compassion. With such a man governing the Reich—a man, moreover, reputed to enjoy Marshal Hindenburg's unqualified support—surely anyone would readily believe it worth his while to attempt to resolve the Franco-German problem.

I myself had been interested in Germany since boyhood; I had traveled and sojourned there frequently and extensively. I had long been familiar with German institutions, language, customs, and thought; I had long grasped the highly paradoxic aspects in the nature of the German people. I knew Germany's qualities and her defects, her virtues and vices, and I was, as I still am, at once attracted and repelled by them. But, like most World War I veterans and like most Frenchmen, I hoped that our relations with our hapless neighbors might improve enough to forestall any possibility of future warfare. And in July 1931 conditions seemed to favor a *modus vivendi,* if not a definitive settlement, whereby the atmosphere might be cleared sufficiently to deliver us from an extenuating period fraught with ever recurring incidents and conflicts.

The Reich at the time was faced with serious difficulties. An economic crisis raged within its borders. The slackening of commercial and industrial activities, the dire indebtedness of agricultural interests, financial disorders, high taxes, and the continuous rise of unemployment had intensified the violence of internal struggles and in one way or another exasperated national feelings. Stresemann's death led to the very swift decline of the Populists and Democrats, and it was upon these parties that political fulfillment of the peace treaties relied. Communism was gaining ground. Hugenberg's National German party, seconded by the organization of the Steel Helmet, kept rousing public opinion to rebel. Finally, Hitler's propaganda, directed with extraordinary vigor, was proving ever more successful. Divided among themselves, these various groups met upon common ground to denounce the Treaty of Versailles and its dictates as the source of all current evils and to accuse the Brüning cabinet of timidity and deference in its relations with foreign powers.

On March 24, 1931, partly in order to reply to the reproaches of the opposition, partly too, perhaps, in order to test how far Germany dared venture in the matter of initiative and liberty, Brüning had allowed his Minister of Foreign Affairs, Curtius, rashly to essay an economic union with Austria, herself at bay. The result proved catastrophic. Both the great and the smaller powers rose in a storm of unanimous reprobation. France reacted with particular force. Germany and Austria were compelled to stand as culprits in the dock before the Council of the League of Nations at Geneva, whence their case was referred for arbitration by the International Court at The Hague.

The damage suffered by the Reich was not only moral. The alarm spread from Europe to America, where the economic crisis was now extraordinarily acute. Bankers in New York and London continued to withdraw, with increasing alacrity, the considerable funds they had invested in Germany. Creditors, lacking confidence, demanded that their loans be repaid. Even those German banks which were reputedly the soundest could not stem the tide. The Reichsbank itself could no longer cope with demands for foreign currency; it was being drained as by a hemorrhage. Thus all Germany was faced with a mammoth bankruptcy. Only an intervention "in extremis" by President Hoover and his proposal for a moratorium saved Germany (June 20, 1931).

The concession of this moratorium should have redounded greatly to Brüning's personal success, for probably no other chancellor could have carried it off. Brüning had managed to win the esteem of the Anglo-Saxons, especially the British. Early in June he visited London, was entertained at Chequers, and was granted an audience by the king. He succeeded in converting the British to his policy of suspension and adjournment of payments.

The British Government was eager to restore calm and confidence throughout the world; it wished to show that the powers, moved by a spirit of solidarity, were studying jointly and in good faith a means to remedy the crisis. Accordingly it invited representatives of France, Italy, Belgium, the United States, and Germany to meet in conference in London on July 20, 1931. This inspired the French Premier to ask Chancellor Brüning to modify his itinerary and to stop off in Paris on his way to the British capital.

At the time the Premier, Pierre Laval, felt his star in the ascendant. Within less than a decade, with ease and dispatch, he had built both his political and his material fortune. He believed stoutly in himself and in his genius. He also felt himself called upon to play a leading role as a French and European statesman. He dreamed of appearing in old Briand's place as peacemaker in a troubled and battered universe. At once bolder and more realistic than Briand, he would not rely solely upon the League of Nations. He was none too fond of this assembly. He professed that the only prompt and fruitful method lay in direct conversations, in personal relations, man to man. According to Laval, a free exchange of ideas, en tête-à-tête, stripped of elaborate terminologies and of such childish timidity as inspires professional diplomacy, must surely lead to the solution of the most complex problems. Laval shared the mob's prejudices against diplomats. To be sure he was not hindered by knowledge of these problems or by the slightest inclination to study them carefully. He was smart, though less smart than he supposed, and his smartness was vulgar. He was pleased to acknowledge what his countless flatterers and obligees repeated daily to him, to wit, that his charm was irresistible.

Convinced that the fate of peace hinged upon Franco-German relations, he was more alive to the importance and scope of the goal than to the number and nature of the obstacles in his way. At any rate he was certain that so novel an event as a visit to Paris by the Chancellor of the German Reich could not fail to heighten his own prestige.

On Saturday, July 18, Brüning arrived in Paris with Curtius, his Foreign Minister, Bülow, Secretary-General of the Wilhelmstrasse, and Schwerin-Krosigck, Director at the Ministry of Finance. Brüning's discretion, moderation, and tact were much appreciated. The public was touched by his desire to attend Mass the following Sunday at Notre-Dame des Victoires. Yet the result of the conversations on fundamental matters was none the less disappointing. The French Government offered to organize measures that might prove of help to the Germans. The Banque de France, the Bank of England, and the Federal Reserve Bank of the United States were prepared to open credits in favor of the Reichsbank to the extent of $500,000,-000, a sum repayable in ten years by means of a guaranteed international loan. In return the Reich was to offer material assurances and political appeasements, to conclude a truce for ten years, and to abstain during this period from any initiative likely to trouble peace. Further, the status quo was to be respected, no attempt at union with Austria was to be made, and Germany was not to increase her military expenditures.

With infinite politeness and gentleness, Brüning declined these proposals. The depression racking Germany rose precisely from the fact that she had abused foreign credits. To his way of thinking, to contract another loan afforded no cure for her ills. Worse, if it were learned that the Chancellor of the Reich had alienated Germany's already somewhat relative political liberty in return for money, a wave of irresistible public indignation would at once sweep him out of office. When invited then to make his wishes known, Brüning made no exact request; he remained evasive. Nor was he more explicit later in London than he had been in Paris.

Truth to tell, what he wanted was the scrapping of reparation payments. That and that alone could allay nationalist agitation within the Reich. But he dared not say so; he feared, quite rightly, that such pretensions must create a scandal and loose a new tempest in France if not elsewhere. He preferred to wait, to procrastinate, to prepare the ground, trying, meanwhile, to gain the sympathy of his interlocutors and to convince them of the honesty of his intentions. In point of fact his game was not so honest as he gave one to believe; it was full of mental reservations which were subsequently to come to light.

For the moment no one knew how to draw up the slender balance sheet of the Paris negotiations. Brüning had rejected the suggested pact of mutual consultation; there remained the affirmation of reciprocal good will. To apply that good will to some tangible object, the negotiators bethought themselves of falling back upon the economic field and of studying what possibilities of co-operation and rapprochement it offered.

Since as Undersecretary of State in the Ministry of National Economy I had been closely in touch with the recent Anschluss and moratorium episodes, since too I had taken part in all exchanges of views with the Germans, it was suggested (Laval and Briand agreeing, Brüning acquiescent) that I might, as French Ambassador in Paris, usefully pursue this enterprise and carry it out.

I arrived in Berlin on September 21, 1931. Within one week I had to take up quarters in the old mansion in the Pariser Platz; I had also to present my credentials to Marshal Hindenburg and to make necessary contacts with higher officials of the Wilhelmstrasse, with my fellow ambassadors and with chiefs of missions, with the French colony, and with the repre-

sentatives of the press; finally, into the bargain, I had to prepare for the forthcoming visit of Laval and Briand on September 27. Brüning had invited them to repay his visit of two
months before; this occasion was to pave the way for economic
co-operation between the two countries.

Faced with great opposition from the Nationalist press,
Brüning would gladly have recalled his invitation if he had
dared to. But he sensed that Laval was eager to make this visit
and was unwilling to risk ruffling his feelings. Laval himself
was quite unruffled. He read little and laid aside any disagreeable tidings that might have given him pause. He was, first
and foremost, curious to tread the pavements of Berlin; he
imagined that his visit constituted a sensational, decisive,
history-making event. He was certain of himself, of his powerful charm, of his great good luck. Briand, more experienced
and more skeptical, shook his head ruefully, but Briand's advice
was rarely sought now, and always superficially, so that he fell
into step, somewhat surprised at the self-assurance of Laval,
the disciple whose ascendancy he had facilitated and who had
now overtaken him.

Because of all this no change was made in the existing arrangements for the Laval-Briand visit. The schedule called for
a luncheon with Curtius, the Minister of Foreign Affairs, a
dinner at the Chancellery, an audience with Marshal Hindenburg, and a dinner at the French Embassy; two working
sessions were to be held in the intervals. This program was carried out without a hitch; nothing untoward occurred. But it
was impossible to dispel a certain constraint, an obscure apprehension, which everyone felt and which lent the meeting a
precarious, artificial character. Curtius, aware that his ministerial days were numbered, was particularly melancholy.

Briand expressed a desire to visit Stresemann's grave. He
found a stone bare of all inscription save only the statesman's
name. He stood over the grave for a long time, moved by
recollections of his former antagonist and partner, perhaps also

touched by an instinct which told him that beneath this stone lay a period of postwar history, its course run out.

The audience granted by the Marshal was short and commonplace. Rain and fair weather provided the theme of conversation. As he escorted his guests to the door of his study, Hindenburg, then eighty-four years old, bowed Briand out before him and, with a glance at Briand and a tug at my sleeve, said: "It must have been a very tiring journey for the old gentleman!"

As for Laval, he had a bee in his bonnet. He could not understand why he had not been served frankfurters and sauerkraut at any of the official banquets. Obviously he was vexed at the idea of facing his chums in Paris when they asked him: "Well, you've probably had some fine frankfurters and sauerkraut, eh?"

There was virtually no discussion at the conference sessions. It was agreed to create an Economic Commission composed of twenty French and twenty German members, each body to include high government executives, representatives of the chief fields of economic activity, and labor delegates. The commission's task was to improve, to intensify, and to extend economic relations between the two countries and thus, in joint endeavor, to attempt to ease world discomfort. Neither France nor Germany had the slightest intention of being locked cheek by jowl; both appealed to other nations for co-operation. They were merely attempting by new methods to set an example and to lay the foundations of a constructive organization, open to all nations.

The visit of the French ministers was concluded by a dinner of seventy covers at the French Embassy. There were no speeches, but I invited our guests to raise their glasses in honor of His Excellency the Chancellor of the German Reich and His Excellency the President of the French Republic. This was the first time (and the last) that such a toast was made. After dinner a muffled noise rose from the street. Going out onto the balcony, we saw a small group of people milling about in the square. Suddenly a cry rose, uttered in French. We thought we understood what its purport was: "*Sauvez-nous!* Save us!" But Briand, whose ear was still keen and whose mind was still shrewd, set us right. "No," he explained. "That voice said: '*Sauvez-vous!* Get out of here!' "

The ministers were to leave next morning at eight. Promptly at seven-thirty I reported at the Hotel Adlon to find Laval had already left, so I went to the station to meet him. He was yellow as a quince, his features were drawn, his face fallen. I learned that when he returned to the hotel after the embassy dinner he had ordered a dish of frankfurters and sauerkraut and made his associates share it with him. But he had cause to rue it. In the middle of the night he was seized with acute indigestion. To shake off the vapors which oppressed him he forced himself to walk up and down Unter den Linden—to the discomfort of the sentries detailed to do him appropriate honors, for every time Laval passed the guard of honor had to present arms.

The very day after the Laval-Briand visit the hopes and illusions which had brought me to Germany began falling away one by one, as so many leaves off a tree in autumn. The cause of Franco-German amity met with no sympathy brave enough to declare itself either in Berlin or in the country at large. Only a few newspapers, the *Berliner Tageblatt* for instance, dared openly uphold it. The new Economic Commission and its subcommissions pursued their task amid general indifference.

The atmosphere in the city was feverish, tempestuous, and unhealthy. To tread its streets was to skim a quicksand. Excitement possessed the people. Large fortunes collapsed, bankruptcies were multiplied, unemployment rose. Paradoxically enough, under a virtuous Chancellor the corruption and depravity that had been flourishing for years decreased but little.

Public vice was flaunted as unrestrainedly as ever. Dubious journals plied their blackmailing trade without compunction. One of them, *Fredericus*, made a point of attacking the French Embassy and denounced it as a center of espionage, sparing neither me nor my wife. I objected to the Prussian Government but without avail; I had to appeal to the Secretary of State for Foreign Affairs, von Bülow, threatening to resign unless the Reich government proved its ability to enforce respect of accredited diplomats.

The intrigues and machinations of nationalistic political parties dominated the scene. Divided among themselves and in constant rivalry, Hugenberg's German Nationalists, Hitler's Nazis, and other chauvinistic groups of like inspiration, were determined to pool all their resources; noisily they vented not their common agreement toward the same end but merely their common hostility toward Brüning's government and toward the "system."

On October 11, a fortnight after Laval's visit, the nationalist opposition held a convention at Harzburg. Hitler was there, arrogant and imperious at the head of his brown-clad militiamen. Then there were the Steel Helmet men, led by Düsterberg and Seldte; despite their uniforms, reminiscent of the Reichswehr, they looked like veterans of another age. Hugenberg moved in and out of their ranks. His gold-rimmed spectacles, his sizable paunch, his bristling white mustache, gave him the comforting air of a humble country doctor, but he was actually a man of the scantiest intelligence, hampered by the most savage stubbornness, a violent sectarian, a ferocious party man, and, in so far as Germany was concerned, an evil genius. Delegates of the patriotic organizations were there, headed by General von der Goltz; of the Pan-German League, headed by Class the lawyer; of the Agrarians, headed by Kalckreuth. Other notables attending the convention included Schacht the banker, Poensgen the industrialist of the Steel Cartel, General von Seeckt with a series of World War

I generals, and various princes, among them the Duke of Saxe-Coburg, Prince William of Lippe, and Prince Eitel Friedrich, son of Kaiser William II.

The Congress of Harzburg will perhaps be mentioned in history only as a minor episode. But in truth it foretold and foreshadowed the future. It marks the first date in the direct responsibility of the ruling classes, if not of the German people as a whole. They were the first to excite public opinion against Brüning, thereby diverting their country from peace, throwing it into the arms of Hitler, and finally plunging it into the abyss.

What resources could the Chancellor muster in order to cope with this raising of shields against him? What elements played in his favor?

First, the parliamentary situation of which his own party, the Catholic Centrists, was arbiter. As it inclined to the Right or to the Left, the majority went to the Nationalists or to the Democrats. Now the Center obstinately refused to move toward the Right. Next, Brüning enjoyed the support of Marshal Hindenburg, who was always ready to sign the decrees by means of which Brüning governed. And third, there was Brüning's skill, his intelligence, his competence in negotiation.

On closer examination, however, these weapons were not so effective as they would seem. Brüning got rid of Curtius and transformed his cabinet by calling in personalities of no accentuated political coloring; but it availed him nothing. His majority remained feeble; it was only by twenty-odd votes that he defeated motions of lack of confidence leveled at him and that (October 16, 1931) he obtained adjournment of the Reichstag until February. So precarious a position could not be prolonged indefinitely. Marshal Hindenburg was himself faced with the early expiration of his mandate. Would Hindenburg be willing to run for re-election as President of the Reich? And if willing, *could* he be re-elected? Again, the Marshal was a man of the Right, a patron of the Steel Helmet, a crony of the old reactionary generals; within his immediate circle his son, Colonel Oscar von Hindenburg, General Schleicher, and Franz von Papen were all Nationalists. It was these men who had recommended Brüning to the Marshal. But with what intent? They had expected Brüning to orient his Catholic Centrist party toward the Right and to form a government of "national concentration" against the Socialists and Communists. Not only had Brüning failed to do this but he was daily moving in the opposite direction. His appeal to the patriotic sentiments of his antagonists, proposing a domestic truce in order better to struggle abroad, did not help matters.

The economic situation was deteriorating. The Chancellor sought to remedy it by means of a rigorous and methodical deflation. He reduced wages, salaries, and pensions, which won him the rancor of workmen, public servants, and retired officials. He established a control of prices which vexed the peasants and a control of banking which estranged the financiers. He offended the industrialists by ordering the prices of materials fixed by the cartels to be lowered. His popularity sank rapidly. Even the Socialists did not conceal the fact that they clung to him only for fear of worse.

Abroad he contented the Allies no better, especially France. The nationalist current, which he wished to fight, was sweeping him along with it. He adopted a firmer tone in order to prove that he was no weakling. Early in January 1932 he made some rash remarks to a foreign journalist. According to a Reuters dispatch Brüning had warned the British Ambassador that Germany was firmly resolved not to resume reparation payments when the moratorium lapsed. The news was denied, but the denial was not convincing. Brüning had let the cat out of the bag. French opinion was immediately alarmed.

Laval's position suffered proportionally. Overthrown on January 13, he formed a new cabinet, but he too was forced to speak in more energetic terms. He insisted that he would not tolerate any prescription of the right to reparations and voiced his determination to defend the Young Plan. The German press thundered. The game was up, the charm broken, ended our idyll with the mild, modest, captious Brüning. Franco-German relations cooled off again; the labors of the Economic Commission were lost in the shuffle.

Would the Disarmament Conference, opening February 2 in Geneva, re-establish contacts and tighten the lax bonds between Germany and France? It seemed unlikely, because Germany then began to needle the Conference to abolish the military inequality imposed upon her by the Treaty of Versailles. She was, of course, secretly and to the full extent of her powers, violating the rules set down. But this very secrecy was humiliating. She claimed "equal rights" with others and that parity which might once more place her among the great powers. "Let every nation descend to the level of Germany," she argued, "or let Germany rise to the level of the others." The Nationalists made of this thesis a war horse which they rode to death; the German people unanimously upheld it; President von Hindenburg set it forth in his speech to the diplomatic corps on January 1; Brüning could not but adopt it. Indeed he presented it to the Conference on February 9, but in prudent, velvety terms, so as not initially and squarely to clash with its opponents. In this he differed from his nationalist enemies, but the difference was one of form, not theme, of means, not ends. "Let us be bold," cried the Nationalists, "and bang our fists upon the table!" "Let us be skillful," Brüning replied, "and flatter our adversaries!"

In this circumstance Germany's adversaries were once more the French, specifically a Frenchman called André Tardieu. Tardieu had laid before the Disarmament Conference a remarkable project for repression and protection through an international police force. Immediately the Reich press fell furiously upon the scheme.

Despite all this Brüning was favorably impressed by his conversations with Tardieu and believed an agreement not impossible. On April 21 another meeting took place; the Chancellor left, filled with hope. A further appointment was set for April 29 at Bessinges. This time Tardieu, suffering from angina, was unable to attend. Brüning, disappointed and offended, imagined the other's absence to be deliberate. For in the interval Brüning's domestic position had grown increasingly critical; it was now extraordinarily fragile.

He managed without too much trouble to persuade the aged Marshal to run again as candidate for the Presidency of the Reich. But he could not assure him re-election without competition and risks. Numerous interviews and interminable palaver did not prevent Hugenberg from turning a deaf ear to all appeals. On the contrary Hugenberg declared that his party would fight the Marshal if the latter persisted in maintaining Brüning as Chancellor. The Steel Helmet, and the Association of German Ex-Officers, adopted the same attitude. Hitler proved as reluctant to bargain as the others. Indeed he went further, not only refusing to concur in Hindenburg's candidacy but deciding to run against him. Accordingly the Marshal had three rivals: Hitler, chief of the National Socialists, Düsterberg, the German Nationalist candidate, and Thaelmann, the Communist.

Throughout the electoral struggle the German Nationalists were considerate of Hindenburg, the veteran soldier, for he was really one of their own; but they fought the more harshly against the nefarious Chancellor who held the old man under his thumb. Hitler, not bothering to take such precautions, cynically played his youth against the senility of the victor of Tannenberg.

The first balloting took place on March 13, 1932. It gave Hindenburg 18,662,000 votes, Hitler 11,338,000, Thaelmann 4,982,000, and Düsterberg 337,000. Hindenburg was supported by 49.6 per cent of the electorate, lacking only 337,000 votes to be elected. The second ballot was held on April 10; its lesson was even clearer. Hindenburg received 700,000 additional votes, which permitted his election, but Hitler was two million more votes to the good. A study of the figures proves that the German Nationalists, who had supported Düsterberg, now preferred Hitler to the Marshal, whereas some four or five hundred thousand Communists preferred the latter. Thus Hindenburg, elected in 1925 by the nationalists of the Right, was now re-elected in 1932 by the democrats of the Left! Who could imagine him pleased with that re-election and grateful to its artificer, Chancellor Brüning? From then on the Presidency was the center for intrigues directed against the Chancellor.

Brüning seemed to suspect nothing. For him the essential was that he had not lost his chief support, the Marshal who, he thought, was still solidly behind him. He had cleared the obstacles from his path; he had beaten Hugenberg, his *bête noire;* he was about to pursue his task and he was satisfied. To be sure, the Hitlerite peril loomed threatening; Brüning understood that he must face it with something more than gentle words or objurgation. A man at his side, General Gröner, Minister of War and of the Interior, understanding this even better than he, resolved to act.

On April 14 a decree signed by the Marshal ordered the dissolution of the Storm Troopers and dependent squads, and the seizure of their matériel, flags, planes, and trucks. Their headquarters were immediately occupied and closed by the police. But it was no more than an ephemeral access of vigor; the Congress of Harzburg had been no vain symbol, nationalistic solidarity prevailed. Amid the protests rising on all sides Hindenburg invited Gröner also to dissolve the Reichsbanner, a democratic organization which afforded the regime and legality their main support. To place the two organizations in the same category was unjust and absurd; for the Marshal even to consider doing so proved how thoroughly he was being influenced by the men of the Right. Gröner tried to resist, but the Reichswehr, his own caste and his clan, opposed him.

The racists soon chalked up a further success. On April 24, 1932, elections were held for the Prussian Landtag, the Nazis proving victorious all along the line. They had held seven seats, they now won 162; the Socialists, with 137 previously, now held only 93. Henceforward the Nazis constituted the most powerful party in Prussia; they could, and presently did, claim the presidency of the assembly; Prussia's parliament was no longer in harmony with the Reich parliament. In Bavaria, in Württemberg, in Anhalt, in Hamburg, the Nazis made like progress.

For Brüning this was a major reverse; having been made to appear weakened and hesitant, he should have retired. But, unwilling to throw up the sponge, he clung to what he had and continued to battle in the Reichstag. Imploring the assembly to permit him to accomplish his foreign task: "We are within one hundred yards of the goal!" he pleaded.

He carried the day with a majority of thirty votes, but scenes of incredible violence, created by Hitlerites, exploded in the corridors of the Reichstag and, on May 25, in the Prussian Landtag itself. The tension was extreme; this sort of thing could not last and Brüning's ruin was determined then and there. But since he always managed to avoid being thrust into the minority, extraparliamentary means would have to be invoked to get rid of him.

The Chancellor submitted to the Marshal several new decrees concerning the balancing of the budget. He also advanced a plan drawn up by Stegerwald, Minister of Labor, whereby the great East Prussian estates, heavily encumbered with debts, were to be parceled out for intensive colonization. The Marshal was readily influenced by his son's coterie and by his old Junker neighbor and friend, Oldenburg-Januschau, especially since Hindenburg, having received the estate of Neudeck as a gift from the nation, had become a large landowner himself, imbued with the feelings and prejudices of that class. Schleicher, Papen, and Meissner on one hand assured the Marshal that his Chancellor had failed in his mission and thrown the country into inextricable confusion; the Junkers, on the other hand, denounced the Chancellor's plan of parceling out large estates as a scandalous collusion with the revolutionary party, i.e., the Reds. Such reproaches, over and above Hindenburg's deeper causes of resentment, won the day.

On May 29 he received Brüning in audience. The Chancellor endeavored to cite the reasons for the new decrees he asked for. Hindenburg cut him short.

"I have heard it said," he grumbled, "that these orders include plans for local colonization which smack of Bolshevism. Kindly explain exactly what this is all about."

Brüning continued to elucidate but again the Marshal broke in: "Hm! These decrees also deal with our financial problems. I was under the impression that Bolshevism was a dead issue in Germany. Things cannot go on this way! Bolshevik plans for colonization and Bolshevik laws on wages are utterly impossible; you and Stegerwald, the two syndicalists, must resign. Naturally it is understood that you may stay in the new cabinet—as Minister of Foreign Affairs."

Swept off his feet by this unexpected outburst, by the aged President's brutal tone, and by the summary rudeness of reproaches that betrayed what influences swayed Hindenburg, Brüning withdrew without protest, mortified to the depths of his soul. He felt himself not only dismissed but executed; next day he submitted his resignation. "Exactly seven weeks after your re-election!" he made a point of telling the Marshal as he took his leave.

Obviously so monstrous a piece of ingratitude amazed Brüning, but what candor in his amazement! Brüning, so subtle in some ways, was not shrewd enough to sense that this re-election, for which he had toiled so hard and on which he counted to bolster up his credit, had occurred under conditions which were to spell his ruin. He had relied too much upon his superiority over his opponents; he had underestimated their tenacity, their boldness, their astuteness, their lack of scruple. He had proved better able than any other Chancellor of the Reich to find favor abroad, principally among Anglo-Saxons; yet he remained a poor psychologist.

More than any other Chancellor he committed errors typically German. He never realized that, far from serving him, the praise he met with abroad rendered him suspect at home. He never conceived to what pitch of blind fanaticism nationalist passions might rise in Germany; he never dreamed that this frenzy was too fierce to be assuaged by any successes he might have won. He attempted a policy of persuasion, and to the velvet glove the German people prefer the mailed fist, the symbol of mastery. Authority and inflexible firmness were the more necessary because the Chancellor was seeking to solve the economic crisis by deflation; but, before producing healthy results, deflation necessarily causes suffering, reversals of opinion, and an unpopularity which only the strongest government can tackle. Brüning neither looked nor spoke nor moved like a leader of the German people. He was repelled by such drastic and brutal methods as would have saved him. He could never resolve to fight the Nazis face to face, wielding the same weapons against them that they used in attacking him. To the end he harbored the illusion that he would finally bring them back into the fold and make use of them.

Twice he had a chance to smash them. Through information supplied by an ex-Nazi in December 1931 the police raided the Boxheim Farm in Westphalia, seizing abundant munitions which proved that Hitler and his party were planning a revolution. This evidence sufficed to establish the existence of a permanent plot against the security of the state. Brüning referred the plotters caught red-handed to the Supreme Court at Leipzig; but instead of developing the case, exposing its ramifications, and reaching up to its source, he allowed the whole business to be minimized and smothered. From that day on I felt he was a doomed man.

Later, when the Marshal was re-elected, the police received information concerning measures which Röhm, leader of the Brown Militia, had decreed if Hitler were elected. These constituted no more and no less than a *coup d'état*. Raids and investigations made by Severing, Prussian Minister of the Interior, proved beyond doubt that Hitler and his acolytes had organized a state within the state and seriously endangered the existing government.

But Brüning could not bring himself to use the weapons placed in his hands; he was satisfied with a mere semblance of repression. Would not Hitler be grateful to him for such mansuetude? Brüning too was by nature calculating, but his calculations erred through ignorance of mankind.

His was a retiring, isolated life, spent amid silence, meditation, and prayer; he took counsel with only few intimates, chiefly with Monsignor Kaas, leader of the Catholic Centrist party. Several times I tried to foster closer relations between us but he gave me no encouragement. He never divined my respect for him nor my good will. He had gone his own way.

When he received me officially he never let himself go; he would raise his eyes to heaven, fetch a deep sigh, and expose in vague terms the difficulties that assailed him, but never once did he enlighten me as to his intentions. He did not know French, he did not know France; his orientation was wholly toward England and the United States. Nothing predisposed him toward my country, in which he saw the instigator and the stubborn champion of the Treaty of Versailles; like all German Catholics he judged France by its reputation for anticlericalism. He mistrusted us. He mistrusted me, too, and he mistrusted any suggestions I might make.

One day, in his presence, I criticized the unanimous hostility of the Reich press toward the French plan of an international police force. I implied that it might be more politic for Germany to favor the project, to offer to join in the formation of this force, claiming the right to share in it equally with the other powers. I added that by so doing Germany could best obtain that "equality of rights" to which she attached such importance. Brüning cast me a dark glance, laden with suspicion. It never occurred to him to examine what was worth retaining in my proposal; he wondered only what ruse or pitfall lay beneath it.

After his downfall, following the German custom, Brüning, as resigning Minister of Foreign Affairs, paid his round of visits to the various ambassadors. When he came to me he looked like a man relieved of an immense burden, free at last but filled with bitterness. For the first time in many weeks he seemed to be somewhat relaxed; there was something human, confident, almost affectionate about him. Not that he was under any illusions as to the future. He foresaw and foretold that if National Socialism came to power it would remain in power for several years and establish a terrible rule. Much as he might apprehend this as a patriot, he was clearly relieved at the certainty of no longer bearing a responsibility which, frankly, was beyond his powers.

Today many a German must believe that it would have been wise to listen to him, and that had he continued to govern the fortunes of the Reich would have followed a more favorable course. Could he possibly have rescued the Reich from the vertigo of nationalism? Can anyone or anything stop a people once it has started its downward course over the slopes of insanity?

This much is sure: Brüning's downfall marked the destruction of the last remnants of parliamentary democracy in his native land. The bridle which had curbed Germany from following the road to adventure was now broken.

II. PAPEN AND SCHLEICHER

B RÜNING gone, the Reichstag consisted of two coalitions each of which paralyzed the other; it could not possibly show a governmental majority. Following an expression then in vogue, the Marshal, calling upon "a man who enjoys my confidence," was to commission that man to form a "presidential cabinet." All Berlin wondered who that man might be. On June 1, 1932, we learned that Hindenburg had chosen Franz von Papen.

The President's choice met with incredulity. No one but smiled or tittered or laughed, because Papen enjoyed the peculiarity of being taken seriously by neither his friends nor his enemies. He was certainly not a first-rate figure. A former cavalry officer, a great steeplechaser, he was best known for his unhappy past as military attaché in Washington, whence he was expelled in 1917. He had also sat in the Prussian Landtag. A fervent Catholic, a heavy shareholder in *Germania,* he belonged to the Center party and to its most rightist wing. The leaders and majority of his group considered him with aversion and mistrust; he had never been delegated to represent them either on the rostrum or in committee. He was reputed to be superficial, blundering, untrue, ambitious, vain, crafty, and an intriguer; his sole asset lay in a certain self-possession and in a winning, almost unconscious daring. Polite, polished in manner, very much the man about town, wealthy, an assiduous member of the *Herrenklub* and of the Union Club, he spoke French and English fluently. He often stayed in the Saar; through his wife, of Sarrois extraction, he was closely in touch with French circles in Lorraine. He declared himself a Francophile and a champion of Franco-German concord. A member of the committee founded by Mayrisch, the Luxemburg industrialist, to foster friendly relations between the two peoples, he did not hesitate to pray day and night for the moment when the German host, victorious in turn, was to enter Paris. His free and easy character admitted blithely of such contradictions; he would have been but a fashionable amateur had not the Marshal appointed him Chancellor. Therein lay his chief title to fame.

The part played by the Reich Presidency in Brüning's downfall has been described (the Presidency, of course, meant Marshal von Hindenburg). But more powerful than even Hindenburg was the clique that surrounded him. There was Colonel Oscar von Hindenburg, square-faced, brutal, and little educated, a man as tall and massive as his father but with nothing of the latter's noble bearing. There was Meissner, the Marshal's secretary, a ruddy, flushed, well-set-up, chubby person always too tightly encased in his clothes, his glance lurking behind goggles, a strange being, at home with all regimes from the Socialist under Ebert, via Hindenburg's where he now was, to finish with Hitler's. There was General von Schleicher,

Chief of the Political Bureau of the Reichswehr (who was often flanked by General von Hammerstein, Commander-in-Chief of the Army), a kindly, placid, blue-eyed giant of a man. And, finally, there was Papen himself. He was the Marshal's favorite and special protégé; he amused the old man by his vivacity and his humor, he flattered him by his respect and devotion, he captivated him by his daring and stood, in Hindenburg's eyes, for the perfect type of the gentleman.

Ensconced in his armchair, Hindenburg would listen to his son's friends as they brought him echoes of the outer world and commented at will on political events of the day. In so far as Hindenburg still retained any personal views, he wished to dissociate himself at the earliest moment from the elements of the Left which had re-elected him. Socialists and Communists were to him just so many Reds and Bolsheviks, enemies of state and fatherland; they must be thrust back into the opposition and fought tooth and nail. To achieve this, all the nationalist forces must be united. The Nazis in their gross turbulence and equivocalness must be brought into line again, especially this shockingly undisciplined and arrogant man Hitler, who during the war had risen no higher than to the rank of lance corporal; and a stable majority with Rightist orientation must be constituted in order to clear up a confusion that was growing worse by the day. For the means to employ Hindenburg relied upon suggestions offered by his familiars, especially Schleicher, the brains of the Reichswehr and its spokesman. The Marshal had never ceased to consider himself the leader supreme of that body; in recommending Papen as Brüning's successor, Schleicher was certain of the Marshal's sympathetic consideration. The new Chancellor and his government would actually be a Reichswehr cabinet.

What of this Reichswehr which exerted so powerful an influence on the destinies of the postwar Reich? And what was it seeking now?

The Reichswehr was essentially the Supreme General Staff

which the Treaty of Versailles had outlawed but which reappeared variously camouflaged. It was the depository and jealous guardian of a military tradition which went back to Frederick the Great, and of a conception of the army's role within the state—and of the officer's role within the army and state—which had been handed down unwaveringly from generation to generation. It was animated by an *esprit de corps* which made it extraordinarily cohesive or, more exactly, had made it so in the past, for its unity was now no longer complete. The rise of National Socialism created rifts which were increasingly to widen and which account for some of the Reichswehr's later shortcomings.

Among the departments of the General Staff a special place was allotted to that known modestly as *Ministeramt* or Ministerial Bureau. This department, under Schleicher's direction, was entrusted with political affairs and with army-Reichstag and army-government relations.

In effect the Reichswehr deemed it to be its traditional right and duty to have its say about everything that concerned the army directly or indirectly. Amid the disorder and crises that marked the existence of the Weimar Republic, the Reichswehr was a remarkable if not an enlightened or beneficent factor of stability and continuity; its persistent action helped most powerfully to reawaken military spirit and national feeling in a Germany disarmed and conquered. In the persons of its great leaders the Reichswehr was monarchist; it remained attached to the Emperor and to the Hohenzollern dynasty. But it had no intention of binding itself with any particular form of government; it accepted any regime which did not cross—and welcomed any regime which seconded—its exact military end. It got on perfectly well with the Leftist government and congratulated itself on the support of Social Democrats like Noske. Anxious to maintain the respectful and affectionate esteem it inspired in the majority of public opinion, it preferred to act under cover rather than show its hand openly. It had a horror of civil war, which leaves the people with a lasting bitterness against the army; in the events to come this horror was more than once to paralyze the Reichswehr. Its sympathies and encouragement went out naturally to patriotic nationalist parties, the German Nationalists and the Steel Helmet which swarmed with reserve officers and aged generals. However, the Nazis were not excluded from its good will; it was grateful to them for enlisting under the swastika an enthusiastic youth which otherwise would probably have swelled the Marxist ranks. It subsidized the Nazis and co-operated in organizing and equipping them.

Immediately after World War I it was the Reichswehr that invented Hitler by charging him to keep it informed about politics in Munich. At first Hitler was its slave, its creature; presently things changed. In various ways Hitler now shocked and worried the Reichswehr because of certain ideas he professed, because of his anti-religious and anti-Semitic propaganda, because of his independence and his pretensions, because of the worse than mediocre character of his fellow workers. Nevertheless the Reichswehr remained in virtually permanent contact with him.

The Elite Guards, Storm Troopers, and Brown Militia pleased the Reichswehr very little; it loathed seeing people playing at soldiers and scorned the pretensions of mock warriors who would form a separate army. It saw in them a force it might use; it had played midwife to them and it still helped them. But it would wish to have them wholly under its power.

Abroad the Reichswehr meant to use the Disarmament Conference at Geneva in 1932 as a means of shaking off the trammels of the Versailles Treaty; wedge upon wedge would be inserted until Germany possessed an army worthy of a great nation, and, like the armies of other great powers, equipped with armored matériel, airplanes and heavy artillery. The Reichswehr goaded the Foreign Office toward that goal in order to obtain this minimum at all costs. Even so the Reichswehr doubted whether diplomacy could bring this off and whether anything positive could ever come out of the deliberations of the League of Nations. It expected more from direct agreement with France and it conceived a plan in this sense.

The Reichswehr's feelings toward France were complex. Certainly it saw in us the *Erbfeind*, the "hereditary" archenemy, upon whom vengeance must be visited. At the same time it held us to be the only enemy of military importance with an army worthy of the name; it entertained feelings of consideration and professional respect for the victors of 1918. Reichswehr leaders such as Hammerstein, Schleicher, Blomberg, and Fritsch always strove to maintain cordial relations with the French Embassy in Berlin and with me.

Was the Reichswehr inclined to war? Did it harbor intentions of conquest and hegemony in Europe? At this particular period it showed no such trend. Its sole grievance seemed to be against Poland, its great dream the suppression of the Polish Corridor; for the rest it argued only of Reich security and of the defense of Reich territory. Conscious of its weakness, it feared and continued to fear any undertaking that might prematurely unleash a general conflict; it knew itself too weak still to face the issue. The Reichswehr was particularly afraid of a conflict with Soviet Russia, for it maintained certain "intelligences" there and cultivated them carefully.

This state of mind and these ideas found their prototype in Schleicher, who was commissioned to apply them and who was closely associated with the events of the period. Previously he had hidden in the wings; now he appeared boldly upon the stage as Minister of War in the Papen cabinet, which he was instrumental in creating. Schleicher passed for a master of political intrigue; he was feared rather than liked, even in military circles, where many resented his rapid promotion earned far from the field of battle. His reputation for realism and cynicism was well established.

He was clean-shaven, his head was shaved too. He was not

merely pale but ashen; his sharp eyes, glittering from a face covered with an unsavory fat, and his tenuous, barely distinguishable lips were unprepossessing. In conversation he was direct, brutal, bantering, caustic, and often witty. He was prone to laugh and to laugh noisily. He has been accused of deceit and treachery. In my dealings with him I never discovered him attempting to trick me; on the contrary such information as he gave me on occasion—rarely, I may add—invariably turned out to be accurate. His intelligence was lively and brisk rather than substantial and deep. He was not the type of soldier whose mind is closed to modern ideas or to the exigencies of the times he lives in. He attached vast importance to preventing any antagonism from arising between the army and the working classes; he dreamed of an alliance between the army and the workers' unions, of a socio-military state which might rob the Nazis of their clientele.

All the members of the Papen cabinet belonged to the old aristocracy. The public immediately dubbed the ministry the "Barons' Cabinet." To me the most interesting of the group was Baron von Neurath, Minister of Foreign Affairs, who was to direct the policy of Wilhelmstrasse for the next six years, until April 1938. Neurath was nearing sixty. He was tall, a whit corpulent, always smartly dressed and impressive in his martial bearing. A *bon vivant*, he was almost always good-humored and simple, but with dignity. He was a southern German. His face, high in color, bore an expression of affability; he was extremely polite, which made all relations with him easy and agreeable. His intelligence was in no way arresting, but he possessed experience, common sense and composure. He was levelheaded, moderate, and sensible. Unfortunately his virtues were marred by serious defects. He lacked frankness, he was crafty, he was something of a liar, and a clumsy liar at that, for he would get flustered as he lied. A weak character, he was wanting in moral courage; he would yield to pressure and, no doubt conscious of doing so, he was prepared to perform or to condone acts he himself condemned so as to avoid the obloquy of slackness or cowardice. Also he was lazy.

But he had an official of worth to support him: Bülow, Secretary of State, who had been Brüning's collaborator, a man assiduous in his profession, as filled with zeal and devotion to duty as he was silent and discreet, a statesman worthy of the traditions of a Prussian family which has given Germany numerous and honorable servants.

The problem Papen and his "barons" had to resolve was not an easy one. Abroad they must obtain adjournment if not suppression of reparation payments and equality in the matter of armaments. At home the reign of Socialists and democrats in Prussia must be liquidated; a Rightist majority must be found in the present Reichstag or one to follow; Hitler and his supporters must be absorbed within this majority or they must be smashed; and of course an ever growing economic distress must be remedied.

From the very first day the reception this cabinet received both from the public and in political circles was the very worst imaginable. Gibes or invective rained down from every quarter. The Left denounced these reactionary country squires obviously destined to scuttle democratic institutions. Hugenberg sulked because he had received no portfolio in the combination. Hitler, who had apparently promised the President to support the ministry, now declared he would do nothing of the sort. To top this, the ministry's most desperate enemies were the Catholics, furious at seeing the government in the hands of a man whom they considered to be a deserter from their cause. All these hazards offered enough pitfalls to give pause to any horseman less rash. But Papen had plenty of pluck. As in the old days, when he was a young officer, he plunged forward at full speed over a course strewn with obstacles.

✦

Abroad he managed fairly well, at least in so far as reparations were concerned. On June 15, at Lausanne, he entered into conference with the Allies, more particularly with Edouard Herriot, who had been named Premier a few days before. Negotiations were laborious, punctuated by ups and downs, crises and interruptions. But they were concluded on July 8. As a result the Reich was granted a new three years' moratorium after which it was to pay three billion marks gold in bonds at 6 per cent to be issued as soon as 90 per cent of their nominal value seemed assured.

If any party to the negotiation consented to make sacrifices, it was certainly France. My country did not complain. For her part Germany, now freed from all worry of immediate payments, enjoyed the prospect of being delivered of her burden for good and all in the near future and at the price of a moderate payment. Here was cause for rejoicing. Ultimately the three billions were never paid and the Lausanne Conference may be said to have buried the whole reparations question.

Far from being elated, Germany was highly indignant! She belabored her wretched negotiator with the most vehement reproaches. Papen should have refused to pay a single mark, said the Germans, he should have left the conference, slamming the door behind him. Such was the extent to which chauvinism had already corrupted the German mind, so general, too, the will to prove that Papen was good for nothing.

At Geneva, at the Disarmament Conference, things were moving less favorably. Here, however, Papen was less involved personally; this affair concerned the Wilhelmstrasse and the Reichswehr. The demand for equality of rights and the German interpretation of the Treaty of Versailles met with the liveliest resistance.

The Reichswehr, which had never believed in the efficacy of international discussions, now carried out its plan for a direct agreement with France; it persuaded its Ministry of Foreign Affairs to second its tactics and on August 23, 1932,

Bülow apprised me of the step about to be taken. In effect, on August 29, Baron von Neurath informed me that in the opinion of the Reich Government the disarmament problem was above all a Franco-German problem, and that any solution adopted by both countries would be automatically ratified by all others. Accordingly Germany wished to hold a conversation with France *en tête-à-tête* in order to discuss a basis for agreement. France, a traditionally military country with a lively sense of honor, must understand that the Reich could not indefinitely suffer the humiliation of a ridiculous army, the caricature of an army unworthy of a great people. What Germany sought, he added, was really quite modest. Grant her no more than equality of rights; she would apply this privilege with moderation, contenting herself with a small number, a few samples of arms which were now forbidden her such as tanks, airplanes, heavy-caliber guns. Her only other request was for authority to raise an additional contingent of thirty thousand troops every year; these would serve but three months and would be employed chiefly in guarding her coasts and borders.

Schleicher confirmed Neurath's explanation. Neurath left me a note embodying the German request; he requested that his action remain confidential. If successful, news of it would be released; if it failed, no one need know of it and public opinion would not be aroused. After obtaining from my interlocutors information that in their opinion the principle of equality of rights included naval forces too, and that the question therefore concerned Britain as well as ourselves, I forwarded Neurath's note to Paris with recommendations for the discretion requested of us.

Unfortunately my dispatch reached Paris during an absence of Herriot, the prime minister; he had gone to visit the Channel Islands with a group of journalists. Alphand, his principal secretary, leaped into a train for Cherbourg, chartered a motor boat there, and raced out to meet the *Minotaure*.

M. Herriot was sitting on deck with his traveling companions; from afar they saw the launch approaching. Alphand waved an envelope he had in his hand, then came aboard.

"What is this, Alphand? News from Germany?"

"Yes, *Monsieur le Président*. A most important message from Berlin."

So, from the very outset, the discretion asked of us was violated.

In Paris a leisurely examination of the German note raised serious objections. Proposals for private conversation were judged to be incompatible with our basic obligations of loyalty to the League of Nations. France publicly contested the thesis that equality of rights might be deduced from the Versailles Treaty; was she now, in privy mediation, to admit it? Again, Germany's intentions were not above suspicion. The principle of equality established, what assurance had we that the Reich would apply it to a minor degree, remaining content, as alleged, with but "a few samples"? It was all too certain that the atmosphere in Germany allowed of no concessions. Nationalism was rampant, and hostile demonstrations grew apace. General von Schleicher himself, at the very moment he was soliciting a friendly solution, broadcast on July 26 in terms that were virtually a provocation. He repeated the offense in a magazine article on August 30; and later, in the interview he granted the Italian newspaper *Resto del Carlino,* he actually exceeded the violence of his previous declarations. In these circumstances it would have seemed rash for France to follow Germany's suggestion.

On September 11, in terms that were courteous and that fostered future relations, the French reply declined the Reich's proposals. The Reichswehr's great plan had fallen through, and far from remaining secret this failure was proclaimed from the housetops. Papen's cabinet immediately decided upon a brutal expedient, such as Brüning would never have considered. It notified Geneva that thenceforward Germany would not attend the meetings of the commission of the Disarmament Conference; simultaneously it announced the laying down of a 10,000-ton battleship which Brüning had postponed. In somewhat less emphatic form the Papen cabinet was giving France and the rest of the world a foretaste of the radical measures Hitler was to take a year later.

Papen's difficulties in the disarmament question were as nothing against his domestic cares and struggles. If the President believed that Papen, a Rightist, could more readily achieve that "national concentration" in which Brüning had failed and in which he, Hindenburg, saw the solution of the crisis, then he was grossly mistaken. Papen's personality served merely to intensify the conflict. He tackled the problem with a will, determined if necessary to resort to drastic measures. He understood that the present Reichstag was hopeless. On June 4 he brought about its dissolution; the new elections were set for July 31. Meanwhile he would try to clear up the Prussian situation.

The Prussian Landtag was also unmanageable. Numerically the Nazis prevailed, but even with the help of the German Nationalists they could not achieve a majority. Nor could the Catholic Centrists, even with Socialist help. The Communists, with fifty-seven members, held the balance of power, but neither Left nor Right would work with them except for negative purposes. Were the Centrists willing to come to terms with Nazi and Nationalist groups, a Prussian premier might be appointed in lieu of the Social Democrat Braun. But the Center refused.

On July 20 Papen dismissed Braun and his Minister of Interior, Severing. An executive decree appointed Papen Reich Commissioner for Prussia, an office which authorized him to suspend ministers, to assume the functions of premier of Prussia and to name whom he willed to cabinet rank. To counteract rising protest, a second decree proclaimed a "state of crisis" in Brandenburg and in Berlin. The army, under General von Rundstedt, was made responsible for the maintenance of order; columns roamed through the streets of the capital, troops camped at Unter den Linden.

Abroad rumor ran rife. The foreign journalists exaggerated matters; not for one moment was public order disturbed. On the contrary, the passivity and docility of the public before this governmental *coup de force* were signally conspicuous. No labor union, no Social Democrat, no Communist lifted a finger in protest. The champions of democracy lay low. Later, opinion seemed to be surprised at the lack of protest Hitler met with when he established his regime; this feebleness was already obvious and measurable under Papen. The "superseded" Prussian Government lodged a complaint with the Supreme Court in Leipzig, protesting that it was still legally functioning. Noisily, but in words alone, the southern German states, Bavaria at their head, backed them up.

Faced with this tumult, the Chancellor wilted. He dared not follow through, and a fantastic confusion resulted. There were now two Prussian governments, one governing without reigning, the other reigning without governing. Tragedy turned into farce again, with Papen once more a laughingstock.

Electioneering for the new Reichstag was progressing throughout the country. Two figures loomed supreme in the public eye. There was Hitler, thundering from the rostrum, surrounded by his immense hosts of Nazis, savagely critical of the existing "system" and passionately evoking what prosperity, glory, and grandeur he would bring to Germany; and there was Brüning, cold, pale, and pertinent, the champion of liberty and legality within the framework of authoritarian democracy. Brawls and bloody conflicts occurred practically everywhere; from June 1 to July 20, 72 murders were listed in Prussia and 322 assaults committed by either Nazis or Communists.

The elections, on July 30, established a sensational Nazi

victory: Hitler won 230 seats, or 120 more than in 1930, and 37 per cent of the total electoral vote. The Communists won 11 seats. In the Reich and in Prussia the Nazis were now the most numerous and powerful party. But they held no majority even with the help of Hugenberg's German Nationalists. The elections had therefore failed to solve the problem: parliamentary government was possible only if the Nazis, Catholics, and German Nationalists agreed to work for the famous formula of "national concentration." This seemed at first glance to be unlikely, but Papen attempted to bring it about.

Their victory did not leave the Nazis without disorder in their ranks. Some believed the time had come to take the last remaining step to power violently, if need were. Others, apparently headed by Gregor Strasser, wished to collaborate in a cabinet including several important Nazi ministers. Still others, such as Goebbels, Goering, and Hitler, favored a continued policy of opposition and obstruction which would eventually allow them to dictate terms.

The issue lay in determining what policy the Nazis intended to follow in the newly elected Reichstag. Papen granted the Storm Sections the right to exist and to wear uniforms. His policy, after all, at home and abroad, differed but little from theirs; would the Nazis be any more conciliatory for that? Papen, Schleicher and Hitler met; their conversations proved complicated and tortuous. Apparently they gave rise to the quarrel, heavy in consequences, soon to estrange Papen from Schleicher.

Nothing came of these conferences. Hitler, intractable, declined all proposals. The Marshal then resolved to hold Hitler publicly to his responsibilities; he summoned him on August 13 and renewed the offers that Papen had made. Hitler turned a deaf ear. This chill interview lasted exactly thirteen minutes.

An official communiqué announced that Hitler, refusing to join a Papen government, claimed the power of government wholly for himself. The communiqué added: "The President firmly rejected this demand; his conscience, he stated, forbade him to entrust powers of government exclusively to the National Socialist party, which was disposed to use them arbitrarily."

His parleys a failure, Papen was determined to dissolve this parliament so recently born. On August 30, 1932, the Reichstag assembled. Traditionally this body inaugurated its activities under the presidency of its oldest member. This time the dean was Clara Zeitkin, the Communist. In any other circumstances the riot the Nazis would have aroused may be readily imagined. Now, however, they avoided any excess that might serve as pretext for the dissolution of parliament. Clara Zeitkin, an old lady, had to be supported under either arm; she climbed painfully into the chair. In thin monotonous tones, she read a long, scarcely audible speech, praying for the day when German soviets might fill this hall. The Nazi deputies, wearing brown shirts with the swastika armband, black breeches and boots, sat in the hemicycle, a very model of good manners, uttering never a comment or cry or objectionable remark. But they were beside themselves with fury. They chafed at the bit, but none budged an inch. When the senior member of the Reichstag had finished speaking the assembly proceeded to the election of its president and executive officers.

Goering was elected by 367 votes, the Catholics supporting him. National concentration, more intent upon playing a trick on Papen than upholding the government, was easily achieved. It eliminated the Socialists from any office. Goering climbed blithely into the chair. His clear voice resounded through the hall. With surprising ease he assumed his functions as though these were long familiar. He promised to fulfill his mandate loyally; he thanked his colleagues gratefully; his authority was immediately established. Adjournment took place without an incident, and from beginning to end the session was edifying. The Nazi game now developed. Under Goering's guidance the Reichstag's officers apprised Marshal Hindenburg of the existence of a majority and begged him receive the leaders of its component groups so as to organize a regular collaboration between himself and parliament. The Marshal reserved judgment; in truth, he had already given Papen a decree ordering dissolution. This news spread rapidly.

On September 12 the Reichstag met for the second time. At outset the Communists requested modification of the agenda. Of the two motions they made, one called for nullification of the latest decrees, the other expressed Communist lack of confidence in the cabinet. They invited the assembly to vote upon these resolutions without discussion. The meeting took a recess, during which the Centrists, Nazis, and Socialists showed themselves ready to precipitate matters and to favor the Communist motions.

Papen, expecting an ample debate, had prepared an important speech for the occasion; now he had barely time to send for the decree of dissolution which he had left at the Chancellery.

When the meeting reconvened, Goering as president reported the agreement arrived at in the interval and asked for an immediate vote. Papen, bobbing up in his seat and brandishing a paper in his hand, requested the floor. Goering was aware of the Chancellor's agitation and plainly understood that the paper Papen was waving was a decree of dissolution. But he pretended he did not see, he looked in the other direction; obstinately he turned his back upon the Chancellor while pressing for an immediate vote. From the eminence of the diplomatic gallery where I was, I caught the minutest details of this singular scene. In despair of attracting the systematically unmanageable attention of the presiding officer, Papen took a few steps toward him, placed the decree of dissolution on one corner of Goering's table, and left the hall, the other government members in his wake. Goering did not turn a hair. Stubbornly keeping his back turned and feigning that he had seen nothing, he declared the ballots closed, and, a few moments later, announced the results. The Communist motion of lack of confidence was carried by 513 votes to 32. Only then did Goering think to discover the paper Papen had left at his elbow. Calmly he read it to the assembly, adding that it was obviously worthless since it was countersigned by a ministry legally deposed.

This victory was without a morrow in spite of Nazi efforts to prolong it before a commission of inquiry. Still it had dealt a sharp blow to Papen's prestige, already quite relative, and made him the butt of much ridicule.

The votes which for once had united to blame the Chancellor were now divided by rivalries and squabbles. On October 25 the Leipzig Supreme Court, ruling on the legality of the Reich's attitude toward Prussia, handed down a verdict of extraordinary ambiguity, justifying each party in turn. Far from settling their differences, it furnished both parties with motives for persevering.

The situation was the more chaotic because measures taken to remedy the economic crisis—the floating of tax bonds, the authorization of unemployment insurance, the reduction of wages and the shortening of the working day—only increased the cabinet's unpopularity, without decreasing the number of unemployed, now seven million.

On November 12 the nation's voters were invited to choose a new Reichstag. Perhaps the government hoped that through such electoral tactics in one continuous stream the country would finally give it an assembly to its taste. But it was exhausting the country's patience and completing the work of discrediting the parliamentary system.

Yet the vote of November 20 seemed to fulfill the government's hopes. This time National Socialism suffered a considerable setback, indeed a veritable defeat; it won only 195, as against 230 seats, and 11,000,000 votes, as against 13,000,-000 previously. The Communists gained 11 new seats but the German Nationalists gained 14. The constantly rising tide of

Nazism seemed to be arrested; already an ebb was setting in. This spelled an undoubted success for Papen. Had he reached his goal? He might well believe so. For the Nazi reverses increased the disorder and discord in their camp. Nazi partisans of collaboration with the government blamed their defeat on the die-hard oppositionists: Strasser's friends inveighed against Hitler's followers. Again, costly propaganda had practically exhausted party resources; the Nazi coffers were virtually empty.

Papen attempted to renew relations with the Nazis, whom he presumed to be wiser and more tractable now. But Hitler refused to negotiate with Papen. Then, with the President and his circle, Papen invented a form of procedure which must overcome Hitler's obstructionism. Papen would resign; the Marshal would invite Hitler to form a cabinet supported by a majority in the Reichstag, and Hitler, doomed to failure, would have to acknowledge his weakness. Papen, recalled by Hindenburg, would then reappear, and this time Hitler would be forced into bargaining with him.

Everything developed according to schedule. On November 17 Papen resigned; on November 19 Hindenburg sent for Hitler. Officially the Marshal commissioned Hitler to seek the bases for a parliamentary majority capable of supporting his cabinet; Hitler was allowed until November 24 to accomplish his task. The Center and the German Nationalists immediately announced that they would not accept Hitler as Chancellor. Among the Nazis themselves dissension ran rifer than ever. Hitler himself began to suspect that he had been drawn into a trap. Was he to be confined within the impracticable formula of a cabinet dependent on a Reichstag majority?

Brüning and Papen had governed by means of decrees, according to Article 48 of the Constitution, which invested the President with discretionary powers. Why should Hitler not do so? He wrote to the President for clarification on this point. A correspondence ensued. Hindenburg concluded it by refusing to grant full powers to the leader of a party which had steadfastly insisted upon its exclusive nature. The Nazi party, he added, had always acted negatively toward him and opposed whatever political or economic measures he had judged necessary. Repudiated by the President, Hitler threw up his mandate, declaring himself to be the victim of an intrigue.

At this point an unforeseen hitch occurred in the President's calculations. Just when he was about to call back Papen, Schleicher raised objections. Schleicher realized that Papen had failed and would fail to dispel the prejudices he aroused; Papen's very personality complicated a problem already difficult enough in itself. Having never for a moment ceased to cover Papen with ridicule throughout the latter's stormy passage as Chancellor, Schleicher now firmly opposed his colleague's recall to power. Papen resented this bitterly. Colonel Hindenburg, Meissner, and the Marshal himself shared his resentment. They decided that since Schleicher was so captious and so critical of others, it was now his turn to assume the direct powers of government and to prove his mettle.

Schleicher invited Hitler, who had retired to Munich, to meet him in conference, for he was confident of clearing the hurdle that had stopped Papen. Hitler actually took the train to Berlin, but on the way, at Weimar, Goering and Goebbels intercepted him on the station platform, made him alight, and then and there dissuaded him from continuing his journey. Hitler wrote to Hindenburg that he would no more support Schleicher than Papen. Under these circumstances Schleicher wished to wriggle out of his difficulties, but he was not allowed to. On December 2 the Marshal forced him to assume the Chancellorship. Papen retired off stage again, but not to confine himself to the role of observer. He was filled with bitterness and rancor; his taste of politics and power, his ambition and his wounded vanity would give him no rest. The Marshal's approval, confidence, and friendship were still unreservedly his; he thirsted for revenge. No, his career was not yet finished!

Had that been the end of it, would he deserve the stern judgment that public opinion has meted out to him?

Of the policy he had been commissioned to follow he accomplished at least the negative part. Abroad he obtained a final and profitable settlement of reparations. At home he drove the Social Democrats out of power in Prussia; his multiple elections doubtless revealed if not favored the progress of Nazism, but he also inflicted a signal defeat upon the Nazis and unsettled their unified front. In the economic field he failed, but it is doubtful whether anyone else, using normal methods, could have obtained better results. Instead of Hitlerian nationalism with its disturbing claims, its brutality and its gangsters, his plan was to bring Germany a nationalism of the Kaiser Wilhelm type, respectful of law and order and managed by aristocrats and capitalists who might presently restore the monarchy. Peace abroad might perhaps not have gained thereby, but the Reich itself would not have undergone the horrible rule it was destined to suffer.

The fierce prejudices and violent antipathy that greeted every act of Papen's during his six months in power may be considered relatively unjust, especially since the Catholic Center, by fighting him so bitterly in order to avenge Brüning, proved none too clearsighted.

Truth to tell, Papen's major mistake—his real crime—began the day when, abandoning power, he indulged his resentment. A turncoat, plotting against his successor, he approached the Nazis, who had done nothing but rebuff and belabor him. Having fought Hitler in the past, Papen now effected a reconciliation and busied himself with paving the Führer's way to power. In this sense Papen may be said to have been a fatal agent in Germany's catastrophe.

Schleicher remained in power barely two months, leaving an impression of complete deficiency, of pitiable collapse. In the course of the few weeks he served as Chancellor, I found him hesitant, at a loss, submerged, paler than ever, exhausted by vigil. Had he been overestimated? Was he to be reckoned among those who shine only in a subordinate position and who, promoted to top rank, suffer an eclipse?

In order to understand Schleicher's adventure we must consider his point of departure. Schleicher was pushed into the Chancellery against his will, not in order to succeed in that office, but to fail. He was to be gotten rid of, to be liquidated, because his own friends were weary of his perpetual interference, of his incessant turns-about-face, of his mordant irony, and of the insecurity of any dealings with him. Papen was the artisan of this operation, but not singlehandedly; he was encouraged and secretly helped by the President's office, which employed every resource at its disposal. After his fall, at a luncheon attended by several official persons, I heard Schleicher cry sardonically: "I stayed in power only seventy days and on each and every one of them I was betrayed seventy times. Don't ever speak to me of 'German loyalty'!" But had he himself always given proof of such loyalty?

The beginning of his ephemeral reign was fairly calm, but this lull was deceptive; it was but a respite and a truce, under cover of which fresh intrigues and new plots were developing.

On December 15 Schleicher made his first mistake, the weight of which was to crush him soon. In an address over the radio he set forth his program. Intent chiefly on dissipating the prejudice his rank as general officer and his reputation as chief of the Reichswehr might arouse among the masses, he was determined to win their sympathies. First he repudiated all notion of exercising a military dictatorship; he would rather be a "social general." Next he announced that he would govern according to the Constitution with the collaboration of the Reichstag, that he was abolishing the decree which had lowered wages, and that he would allocate 750,000 acres belonging to large bankrupt estates in eastern Prussia for purposes of interior colonization for the benefit of small landowners and

minor exploitation. . . . Here was a piece of supreme temerity! He was touching a highly explosive matter on which
Brüning had already burned his fingers. Indignant at his behavior, the Conservatives and Hugenberg's German Nationalists nicknamed him "The Red General." Yet he was unlikely
to recruit followers among Leftists.

In his attitude toward National Socialism, Schleicher did
not exceed the President's intent, which Papen had but half
executed. The problem was to soften up the Nazis and, if they
persisted in being stubborn, to smash them. For some time
Schleicher had been attempting to iron out the differences
among their leaders; he favored Gregor Strasser, who was more
reasonable and less excitable than Hitler and who enjoyed
great popularity in the party. Strasser, considered to be the
Führer's chief lieutenant, incurred the jealousy of men like
Goering and Goebbels; he went so far as to break with Hitler,
to resign obstreperously and to join the dissident group.
Schleicher was ready to give Strasser a portfolio in his cabinet
or to place him at the head of the Prussian Government.

This was a smart move and it might have succeeded if only
Papen had not opposed it. Papen's friends, the bankers and
industrialists, prevailed upon him to compound his differences
then and there with Hitler and the Hitlerites. The National
Socialist current was too strong to be assimilable; so long as
the Nazis remained the opposition party, the domestic crisis
would continue and Germany would remain ungovernable.

Now the November elections had given Hitler fair warning; he realized that he must not venture too far. His financial
difficulties were serious; the government thus held the advantage over him. He could no longer flaunt the claims he had
made yesterday. For Papen the moment was opportune. The
Papen-Hitler tandem had proved impossible; the Hitler-Papen
combination might well succeed. Vice-Chancellor Papen could
be counted upon to keep an eye on Chancellor Hitler; besides,
only one or two of Hitler's acolytes need enter the cabinet.

Their fellow ministers, aristocrats and nationalists of good complexion and familiars of Hindenburg and Papen, could be relied on to form a stout guard about Papen. There would be no more abuse of force and no more nonsense.

Papen lent a willing ear to this argument. The prospect of returning to power and turning the tables on Schleicher, who had driven him out of office, was beguiling. Papen agreed to meet Hitler in Cologne on January 4, 1933, at the house of the banker, Kurt von Schroeder.

Their conversation took the exact turn its instigators desired. But certain newspapers, getting wind of the interview, denounced its equivocal character. Papen pleaded that he was simply continuing to seek means whereby the Reich might emerge from the political stalemate. Actually he had been won over to the suggested policy; he was thenceforward to devote his every effort to influence the Marshal. The old man must get over the aversion and mistrust he harbored for Hitler; he must gradually be persuaded to adopt the formula to which Papen himself was converted. Papen's friends, acting likewise, spread their webs here and there; Schacht, Silverberg, Thyssen, and Vögler were very active. Hugenberg and the Steel Helmets snapped at this bait which seemed to offer them a place in the sun.

Amid this maze of Byzantine intrigue one circumstance was to play a capital part. On January 15 the tiny state of Lippe-Detmold was to hold elections for the renewal of the local assembly of twenty-one deputies. The election itself was trifling, but within its paltry frame it was declared to figure as a kind of supreme test, a divine judgment. Were Nazism to be defeated in Lippe-Detmold, it was irremediably doomed; were it to emerge victorious, it was destined to conquer. Hitler summoned all the remaining forces of Nazism, utilized every available resource, and put the whole machinery of his propaganda into action. The results fulfilled his expectations; the Nazis who had previously held but a single seat now boasted nine. An immense clamor of triumph arose among them. Exaggerated out of all proportion, the Lippe-Detmold victory was touted by them as an illustration of the party's irresistible surge. Amid the atmosphere thus created—it did not escape the President and his followers—Schleicher's ruin was determined.

The Reich had relapsed into its chronic state of confusion. Throughout the Reich battles between Nazis and Communists grew ever more frequent and bloodier. Of what use, people kept asking, to have a government directed by a general if, incapable of keeping order, it allowed all notion of authority to be jeopardized? On economic grounds Schleicher was most vulnerable, for here he possessed neither experience nor competence nor an enlightened and reliable adviser to guide him. Dazed by the tumult caused by contradictory demands, Schleicher wavered in perplexity.

On January 11 the powerful Agrarian association, the Landbund, headed by Count Kalckreuth, after a visit to the Marshal at which the Chancellor had been present, published a fiercely hostile statement against Schleicher in the press. On January 20 Centrist deputies in the Reichstag Budget Commission brought up the explosive question of *Osthilfe* or aid for large landed proprietors in eastern Germany. One deputy revealed that Oldenburg-Januschau, Hindenburg's crony, had received 60,000 marks; another declared that many beneficiaries of state subsidies used these not to pay their debts but to purchase automobiles and go on tours to the Riviera. To a man, the Junker clan, shuddering with anger, held Schleicher's demagogy responsible for the insolence of the Reichstag. Finally, on January 21, Hugenberg's German Nationalist party, now on good terms with the Nazis, launched its own public attack upon the Chancellor. There was open talk of an imminent ministerial crisis. Indeed, Schleicher's enemies had managed to rouse against him the chief industrialists, the large landowners, the bankers, the peasants, the Nazis, the Nationalists, the Steel

Helmets, and the monarchists. Papen had at least kept the President's support; Schleicher now lacked even that. He was in exactly the plight to which he had reduced Brüning eight months before.

Imposed upon and solicited from every quarter, the Marshal finally accepted the palinode proposed by Papen. He admitted that there was no other solution, he must try out Hitler once and for all, with of course the necessary precautions. If this test succeeded, so much the better; if it failed, then Germany would be delivered of a most vexatious figure. As for Schleicher, Hindenburg got rid of him with as little ceremony as he had shown in liquidating Brüning. On January 28 he refused to sign the decree of dissolution which Schleicher requested in view of the forthcoming meeting of the Reichstag; the General had therefore to resign.

Hitler, reaching Berlin the day before, had settled at the Kaiserhof Hotel, his usual residence in the capital, a few steps from the Chancellery and from the Palace of the President. A considerable throng filled the square, watching the comings and goings and cheering whenever Hitler appeared. A fever spread over the capital, everyone waited for news, everyone felt that a supreme hour in the Reich's destiny was about to strike. Goering, Hitler, and Papen negotiated with the representatives of the parliamentary factions; at last, on the morning of January 30, the Marshal summoned Hitler. Meanwhile strange rumors ran rife through Berlin. The Potsdam garrison, said to have been alerted by Schleicher and the generals, was marching upon the capital; to avoid a *coup d'état* speedy action was essential. Probably there was not a word of truth in the story intended, as it was, to sweep away Hindenburg's last scruples.

At noon special editions, hastily printed, officially announced Hitler's appointment as Chancellor. The tramp, the pre-1914 failure, the shady character, the "unknown soldier" of World War I, the semi-ridiculous orator of the postwar Munich beer halls, the member of a party then numbering only seven members, was at the helm, and behind him the movement which he had created now totaled thirteen million Germans.

That evening the National Socialists organized a torchlight parade. In massive columns, flanked by bands that played martial airs to the muffled beat of their big drums, they emerged from the depths of the Tiergarten and passed under the triumphal arch of the Brandenburg Gate. The torches they brandished formed a river of fire, a river with hastening, unquenchable waves, a river in spate sweeping with a sovereign rush over the very heart of the city. From these brown-shirted, booted men, as they marched by in perfect discipline and alignment, their well-pitched voices bawling warlike songs, there rose an enthusiasm and dynamism that were extraordinary. The onlookers, drawn up on either side of the marching columns, burst into a vast clamor. The river of fire flowed past the French Embassy, whence, with heavy heart and filled with foreboding, I watched its luminous wake; it turned down the Wilhelmstrasse and rolled under the windows of the Marshal's palace.

The old man stood there leaning upon his cane, struck by the power of the phenomenon which he had himself let loose. At the next window stood Hitler, the object of a very tempest of cheers, as wave upon wave kept surging up from the alleys of the Tiergarten. The parade, which lasted until midnight, was conducted amid perfect order. But there had been so little time to organize it that no one had thought of summoning photographers. On the morrow, therefore, the ceremony was repeated with unabated fervor in order that the memory of this historic night might be perpetuated pictorially.

III. HITLER IN POWER

THE REICHSTAG FIRE

O N THE morrow of January 30, 1933, the Storm Troopers set the tone for what the new regime was to bring. Throughout Germany these gangs took possession of the streets, molested passers-by, arrested whom they pleased, broke into private houses, commandeered what they willed, drove the mayors and officials of the late government out of public buildings, indulged their rancor, and vented their private vengeance. Their attacks were directed chiefly against Communists, Socialists, Liberals, and Jews. But they did not spare foreigners; consulates and embassies worked day and night answering calls for aid from nationals of theirs who had been

49

maltreated. Papen in his optimism had said: "Let the militia-men have their fling." They were "having their fling" and were to continue to do so for a long time: indeed, with them law and order were never to be re-established.

Meanwhile Hitler was feverishly active. With a promptness, resolution, and self-assurance that were extraordinary—not to speak of his skill and cunning—he exploited his victory to the full. Given an inch, he took an ell. He harassed this and upset that; he overturned obstacles, he heaped law upon far-reaching law, and in every field he laid the foundations for his major plan. In the rush of events that stampeded the year 1933, it was a shrewd observer who could tell what it all meant. But Hitler's dash and temerity fascinated rather than shocked the German people; they quivered as a horse quivers when suddenly it feels the master's hand and spurs.

Hitler proposed to accomplish many things at once. He would establish his dictatorship by means of a plebiscite, thus proving that he had the country behind him. He would enlarge the cabinet in which certain wishful thinkers had sought to confine him. By expelling his provisional allies and introducing his friends he would suppress the opposition parties, one after another, to the greater advantage of the National Socialist party, which was to reign alone. He would, in the same operation, break down Prussia and the southern *Länder*; he would proceed to eliminate Jewry altogether; he would use the machinery and basic institutions of his regime; and finally, step by step, he would reintegrate the foreign policy of the German Reich.

On February 1, 1933, forty-eight hours after taking over, Hitler dissolved the Reichstag; on February 4 he dissolved the provincial (*Länder*) and municipal assemblies. The Marshal had granted Hitler what he had denied Schleicher. Once again Germany was in the throes of balloting.

The stake was more serious than ever, but this time a new

dispensation placed the police in command of party competition. There were only three authentic Nazis in the cabinet: Hitler, Goering, and Frick; but Frick was Reich Minister of the Interior, and Goering had had himself appointed Minister of the Interior in Prussia, so that between them they controlled the entire police force of Germany. This advantage they used shamelessly to effect a purge whereby officers and ranks the Nazis were not sure of were either broken or arrested, to be replaced by henchmen of Nazidom such as Diels, Lewetzow, and Daluege.

On February 4 Hindenburg, with surprising docility, authorized the government to take steps "for the protection of people and State," to forbid public assemblies, to suspend the freedom of the press, and, if necessary, to ride roughshod over the opposition of the individual *Länder*. Goering and Frick made the most of this unconditional privilege. Alleging that the police required the support of the Brown Militia, they appointed troopers as auxiliary policemen, a step which legalized the lawlessness of the Storm sections and entrusted the maintenance of order to the very forces that were disrupting order.

The electoral campaign was immediately affected. The Communists were hunted down, their headquarters in Berlin occupied, and when they made a show of resistance they were quelled by grenades and machine guns. The Liebknecht Haus was raided twice within a week. After the second raid a communiqué published in all the newspapers announced that the police had discovered not only secret shelters, trapdoors, mysterious hiding places, and stores of weapons, but also a wealth of documents proving that the Communists were hatching a general plot. The government identified Socialists and Communists by confounding them under the single term "Marxists"; it proclaimed its determination to stamp out "Marxism."

The Catholic Centrists escaped such abusive violence, for their hour was not yet struck. But their meetings were invaded by hecklers and their debates universally obstructed. Military detachments had seized all radio stations, allowing only such orators to broadcast as would give the Nazis no umbrage. Despite these vexations and frequent clashes, often resulting in men wounded and killed, the opposition stood its ground bravely: Brüning, Kaas, Schaeffer for the Catholics, and Loebe, Stampfer, Sollmann for the Socialists, campaigned as best they could. Police reports testified that opposition propaganda was not unsuccessful; the Nazis were proportionally vexed and nervous.

Against this background the Reichstag was burned on the night of Monday, February 27, 1933.

That night there was an official dinner at the French Embassy. The Reich Minister of Finance, Schwerin von Krosigck, was present. Halfway through the meal, at about nine, the embassy porter passed me a note which read: "The Reichstag is on fire." I immediately excused myself and moved to one of the windows overlooking the garden; from there I could see the dome of the Reichstag. Its glass cupola blazed as scarlet as though fireworks were being set off below. I returned to the dining room to inform my guests of what was happening. Their reception of this news betrayed their stupefaction. But Krosigck, who was not a Nazi—at least not at the time— could not disguise his joy. "*Gott sei dank!*" he exclaimed. "Thank God!"

The earliest information I heard was that passers-by, seeing flames bursting from the building, had spread the alarm. Firemen reported that the fire was blazing in the Hall of Parliament; the fire chief, interviewed by journalists, declared that incendiaries had set the fire at many points. Here, beyond all hazard, was a clear case of arson. The culprit had been arrested inside the Reichstag building, wandering about, obviously in search of a way of escape. Papers found upon his person disclosed the fact that he was a certain Van der Lubbe, of Dutch origin, an associate of the Dutch Communist party, a strange fellow, apparently not in full control of his mental faculties. He could not possibly have acted singlehandedly. The fire chief stated that the elaborate preparations he had discovered must have required about ten men.

Next morning the press recorded the reporters' stories, with eyewitness evidence from policemen and firemen; but this type of testimony was speedily banned by government order. An ironclad cordon was flung about the Reichstag, and from then on only the official version obtained.

The Reichstag fire, it said, was an act of terrorism, a Communist crime. The culprit had made a complete confession. Here was no individual crime but a party crime. Recent documents, previously seized at Liebknecht Haus, explained everything; they established the existence of a vast plot, on Bolshevik lines, designed to spread terror by setting fire to public buildings. The Communists had also planned mass poisonings in the mess halls of Hitlerian and Steel Helmet units. Van der Lubbe's accomplices had been able to escape only because they were thoroughly familiar with the Reichstag building. This familiarity they could have obtained only from Communist deputies. Incidentally a Communist deputy, Torgler, had been seen in the corridors in company with Van der Lubbe the evening of the crime; also, Torgler and his colleague Kuhn had been the last to emerge from the Reichstag building. Both were now under arrest, together with two Bolshevist agents, Bulgarian nationals, named Dimitroff and Popoff.

Meanwhile the government had taken appropriate measures. All Communist members of the Reichstag and all notorious Communist party members were under lock and key; all Socialist publications, including newspapers, had been suppressed despite vigorous protests from the Executive Committee of the Social Democratic party which loudly denied any connivance with the Communists.

Diplomats, foreign journalists, and liberal German circles

greeted the official report with much skepticism and numerous objections. What puzzled me was that the documents which had been seized at the Liebknecht Haus and which allegedly revealed the existence of plans to fire the principal public buildings had not prompted the police to guard these buildings properly. The insistence with which the official communiqué strove to implicate the Socialists by reporting their patent collusion with the Communists obviously inspired mistrust in all who knew that Socialists and Communists had never been able to get along together. Further, if the Reichstag fire was the agreed signal for insurrection and civil war, how did it happen that, the signal given, no attempt at any sort of uprising was reported at any point throughout the Reich? Further still, if the Reichstag was but one incident, could the Communists have been so witless as to commit it on the eve of an election? Surely this could not have failed to bring down upon their heads the most ruthless governmental reprisals and the high moral indignation of the electorate? The more the Reichstag fire appeared directly adverse to Communist interests, the more it proved manifestly opportune to the government. Hitler had considered outlawing the Communists but he had not made up his mind, perhaps because he lacked a valid pretext for doing so.

These observations and thoughts struck me and many others forcibly. For the most part my fellow diplomats and the French and Anglo-Saxon press correspondents stoutly denied the official version and believed a Nazi plot more likely. On February 28, 1933, at 8:00 P.M., I questioned Baron von Neurath about the event. He stated that the culprit was certainly the Dutchman, Van der Lubbe, and that Torgler, chief of the minority Communist party in the Chamber, had admitted Van der Lubbe into the building. Quite obviously the Reich Foreign Minister was reciting a lesson. As early as 3:00 P.M. I submitted my own opinion by wire to the Quai d'Orsay. I cannot certify that the Reichstag fire was actually created out of whole cloth by *agents provocateurs;* but I *can* say that every happening, before and after, would lead one to believe so.

On March 4, 1933, a piece of information supplied by the Soviet Embassy enlightened me considerably. It appeared that an underground corridor linked the Reichstag to the residence of the Reichstag President, Goering. The incendiaries must have taken this corridor. The source of this item was no less interesting than its substance. It emanated from "a member of the Reichswehr" who wished so to inform the Soviet diplomats lest the Reichstag fire occasion a breech in relations between Russia and Germany. (Many ranking officers in the Reichswehr remained attached to the tradition of friendly relations between the two countries.)

Today nobody, save in Germany, can possibly doubt that the Reichstag fire was set by a dozen Brown militiamen, who entered and left the building through the secret corridor linking it to the residence of Goering, the Reichstag President. The trial held in late 1933 at Leipzig failed to reveal this, but it did at least establish the innocence of Torgler and of the Bulgarians indicted. It also proved that the luckless Van der Lubbe, so prone to acknowledge his guilt, was a moron, a human wreck, and had probably been drugged in order, as decoy, to divert suspicion from the true criminals. The press announced that he had been sentenced to death and executed, but rumors in Berlin asserted that his family, claiming his body, had never been able to obtain possession.

Much to the fury of the Nazis, further facts about the whole business were aired in the countertrial held in London. Yet it is curious that none of the Nazis involved in the crime was ever to testify. Some assert that they were all subsequently and successively put to death; others, that their leader was Count Helldorf, chief of the Potsdam police, a sinister adventurer later hanged for his part in the plot of July 20, 1944.

Either supposition is plausible, but as far as I know today neither has been confirmed.*

Like the murders of June 30, 1934, the Reichstag fire was to become one of those subjects not to be mentioned in Hitler's presence. But Goering discussed it freely, mostly, of course, in order to repel, with an irritable and sarcastic breeziness, the insinuations and accusations he knew lay at his doorstep. In this connection I have heard him compare himself with Nero. Just as the Christians once set fire to Rome in order to accuse the Emperor of it, so the Communists had set fire to the Reichstag in order to impugn Goering.

Nevertheless the memory of it tormented him. One evening during the Berlin Horse Show he was entertaining the horsemen and foreign visitors of note, including a Swedish prince and his wife. Goering's guests waited in the drawing room in vain. After perhaps a half hour he came down to welcome them. His brows were knit, his air worried. When I asked him the cause of his trouble he replied in a whisper that the Prussian Landtag was on fire. Investigation revealed that it was but the reflection of flames from two cressets at the door of his palace.

THE POTSDAM COMEDY

The notion that the German Government can possibly utter falsehoods is difficult of conception by the German brain. Germans bear an innate respect for lawful authority; this makes them accept anything official with the utmost docility.

---

* A certain Kruse, declaring himself to have been Röhm's orderly officer, addressed a letter to Marshal von Hindenburg which was found later by British or United States Intelligence officers. In it he stated that twenty-three SS troopers, acting on Röhm's orders, approved by Goering and Goebbels, set fire to the Reichstag. Kruse alleged that he had taken part in the operation. It is further alleged that Kruse managed to take refuge in Switzerland and thus remains the sole survivor of the team of incendiaries reputedly exterminated during the massacres of June 30, 1934.

It proved the more true in the case of that strange statesman whom the Marshal had appointed Chancellor and who set himself up for a corrector of past wrongs.

Abroad the Reichstag incident was judged to be a suspicious machination; in Germany an overwhelming majority of the people swallowed the government version and saw the fire as a Communist crime. The incident roused the entire country; a wave of emotion broke over the people. Peasants were reported to have set up guards over wells and springs for fear of the mass poisonings mentioned in the official reports. Foreign skepticism met with like fury in Germany, rousing in the populace a violent xenophobia. The gap between Germany and other nations was widening.

Hitler had the country behind him and he struck while the iron was hot. On March 7, 1933, a second statute "for the defense of people and State" reinforced the first one. Since the Nazis were none too sure of the Reichswehr, that statute created a special state of siege without calling for army intervention. It empowered the central government to act for the governments of the *Länder* and it further restrained what was left of individual liberty, of the freedom of the press, and of the right of assembly. The privacy of postal, telegraphic, and telephonic communication was abolished. Crimes of high treason—a term the Nazis neglected to define exactly—of arson and of assault upon the persons of the President of the Reich and of cabinet officers were made punishable by death. Not only the Communists were systematically decimated, with Thaelmann their leader clapped into jail, but also the Socialists, Nazism's outstanding foe.

Within a few days five thousand people were arrested in Prussia and two thousand in the Rhineland. At this time also two new institutions, characteristic of the Third Reich, came into being: concentration camps and the State Secret Police, *Geheime Staatspolizei*, that Gestapo which was soon to become one of the most powerful organs of the regime. Sinister rumors ran rife about both. Liberals and Jews fled the country in ever increasing numbers, they besieged foreign consulates in order to obtain passport visas and they departed to swell the tide of immigrants in Britain, in America, and in France.

Meanwhile the Nazis intensified their electoral campaigning. They multiplied their marches through the streets to the blare of bands, their parades, drills, torchlight tattoos, and spectacular public meetings. Hitler made addresses in all the great cities. Loud speakers were set up in squares and at street corners where compact groups stood devotedly absorbing the echoes of his raucous cries.

On March 5, amid the highest excitement, Germany went to the polls. The booths were of course presided over by Nazis, and SA platoons filled the halls. The number of voters was very large; only 11 per cent of the electorate refrained from voting. The result of the ballot gave the National Socialists 288 seats in the Reichstag as against a previous figure of 195. In the last election Hitler had polled eleven million, today he polled seventeen. He could well congratulate himself upon a success and his followers could well celebrate their triumph noisily. But this success was actually less striking and, more important, less decisive than Hitler had hoped. The votes he won amounted to no more than 43.9 per cent of the electorate. To be sure, his party was much the strongest of all parties; but it did not enjoy an absolute majority. It was only by allying itself with the German Nationalists—the sole group upon which Nazism could count and a group which comprised but 8 per cent of the Reichstag—that Nazism barely managed a majority of 52 per cent.

Thus the most striking feature of the election lay in the extraordinary steadfastness of the opposition parties. Despite the vexations to which they were subjected, their electors remained faithful to them; these parties maintained their positions; even the Communists lost but 19 seats. This fact proves that the last time Germany was free to vote—amid a thousand obstacles, true, but nevertheless according to approximately democratic processes—she gave the foes of Nazism as many votes as she gave the Nazis. It also proves that but for the support of the German Nationalists (the party to which the Marshal, Hugenberg and the conservative barons belonged) Hitler would have been in the minority in parliament. On March 12 elections to the various *Länder* parliaments and municipal elections yielded practically the same result. Everywhere the Nazis gained votes and seats, everywhere they formed an imposing aggregation; yet nowhere could they have been in the majority had not the slender help of the reactionaries tipped the scales in their favor.

Knowing that forceful affirmation invariably impresses the flabby mind, Hitler began by celebrating his relative gain at the polls as a total and final triumph. To make the public conscious of this, he promoted the red, swastika-crested flag of the party to the rank of a national ensign, side by side with the former imperial standard of black, white and red. The flag of the Republic was tossed overboard.

Far from slackening, official terrorism reached new heights. Raids on private domiciles, sequestration of goods, and personal arrests gathered increasing momentum. Jews were savagely hunted down. At Kiel a Socialist lawyer was murdered by night; at Magdeburg a town councilor suffered the same fate, and at Königsberg the Nazis occupied the offices of the labor unions. Questioned about such excesses, Goering calmly announced over the radio: "When you plane a plank, the shavings must fall somewhere."

Squads of SA men having paraded and occupied a barracks in the demilitarized zone at Kehl, I complained to Neurath. The Minister offered his excuses, but this did not prevent him from issuing a vainglorious statement to the press in which he declared that I had been *"abgeblitzt,"* or rebuffed and routed. Even a weakling like Neurath deemed it opportune to adopt the fashion of the day.

Commissioners charged with executive police functions were sent into the *Länder*. When Bavaria gibed, General von Epp was at once detailed to take office as Reich Commissioner for Bavaria. He proceeded to depose the lawful government of Bavaria, to seize its ministries and to set up Nazi leaders like Röhm and Wagner in them. Held, the Bavarian prime minister, and his colleagues gave way without a struggle. One, the Minister of the Interior, was seized in his bed and was marched barefoot to the Brown House, the SA headquarters.

All this was simply a foretaste of what was to come.

The inaugural session of the newly elected Reichstag was scheduled for March 21. But with the imperial parliament building burned, where were the deputies to meet? Hitler decided that the first session of the assembly should be held in the Garrison Church at Potsdam. That church is a kind of sanctuary of Prussianism. There, in a bronze casket, rests the body of Frederick the Great; there, addressing the dead monarch, Napoleon is said to have declared: "Were you not in this tomb, I should not be here!" Architecturally the church is rather sober, considering the period at which it was built, sober as was old Prussia, but harmonious and luminous as was the organization of the old Prussian state. It conjures up memories of glory and of grandeur. It evokes a Germany austere and military, fraught with martial and civic virtues, and it brings to mind a dynasty which raised Germany to the status of a great nation and which led her to the apex of power. No German enters this place but, possessed by such thoughts, feels his breast swell with emotion and pride. When Hitler summoned the Reich deputies there for a *Staatsakt*—a solemn state ceremony—he was certain of offering to the romantic imagination of his people a symbol whose significance was clear and certain to arouse high enthusiasm. The day too, March 21, was of good omen, for it marked the anniversary of the summoning of the first Reichstag by Bismarck in 1871. The shade of the Iron Chancellor would thus join with that of Frederick the Great to welcome under these hallowed arches the man whose ambition it was to carry on their work.

How could that idea fail to win the hearts of the men who considered themselves depositaries of the true Prussian tradition? How could it fail to win the hearts of men like Hindenburg and his friends, the Junkers and monarchist barons, of men like Hugenberg and his German Nationalists, of the officers of the Reichswehr? To them the Potsdam ceremony was specifically addressed with the purpose of winning them over and of inspiring them with the most reassuring of illusions. After the dazzling pledge made by Hitler at Potsdam, how could such men fail to dismiss the apprehension with which they had begun to view the excesses and abuses of his party? Could they now hesitate to grant him their entire confidence, to meet all his requests, to concede the full powers he claimed?

On March 20 there was a steady downpour of rain all night into the morrow; but on the morning of the twenty-first a wind scattered the clouds. Patches of blue appeared in the sky and the sunlight glittered in reflection in the puddles. The brisk tonic air heralded the coming of spring. The citizenry had decked the houses with flags and bunting. Huge swastika-crested banners hung from the rooftops side by side with the black, white, and red flags of the former Empire. The bells rang out in full peal as the official automobiles sped down the road between two lines of Brown Shirt militiamen.

At the Garrison Church the public was admitted to the gallery only. In other words the audience, necessarily reduced and compressed within too narrow a space, consisted wholly of high officials, party dignitaries and their families. The central gallery was reserved for the imperial family: in the foreground stood the chair of Kaiser Wilhelm II, empty, and immediately behind it the Crown Prince in the uniform of a colonel of the Death's Head Hussars. Beside him I noticed his wife, the Crown Princess Cecilie, his brothers, and his sons.

The diplomatic corps, bemedalled and beribboned, sat in an adjoining gallery. The entire nave was occupied by the members of the Reichstag. The Communists of course did not attend; they were in prison and thenceforth practically, if not legally, excluded from political life. The socialists were also absent; they had preferred to abstain. But the Catholics filled every seat assigned to them in this Protestant chapel. This whole crowd was relatively silent; people dared but exchange whispers, awed as they were by the austerity of the place and by the solemnity of the hour.

Suddenly the door opened; the audience rose to their feet as one man as Marshal Hindenburg entered, wearing military uniform, spiked helmet, and the grand cordon of the Black Eagle. Although grown stouter and obviously laced tightly into a tunic which no longer fitted him, he still possessed all the dignity of a veteran leader. The audience admired his high stature, his calm, his poise, the grandeur that stamped his melancholy face. He advanced slowly, leaning heavily on his cane. As he reached the front of the imperial gallery, he turned to face it squarely and raised his marshal's baton to salute his master's empty seat and the princes of the blood gathered about it.

Hitler, advancing by his side, looked like a timid newcomer being introduced by an important protector into a company to which he does not belong. Who could have believed that this wan man with such vulgar features, dressed in an ill-fitting coat and in appearance so respectful and so modest, was the more powerful of the two personages? A multitude of uniforms streamed by behind the Marshal and his Chancellor. Goering and Goebbels in their turn saluted the Imperial Highnesses, but in a breezier way, with the back of the hands.

Hindenburg and Hitler sat down facing each other in a vacant space in the center of the choir. The Marshal put on his heavy tortoise-shell spectacles and read a speech which may be summed up exactly as follows: "The place in which we are gathered invites us to contemplate ancient Prussia, a god-fearing nation which owed her greatness to her labor, to her consciousness of her duty, to her firm courage and to her love of the fatherland. May that ancient spirit enliven the present generation too!"

Hitler's reply was more abundant. In a voice at first muffled but gradually gathering volume, he sought to whitewash the past generation from undeserved reproach. Neither the Kaiser nor the government nor the people had sought war. Only the decadence of the nation and the general downfall forced Germany to acknowledge against her most sacred convictions that lie which constituted her a guilty party. Having stigmatized the scandalous exactions of the Versailles *"Diktat"* and the folly of reparations, Hitler went on to exalt that youthful Germany which, in the elections of March 5, had re-established the honor of the nation. Next he uttered a fervent apologetic of Hindenburg, to whom he gave all thanks in the name of the youth of Germany. And since he realized that the Nazi regime caused apprehensions abroad which the Potsdam ceremony was not calculated to diminish, he finally declared himself resolved to govern authoritatively but as a sincere friend of peace.

Hitler's hand and the Marshal's met in a firm grip as the deputies rose to their feet. The image of Kaiser Wilhelm II dominated the scene. It was as though the Third Reich, bent upon continuing the labors of the Second, intended, before burying the Weimar Republic, to bring back the imperial exile of Doorn so soon as circumstances permitted. At the end of the ceremony a military parade took place before the doors of the Garrison Church. The Crown Prince, standing in the first row of spectators, looked for all the world as though the review were being given in his honor and he inspecting his own troops.

The Potsdam *Staatsakt*, though an impressive national ceremony, was no more than a prologue; it served merely to set the background for the main action whereby Hitler was to be invested by the Reichstag with full powers. Since no parliamentary building was available this drama was to be enacted two days later at the Kroll Opera House.

SA and SS platoons swarmed in the corridors as the new Reichstag convened. All the Nazi deputies wore uniform; the other deputies, in dark civilian dress, looked like poor country cousins. The assembly proceeded to elect its officers. Goering won the presidency unanimously save for the Socialist vote; election of the vice president and of the twelve Reichstag committee chairmen was negotiated by a standing vote; there were no interruptions and no protests. Within five minutes the proceedings were over.

On March 23 the assembly was charged to consider the law whereby full powers were to be granted to Hitler. This was the decisive meeting. Hitler opened it with a long speech in which he set forth his policy and program; he read it with brows knit and in a dismal voice. It was, incidentally, a prudent speech, calculated to embarrass the Catholics and to force them to come to heel since the Communists were excluded from debate and the Socialists already expelled from the majority. First Hitler recalled the Reichstag fire and thundered against the incendiaries. Then he reaffirmed his determination to unite all Germans. To the *Länder* he would leave a certain autonomy but he announced that in future their differences must not be aired in public. Parenthetically he dashed all monarchist hopes to the ground when, alluding to possible reforms of Reich and Constitution, he stated that the return of the monarchy was for the moment impossible. How speedily the Potsdam ceremony was relegated to the background!

Hitler declared that he would of course protect the twin religions which everybody held to be important factors in the preservation of Germany. He would respect property and individual initiative. He would abstain from any monetary expedient; he would grant debtor peasants the necessary moratoria; he would give the middle classes what aid they needed.

Without explaining how, he promised to find work for the jobless. The Reichswehr came in for his high praise and particular regard. Concluding, he affirmed his attachment to the cause of peace, but to a peace which must not distinguish between victors and vanquished. He added that he was eager to live on friendly terms with Britain, France, the Holy See, and even Russia. His peroration was clearly aimed at the Catholics; they would be treated according to what attitude they adopted. The House rose to sing "*Deutschland über alles!*" During the recess I heard the echo of Hitler's platoons in the street as they shouted in chorus: "We want full powers. If not, look out for trouble!"

When the session reconvened, Wels asked for the floor in order to speak for the Socialist party. The Socialists, he said, had assumed their part of responsibility during the tragic days following the defeat. Though the Weimar Constitution was not a Socialist constitution, the Socialists nevertheless remained true to liberty, equality, social law, humanity, and justice. Let the government persecute them and strip them of their power, the Socialists could not be stripped of their honor. They would not vote for full powers. Wels spoke with extreme moderation in an apologetic and pleading tone, much as a spanked child might speak in the expectancy of future spankings. Under the circumstances here was a very brave, worthy, and honorable address.

As he spoke, I watched Hitler taking notes feverishly. Hitler at once asked for the floor and, when it was granted him, betrayed himself for exactly what he was: a polemicist, an agitator in public meetings, an ungenerous fanatic. "Do not mistake us for bourgeois," he wound up with biting, sonorous passion. "The star of Germany is in the ascendant, yours is about to disappear, your death knell has struck."

Hitler done, Monsignor Kaas, representing the Center party, proved to be humble and deferential. He was skating on very thin ice. He recalled how important was national unity; the

Center, he said, was above party politics; for his part, he would gladly shake hands with his former adversaries. Brüning was present but remained silent.

Hitler had won; he was given full powers to the tune of 441 votes for and 94 against. Two-thirds of the assembly voted for him, the Socialists alone dared vote against him. Thanks to this dispensation, valid for four years and based upon a semblance of legality, Hitler had become absolute master of the Reich. He could legislate as he listed in every walk of German life. The way lay open before him. There was no longer need for either the Reichstag's sanction or Hindenburg's signature to legalize his decrees.

The Marshal had been ousted with, for only recourse, the faculty of expressing lack of confidence in the cabinet. This he could not do without risking the horrors of civil warfare. Hindenburg's Chancellor was stronger than Hindenburg himself; very soon there would be no single instrument of government that Hitler had not seized. The *Völkischer Beobachter* exulted: "The day of the Third Reich is at hand!"

The Communists eliminated, it was soon to be the Socialists' turn. The Catholics were granted but a breathing spell. Hugenberg, the Steel Helmet, the reactionaries, and the monarchists, having been flattered so long as their collaboration was indispensable, were to be discarded in good time like so much rubbish. The ceremony at Potsdam did not mark an alliance between two generations, it allowed the younger to evict the senior. Youth bowed, scraped, and made a show of reverence but thumbed its nose behind the backs of the oldsters. And so, in sum, the solemn act in the Garrison Church proved to be no more than a solemn swindle.

MAY 1, 1933

The Reichstag fire had provided too flimsy a pretext to annihilate the two rival and comrade parties at one blow. Hitler's accusation that Socialists had participated in this arson was too thin to justify any immediately radical measures, but it served him for a pretext to pack off a round number of Socialists into concentration camps. The rest were kept under surveillance, subject to abuse and dogged by threats, as the last Marxist reprobates. Hitler proposed to destroy them in two stages, the first of which, as hypocritical and cynical as the Reichstag fire and the Potsdam comedy, was to deprive Social Democrats of the support of the labor unions.

A "Labor Day," intended to supersede the traditional revolutionary holiday, was appointed for May 1. Hitler, Goebbels, and their henchmen were bent on setting up a spectacle of proportions hitherto unknown. The main feature of this demonstration was to be a mammoth rally on the Tempelhof parade grounds, held at night amid a dazzling display of fireworks. Owners and employees from factory, workshop, warehouse, office, and neighborhood store were invited to participate in the procession, trade by trade, the bosses at the head of each unit.

The leaders and members of the "free syndicates," which were mainly Socialist, were the object of particular strenuous solicitation by the government, which led them to believe that it would be grateful to them for this proof of their good will. They were assured that their participation was not a political act but rather the affirmation of a social faith. The theme of this festival, said the government, was solidarity among workers, the union of one and all in the religion of labor, the brotherhood of all Germans who toiled. It would therefore be disloyal to socialism and its standards for Socialists to disassociate themselves from a demonstration of this sort.

The Socialists allowed themselves to be convinced. They were promised per diem pay at the usual scale and, in addition, the double bait of a bonus for transportation and rations. At dusk the streets of Berlin were packed with wide columns of men headed for the rally, marching behind banners, with fife and drum units and regimental bands in attendance.

Stands had been set up at one end of the field for the guests of the government, among them the diplomatic corps, compulsory spectators, bidden to be awed into respect and admiration. A forest of glittering banners provided a background for the spectacle; a grandstand, bristling with microphones, cut forward like a prow looming over a sea of human heads. Downstage, Reichswehr units stood at attention with one million civilians assembled behind them; the policing of this stupendous rally was effected by SA and SS troopers. The Nazi leaders appeared in turn as the crowd cheered. Then came Bavarian peasants, miners and fishermen from other parts of Germany, all in professional garb, then delegates from Austria and the Saar and Danzig, the last being guests of honor of the Reich. An atmosphere of good humor and general glee pervaded the assembly, there was never the slightest indication of constraint; these masses were obviously proud and happy to participate in the pageant they were presenting.

At eight o'clock the crowds backed up as Hitler made his appearance, standing in his car, his arm outstretched, his face stern and drawn. A protracted clamor of powerful acclaim greeted his passage. Night was now fallen; floodlights were turned on, set at spacious gaps, their gentle bluish light allowing for dark interjacent spaces. The perspective of this human sea stretched out to infinity, moving and palpitant, extraordinary when at once sighted in the light and divined in the darkness.

After some introductory remarks by Goebbels, Hitler took the stand. All floodlights were turned off save such as might envelop the Führer in so dazzling a nimbus that he seemed to be looming upon that magical prow over the human tide below. The crowd lapsed into a religious silence as Hitler prepared to speak. Having never seen him officiate out of doors, I watched him steadfastly. He held a batch of small paper squares, as one might hold a hand at cards; on each he had noted a single key word, and, as he developed the ideas it suggested, the small squares passed in rapid succession through his fingers. He exalted labor and the nobility of labor, the role of the worker within the framework of society, and the fusion of all classes in the practice of work. Next he outlined the program whereby the nation was to be regenerated through work. Participation in National Labor groups, he announced, was soon to be made compulsory so that each and every German might learn the salutary lesson of manual labor. Public works would be undertaken on a huge scale in order to abolish unemployment. . . . The new Germany would no longer be subject to social conflict. From now on she would form a single family, working with might and main, all its members harnessed to the same task. Thus Germany would once again become a powerful and respected nation, once again she would follow the way of her true destiny toward the goal of her grandeur and glory. . . .

What struck one most in this speech was not the content, which was after all quite vague, but rather the orator's action: his voice, warm, harsh, trenchant, and fierce, the passion that carried him away, the breath that animated him and, quite literally, dilated his nostrils. I could not help recalling the testimony of that Greek who declared that to appreciate Demosthenes one must have known "the very beast itself." Doubtless many among Hitler's listeners eyed him with feelings of mistrust or of hatred; but even they were troubled and attracted as the boatman was troubled and attracted by the song of the Lorelei.

The end of Hitler's speech met with a veritable ovation. The national hymn was followed by the party song, the *Horst Wessel Lied,* throbbing across a night which, immediately afterward, was punctured by the skyrockets and illumined by the mines and flares of varicolored fireworks. It was indeed a brave, a magnificent fête. The German participants and the

foreign guests left with the conviction that a wave of reconciliation and of concord had swept over the Third Reich.

But next day, May 2, 1935, at 10:00 A.M. all independent
labor union offices, clubs, meeting places, co-operative centers,
and lodging houses were occupied by police and Storm Troopers. So too were independent labor newspapers, the Workers'
Bank and its many branches. Fifty-eight labor leaders were
arrested at their homes; files and bank accounts were confiscated in an operation directed by a "Committee of Action
for the Protection of German Labor," whose president, Robert
Ley, one of the most vulgar of Nazi leaders, was famed for
his crapulousness and evil habits. The operation extended
throughout the Reich.

At one blow the whole enormous structure and organization which was so heartily admired abroad—a union four
million strong with 184,000,000 marks at its disposal—crumbled into dust. Nowhere was there the slightest reaction, let
alone resistance; German syndicalism disappeared as through
a trapdoor. It was deprived of its leaders, discouraged by their
feebleness, and demoralized by accusations of corruption
launched at some of them; it was harassed by Nazi agents who
had filtered into its ranks, and it was tempted too perhaps by
the promises of a better future held out to it by the new
regime. Inevitably its supporters, yielding to Nazism, were
swept away by a flood which disconcerted and paralyzed them.

Stricken just as mortally as labor, Social Democracy resigned
itself to the lot in store for it. For a time Hitler remained
considerate of it, for he needed the help of the Social Democrats in order to prove to the world and to the Disarmament
Conference at Geneva that the entire German people, including the last representatives of Marxism, supported him in his
claim for equal rights. On May 17, 1933, the Socialist deputies
in the Reichstag, applauding Hitler's statement of the German
thesis, joined in the unanimous vote he obtained from the
subjugated assembly. A few weeks later the Socialists were to

be excluded from Parliament, banned as an organization, and forbidden the rights of assembly and propaganda.

By similar means the German Nationalists and the Catholics were subjected to daily vexations that grew increasingly harsh, and their whole movement, undermined by perfidious machinations, fell to pieces. The German Nationalists centered around the Steel Helmet and its many subsidiary groups; Seldte, the Steel Helmet leader, was Minister of Labor. The German Nationalist leader, Hugenberg, was both Minister of National Economy and Minister of Agriculture in the cabinet of January 30. These bastions were marked for annihilation.

Relations between the Brown Shirts and the Steel Helmet had never been cordial; they now gathered fresh venom day by day. The Steel Helmet men were disgusted at the brutalities of the SA and they frowned upon the anti-Semitic campaign. Thus they became the refuge of many malcontents, a fact which caused the Nazis considerable alarm and anger. Street fighting between the rival groups grew more frequent. As early as March 27, 1933, six days after the Potsdam ceremony, the National Socialist leader in Brunswick, Klagges, ordered the disarming and dissolution of the Steel Helmet in that state. Shortly after, the Rhineland was to enact the same measures. On April 27 Seldte, eager to retain his ministerial post, repudiated his colleague Düsterberg, co-leader of the Steel Helmet. Joining the National Socialist party, he invited his fellow veterans to do likewise.

On June 19 the Scharnhorst Association—the most important offshoot of the Steel Helmet because it recruited followers among the German youth—was suppressed. On June 26 the Steel Helmet, having been dissolved, vanished willy-nilly into the maw of the Nazi party. For Hugenberg this represented not only an affront but also a substantial and irreparable loss. This was by no means the first time Hugenberg had been insulted; Hitler had used Hugenberg and Hugenberg's stupidity as steppingstones to power. Hitler had never entertained the slightest feelings of amity toward him, and Hitler's Nazis considered it exorbitant that this aged, obstinate, narrow-minded man, this wild boar of politics, this confederate of Germany's leading capitalists, should hold two important cabinet portfolios. Hugenberg protested to no avail; he was fobbed off. On June 18 at the London Economic Conference he took it upon himself to read a paper of his own making wherein he demanded colonies for the German Reich, a blunder which called down mockery and scandal upon his head. He was now at the end of his tether; at length, on June 28, he gave up. His personal eclipse marked that of the German Nationalist party.

Curiously enough not one of those who should naturally have risen to defend him lifted a finger in his behalf. The conservatives in the cabinet—Neurath, Krosigck, Papen and the like—washed their hands of him, though they too were German Nationalists or closely akin to German Nationalism. In the make-up of the government on January 30 they represented the contribution of a small group without which Hitler would have been in a minority. Hugenberg's fall made them vulnerable, it diminished their strength and left them more than ever at the mercy of the Nazis. This they seemed not to suspect nor to consider to be a cause for alarm. They meekly accepted the resultant situation.

Hindenburg, patron and protector of the Steel Helmet and linked by his past and by all his friendships with the German Nationalists, set the example. Harassed on all sides, Hugenberg had insinuated that were he to leave the government, Hindenburg might well withdraw his support of the cabinet since the coalition, which was the raison d'être of that cabinet, would have ceased to exist. But this had never occurred to the Marshal and he turned a deaf ear to the suggestion although he must have realized what was going on. Surely he could not but know that the alliance formed at Potsdam amid a tolling of bells was already dead? Surely he must have realized that he was no longer the master but rather the captive of his Chancellor? Did he consider himself placed in a position in which he could not shake off this yoke? Did he prefer calm to a crisis of dubious outcome? The Marshal was a miser who had developed a taste for landowning and felt happy at the idea of restoring the family fortunes. On August 27, the anniversary of the Battle of Tannenberg in which Hindenburg had defeated the Russians in 1915, Goering announced that the Prussian Government had added considerable acreage to the estate of Neudeck, where Hindenburg lived. By national subscription the Marshal was to receive the adjoining estate of Preussenwald, free of all charges, for so long as he continued to have male heirs. Here certainly is a point calculated to embarrass such historians as are apt to view the Marshal's career indulgently.

The Communists, Socialists, and German Nationalists having been disposed of, Hitler had now but the Catholics to cast off. In vain they had fallen in line, had voted the law of full powers by which Hitler was to crush them, and had proclaimed their patriotism second to none. Attacked at once from without and at the mercy of spies from within, subjected to individual arrests, beatings, outrages, and dishonoring accusations, they steadily lost ground, resigning themselves to the prospect of their disappearance from the political scene. Yet they continued to hope that by clearing the ground they might stop the fire from spreading, or, in other words, that by sacrificing their political existence they might perhaps prevail upon the Nazis to assure them the minimum of freedom indispensable for the practice of their religion. The bishops sought to pave the way for an acceptable *modus vivendi.* They did not condemn the new regime; on the contrary they declared that there was no discrepancy between Catholicism and National Socialism. Papen encouraged them in this direction, going so far as to found an organization of Catholic National Socialists called "Eagle and Cross."

An amazing spectacle ensued. Within Germany, while prelates were being arrested, while scores of organizations, affiliates of the Center party, were being dissolved and their property confiscated, and while in Munich members of a Catholic congress were brutally beaten, Papen was at Rome discussing the bases for a concordat. By its terms the Vatican recognized the Nazi State, agreed that the bishops pledge their allegiance to it, and forbade priests to engage in politics. In exchange the Nazi Government promised the Vatican to respect the liberty of the Church, its properties and possessions, the garb of its clerics, and the existence of its congregations. But agreement or no, the Nazi campaign against the Catholics continued just as before, taking on increasingly brutal and odious forms. Nazism, inspired by Goebbels, himself a Catholic, went so far as to organize a series of sensational trials in which priests were indicted for indecent assault and nuns for trafficking in foreign currency, the whole with a view to producing the impression that Catholicism was an abyss of immorality.

Like the labor unions, like the German Nationalists, the Holy See was cynically duped, or, to put it bluntly, was swindled outright. On July 8 the Concordat was signed; it was to come into effect on July 10. But already on July 5 the Center party had itself brought about its own dissolution, and such of its deputies as sought to join the National Socialist party in the Reichstag had suffered the added mortification of being rejected. Hitler seems to have been astonished at such docility. "Who would even have believed in such a collapse?" he asked in a public meeting on July 9 at Dortmund. "Who would have believed that a party like the Center could disintegrate, as it has today, and vanish completely?"

One of the tasks Hitler had set himself was now accomplished. On July 14, 1933, in a list of nineteen new laws, there appeared one which forbade the formation of any political party in Germany and which decreed confiscation of the property of former parties. From then on there was to be but a single party in the Third Reich, the National Socialist party.

From then on the Reich Cabinet had nothing in common with the initial cabinet of January 30. Nazism, storming in through window and door, completely transformed its character. On February 15 Goebbels had caused himself to be appointed Commissioner of the Reich; on March 12 he received the portfolio of Propaganda, a cabinet post created especially for him.

In the weakly person of this youthful man, one of the most frightening of Hitlerites entered the government. Goebbels was short, almost deformed, afflicted with a club foot and an abnormally large head; his face, slashed by an enormous, scarlike mouth, was illumined by magnificent black eyes and its expression bespoke a lively intelligence. He was undoubtedly among the most cultivated of them, perhaps the only cultivated one. He was usually called "the doctor," for he was a Ph.D. in philology. As orator and writer he was remarkably gifted. Goebbels may be considered as the archetype of those warped intellectuals who, in order to escape from their own nihilism, threw themselves into the arms of the National Socialists. His mind, highly resourceful and fertile in ruse and sophistry, possessed something about it that was perverse and diabolic. His imagination, fed upon romanticism and of an inventive turn, delighted in majestic visions and fantastic spectacles. He was unparalleled in the art of moving between falsehood and truth, of lending to those facts he deformed the aspect of accuracy, of interpreting events in the sense which would most profit his cause; he was unparalleled too in his talent for explaining a complex problem to simple crowds in clear yet never vulgar terms. He excelled in polemics, in superior irony and in invective. He was probably too intelligent to harbor any illusions about the worth of most of his colleagues or the nonsense they uttered or the errors they committed. But he was moved by a fanatical ardor which lifted him high above any feelings of repugnance. He was an extremist, a man of fundamentally revolutionary temper who dedicated himself body and soul to Hitler. Under his impetus the Ministry of Propaganda, enjoying funds which amounted to some hundreds of millions of marks, was to prove itself one of the most effective and powerful bodies in the Reich.

Goering, who was jealous of Goebbels, did not hang back. Retaining the Prussian Ministry of the Interior, he also became Prussian Premier on April 11 and immediately surrounded himself with Nazi collaborators: Kerrl at the Ministry of Justice, Rust at the Ministry of Public Instruction, Popitz at the Ministry of Finance. Besides holding these offices he was also Reich Minister for Aviation. Hugenberg, having resigned, was replaced at the Ministry of Agriculture by Darré, the Nazi expert in such matters, and at the Ministry of Economy by Schmitt, a top-flight man in the field of insurance. On June 30 Rudolf Hess, the Führer's deputy as leader of the party, was authorized to attend cabinet meetings until such time as he and Röhm, chief of the Storm Troopers, were named ministers of state.

The barons had wished to isolate Hitler; it was they who were now isolated. Papen, who originally was to act as a sort of brake on the Chancellor's movements, was now of virtually no consequence. He had been compelled to relinquish his post as Reich Commissioner for Prussia so that the true Vice-Chancellor today was no longer Papen but Goering. Papen's role now was merely to execute special missions, that to Rome, for instance, where he laid a trap for the Vatican. But this suited his vanity perfectly. Blomberg, Minister for War, like the dilettante he was, fell under the spell of the Führer's personality. Neurath and Krosigck were chiefly interested in retaining their posts; when Hitler requested them, as a matter of official routine, to join the party, they offered no objection. As for Bavaria, General von Epp set up a completely Nazi cabinet there. It had required only six months for Hitler to sweep away all parties; it required no more for him to turn his government inside out, as one might turn a glove, and to make his dictatorship supreme within the cabinet and throughout Germany.

But Hitler's clean sweep would have been incomplete without the systematic elimination of the Jews. His notorious hatred of Jewry had been clearly set forth in *Mein Kampf*, a work in which its paroxysms took on aspects of a ferocity so hideous as to reveal downright insanity. Throughout the course of the years Hitler was in many ways to attenuate or to modify certain ideas and feelings which he had voiced in *Mein Kampf*. But on the Jewish question he never once budged one inch. According to him the only satisfactory solution was to exterminate the Jews wholesale, There can be no doubt that this notion of total extirpation, rooted deep in his mind, inspired his own conduct and that of his party.

Anti-Semitism was always widespread in Germany; it had strong, ancient roots in that land, it was a popular prejudice and a popular passion. Violent even before 1914, it developed considerably because of the part played by Jews in the Weimar Republic and in the Leftist parties, because of their tenure of public posts from which they had been excluded a short time previous, and because of the wealth they displayed during the years when speculation ran wild. By proclaiming his hatred of the Jews, far from parting from his people, he grew much closer to them, he became their reflection. His frantic anti-Semitism did not damage his popularity; it was on the contrary one of its factors.

If Jew-baiting had been a favorite sport of the Nazis even before their leader assumed power, it became legal after January 30. In fact it assumed such proportions and such odious forms that foreign opinion, revolted, rose in noisy reprobation. Now nothing exasperated the Nazis so much as to find themselves blamed abroad. Their fanaticism made them indignant at any who dared criticize them; to them foreign disapproval was an infringement of their sovereignty. They accused the Jews of exciting foreign opinion against them, of instigating this movement of protest. Reprisals were imperative.

With government approval a committee was formed under chairmanship of the ignoble Streicher for the purpose of organizing a general boycott on April 1. That day SA columns covered the capital, arresting or beating such Jews as they encountered. They broke into the most frequented cafés and restaurants of the Kurfürstendamm, and, wielding their blackjacks, expelled all Jewish clients. Militiamen were detailed to stand outside shops and prevent anyone from entering. Inside, the shopkeepers were soundly drubbed, their stock rifled and money extorted from them under threats of future brutality. These operations continued all day long at the tune of *"Juda verrecke,* let Jewry perish!"

In point of fact such persecution was never to end, for it was inherent in the very nature of National Socialism. All private industrial or commercial businesses were compelled to dismiss any directors, members, or coworkers of Jewish blood. The medical and legal professions were expurged in the same fashion. By virtue of the law of April 7, which introduced the Aryan clause into the new statute for public officials, all such with a single Jew or Jewess in direct ascending line were forced to abandon their posts. The magistrature, the universities, the various teaching bodies did not escape this implacable law. At first Jews were allowed to emigrate, but soon they were refused passports, their possessions were confiscated, and they were forcibly included in a society which made life unbearable for them. It seemed as though they could never be manhandled harshly enough. Blow succeeded blow with no end in sight. The Third Reich reproduced a ghetto infinitely more evil than its model in the Middle Ages.

By so doing it deprived itself of one of the most useful and industrious units of its population, and, specifically, the one unit which kept Germany in touch with the main currents of the outer world. Nazism claimed that it was purifying Germany; it was debasing her. Nazism believed it was freeing Germany; it was isolating her. It was unleashing her sorriest instincts, her latent barbarity; it was confining her within the pitiful limits of her own stubborn blindness; it was creating, between Germany and the conscience of the world, a conflict whose remote, fatal consequences it did not even suspect.

NAZISM IN THE SADDLE

Expulsion from public life of Communists, Socialists, German Nationalists, Catholics, and Jews marked but one aspect— and that negative—of *"Umbruch,"* the great upheaval of society which Hitler proceeded methodically to create. With one hand he was, so to speak, clearing the ground, but simultaneously, with the other, he was setting up the Nazi order.

It was really arresting to see him pass from theory to practice, apply his doctrine and coolly crush whatever stood in his way. Watching him I felt as though I were witnessing a change of sets on a stage over which the curtain had not fallen. Stalwart teams of stagehands moved to and fro. Some bore away the units of the former décor quite roughly; others put up the framework of the new flats; still others emerged from the wings, their backs laden with unfamiliar furniture, as canvas sections disappeared under the stage and new ones fell from the flies.

The spectator sometimes wondered whether chips of wood or slivers of steel, flung by too lusty a hand, might not ricochet into the house and strike an innocent bystander. Time and again I was called upon to protest against some demonstration insulting to my country, to free some fellow countryman from jail, to save some rash journalist from expulsion, or to help some unfortunate victim of persecution to cross the border. But when all was said and done, jolt and unpleasantness notwithstanding, the new order was set up and in the space of one moment one world succeeded another.

Among Hitler's chief aims was the building of a strongly unified and strongly centralized Reich. Differing from its predecessors, the Third Reich was resolved to finish with regional particularities once and for all, not factually alone but legally. It considered regionalism to be an open wound, the cause of Germany's inferiority as compared with her neighbors Britain and France.

On March 31, 1933, a law called the law of "reduction to discipline" or of "uniformization" (*Gleichschaltung*) invited the Nazi governments of the *Länder* to pattern their legislation on Reich legislation and in harmony with Reich ideas. Further progress was made by the law of April 7, 1933, which created *Statthalter*. These, the direct delegates of the Chancellor, were entrusted with supervising the execution of Reich laws and of the Führer's orders in the *Länder* or groups of *Länder* to which they were appointed. Within their jurisdiction they enjoyed the same powers as did the Chancellor in the Reich. In case of trouble they had the armed forces at their disposal; their authority extended to all walks of German life. In the Reich generally there were to be eleven such *Statthälter*: in Prussia the Prussian Premier, appointed by the Reich Chancellor, exercised these functions. Hitler naturally entrusted these new posts to proved Nazis: von Epp in Bavaria, von Killinger in Saxony, Sauckel in Thuringia, Hildebrandt in Mecklenburg. The municipalities of the large cities were to lose their autonomy too and to be ruled by commissioners or handpicked mayors.

On February 14, 1934, the *Reichsrat* or Council of the *Länder* was abolished. There was no reason left for its existence. What remained now of the old regionalism? Practically nothing! Hitler had razed the edifice he had inherited from Bismarck and erected a rigorous centralization upon its ruins. From that day on everything emanated from Berlin to end, via a serried hierarchy, boomerang fashion, in Berlin. The government and its administrative apparatus formed a group without counterweight, wholly free from control by public opinion or by any other exterior force. Hitler could congratulate himself upon having accomplished without a struggle, indeed with the most consummate ease, one of the most important revolutions in the history of his country.

Because, according to National Socialist concepts, the party should animate and supervise the functioning of state machinery, the party must itself be built upon an appropriate structure. During the early months of 1933, therefore, the party was the object of reorganization and readjustment. The Reich was divided into thirty-two *Gaue* or regions, each region was divided into *Kreise* or circles, each circle into *Ortsgruppen* or local groups, each local group into cells, each cell into units. Above the *Gauleiter* or regional leaders and the inspectors appointed by the Führer sat a general staff comprising the leaders of the party's multiple departments: the Chief of the Central Political Commission, the Chief of the SA, the Chief of the SS, the Treasurer of the party, the President of the Disciplinary Committee, the Chief of the Agricultural Section, the Chief of the Juridical Section, the Chief of Propaganda, the Chief of the Youth Movement, and the rest. All these chiefs of course possessed offices and staffs of their own, the whole organization headed by Rudolf Hess, as the Führer's Deputy Leader of the Party.

To these units we must add Hess's own staff and that of the Chief of Co-ordination, Philipp Bouhler, with the numerous sections attached to both. There were also numerous affiliates such as the Motor Corps, the Youth Movement for Boys, the Youth Movement for Girls, the Women's Union, and professional associations of students, physicians, lawyers, and teachers; there were the Labor Front and, of course, the Brown and Black militias. The immense range and complexity of the system was striking. To be sure it neither simplified nor sped the transaction of business; more than one clash rose between state officials and party officials and there was more than one instance of rivalry between members of various departments. Yet, such as it was, the system did offer two advantages. It furnished employment, rank, and salary to a great many persons, feeding a sizable clientele whose private interests, strengthening their ideological convictions, integrated them into the system. And it spread tentacles everywhere, applying orders received from above and, in turn, keeping the upper echelons informed of popular reaction and behavior; it supplied information on things but, more important, on persons; it formed an outstanding auxiliary for the constabulary and Gestapo; in a word it made of Germany a police state.

The fundamental importance attributed by Hitler to his race theory was to lead him to take strictly racist measures without delay. The anti-Semite laws were but one chapter in this volume. On July 14, 1933, a law instituted compulsory sterilization for individuals suffering from hereditary illnesses or from incurable diseases. Further laws were imposed to protect "the hereditary health of the German people" by defining cases in which marriage was forbidden and by imposing the premarital certificate. By the same token "healthy" marriages were favored. The institution of "marriage loans" helped young men eager to marry by supplying them with the indispensable furniture and a sum of money, to be repaid on a sliding scale, governed by the fecundity of the parents.

The German birth rate, stationary or falling under the Weimar Republic, now rose under the Nazi regime. In 1933, in the first year of its reign, National Socialism, hostile to prejudice against bastards, established a powerful movement, known as "Mother and Child," with a view to giving youthful mothers and their offspring all imaginable aid. Among the Black Shirts, the Elite Guard of Nazism, rationalized selection was actually practiced; model couples were brought together for perfect mating.

The same desire to improve the race was closely linked to the German effort for the organization of youth and the generalization of athletics. The party youth groups, already very numerous when Hitler came into power (the *Jungvolk* for children from the age of eight up, the *Hitlerjugend* for their elders, and the *Bund der Deutschen Mädchen* or Association of German Girls, all of them under the direction of Baldur von Schirach), soon gathered enormous momentum. No effort was spared to strengthen the youngsters' health, to instruct them, and to let them learn self-reliance under the guiding principle that their immediate leaders rose from their ranks. Obviously they were at the same time being impregnated with Hitlerian doctrine, molded according to the patriotic, pan-German, brutal, and warlike ideal of National Socialism; they were being trained in discipline, obedience, leadership, and raised in the cult of the regime and of the Führer's person.

Under the impetus of Tschammer-Osten, promoted to Reich Chief of Athletics in July 1933, physical culture developed throughout Germany no less swiftly. Each individual sport led to the formation of its particular group under an appointed leader. No modest town or even village but was soon eager to have its own stadium and swimming pool. At first physical education was applied along the most modern lines to school children, but later it was also diffused systematically among the working classes.

Similarly the National Work Program contributed to rear in Germany generations which, being stronger, tougher, and more clearly conscious of the "national community," would provide the Reichswehr with trained recruits. On May 1 Hitler announced that National Labor, hitherto voluntary, was now compulsory. The execution of such a decision once more presupposed organizational effort. By the close of 1933 the system was established and working soundly with some 250,000 young men; Germany was divided into thirty regions, each region into several groups, each group into several *Arbeitslager* or work camps. The program called for the opening up and draining of certain areas, the building of roads and railbeds, the clearing and replanting of forests, the improvement of waterways, and so forth.

Special schools were set up for the training of leaders. In these camps the young were subject to military discipline. They constituted a hierarchy with special titles that corresponded to ranks in the army. They wore uniforms and bore spades and shovels which they handled like rifles. They marched in formation like soldiers, and their annual parade was later to present one of the most impressive features of the Nuremberg Congress. As they graduated progressively to camp and yard, the political education they had previously received in the *Hitlerjugend* was intensified. Nazism's goal was to make them into men who were healthy, free of the old social prejudices, and aware of what it meant to have callused hands. Also they were to be good Nazis.

This religion of work, preached so ardently by Hitler on that memorable holiday of May 1, found its fulfillment not only in the extension of the Work Program but in a series of other endeavors. The first problem was unemployment, for the government was urgently challenged to find the means of solving an acute crisis. A law promulgated early in June called for considerable public works of all sorts to be undertaken by population groups, districts, and groups of districts, the whole program to be financed by a Reich Treasury issue of Work Program Bonds.

In August 1933 it was decided to build the national automobile highway network according to the Italian pattern but on a far greater scale. Reich railroads supplied the necessary funds, swelled by state appropriations. A first unit of almost four thousand miles, initiated under the direction of Todt, the engineer, called for the labor of two hundred thousand men. In September, in a ceremony in which he solemnly distributed tools to the workers, Hitler inaugurated the laying of a superhighway linking Frankfurt and Heidelberg. Four years later the blueprint was a reality and Germany was covered by splendid rectilineal roads, as favorable to economic traffic as to military movements. Also the Reich rearmament, begun immediately by the Nazis and secretly pursued, absorbed many more of the unemployed. Primed by a flow of orders, industry put its machines to work again, and its factories hummed with busy workers.

Presently a statute laid down utterly new bases for labor. The fundamental unit was now to be the *Betrieb*, i.e., factory, plant, or office; its members, comprising the *Führung* or directors and *Gefolgschaft* or coworkers, formed a whole, much as the captain and crew of a vessel. Every morning an assembly brought the entire personnel together. Directors, workmen, and clerks were allotted duties and privileges which were strictly defined. From a list drawn up by management the personnel chose "trustworthy men" to represent them, delegates who, from the Nazi point of view, obviously offered all desirable security. Any conflict was submitted to a special "Labor Court."

On the morrow of the brutal coup of May 2, 1933, the Third Reich instituted a single, gigantic organization, the "Labor Front," to replace the unions which had been suppressed. A small board and a general council directed the whole system, headed by Robert Ley, who appointed the group leaders. The Labor Front, itself a branch of the National Socialist party, dealt with anything which concerned the social policy of the Reich; it controlled social insurance, co-operatives, workers' banks, apprenticeship, handicrafts, and wages. It took over the property of the unions which had been abolished; it collected dues and it grew ever more important.

In November 1933 the Labor Front created a special unit, called *Kraft durch Freude* or Strength through Joy, in order to organize the workers' leisure moments. Amid much noisy publicity it promoted dramatic and musical performances, it established beaches, and it built vessels of heavy tonnage which took the workers and their families on vacation cruises, and which, in time of war, could be converted overnight into auxiliary cruisers and transports.

In October 1933 a new activity appeared for the first time, the "Winter Aid Movement," sponsored by the party. Its mission was to help the poorest and most unfortunate strata of the population, to furnish them with clothing, food, fuel, and shelter, thus expressing the social consciousness and the sense of national community which were to inspire the new system. From October to March collections were taken in house-to-house and street campaigns in which all the Nazi leaders personally took part. The Winter Aid Movement invented the "one-dish meal," compulsory on certain days and representing the contribution of a sum that made the difference between this frugality and an ordinary diet.

As everyone knows, the Hitler doctrine stressed agriculture as much as industry, if not more. Nazism was perhaps keener to win the peasant than the worker because the former bred a "sounder" racial stock which provided excellent soldiery; again, Reich independence of foreign countries depended mainly on the production to be drawn from the soil in order to feed the nation. Profiting from the experience of World War I, the Nazis proposed to permit Germany to resist a future blockade; for this she must virtually become autarkist.

The mission of realizing this program fell upon Darré, Führer of Agriculture after Hugenberg's departure. An agricultural engineer by profession, Darré, an intelligent, patient and tenacious man, was surely one of Hitler's ablest lieutenants. As in this field it was impossible to overturn existing habits and to implant new ones overnight, the Nazis were careful not to go to work too quickly. Yet as early as May 1933 an institution dear to Nazi hearts, the *Erbhof* or Hereditary Farm, was introduced in Prussia. By its regulations an area of land as large as 320 acres, tilled by its owner, his family, and his help, was made indivisible, unassignable, and transmittible, by bequest only, to that son whom the father designated. The owner of an *Erbhof* must be of German blood, devoted to National Socialism, and capable of administering his property. In September 1933 the law was extended to embrace the whole Reich. In so far as one can judge, it seems to have operated successfully; at all events those concerned welcomed it.

For the rest of the program the Nazis merely gathered under a single head all the existing agricultural unions, created a "Peasant Front" after the fashion of the Labor Front, and laid the ground for future reforms. On October 1 a Harvest Festival, comparable to the May Day Labor Festival, was held at Bückeburg near Hameln. An apotheosis of rustic works, it featured symbolic pageants, choirs, dances, and speeches, the whole crowned by a Reichswehr military parade, equally symbolic. It was thereafter to rank high in the calendar of the great national holidays of the Third Reich.

But the big structural reform, the *Reichsnährstand* or Government Food Administration, was not set up until 1935 and 1936. Its object was to associate closely all activities concerned with the feeding of the nation; firms supplying fertilizers and agricultural material, producers of foodstuffs, cattle raisers, butchers, bakers, pastry cooks, truck gardeners, warehousemen, and shippers, as well as the farmers themselves, were brought into one common organization. The competence of the *Nährstand* was boundless. It regulated the general and particular dispensations affecting production, transport, and retail disposal of agricultural commodities; it determined what crops should be sown and attributed them here and there according to the preponderant interests of the Reich; it stepped up the yield, it regimented distribution, it reduced the number of middlemen, and it assured a steady flow of goods into the market. Its chief task was to determine prices, leaving a reasonable profit to all concerned; it also saw that these prices remained firm so as to stabilize the cost of living in the Reich.

At the outset the Government Food Administration, whose members were all party affiliates, roused much conflict. The peasants were irked by the orders given them, by the bureaucracy, and by the tyranny of red tape. Presently, growing accustomed to the system, they heeded its injunctions. Just before the war, imports had fallen conspicuously, as the production of native textiles, of sugar, milk, poultry, and cattle of all sorts had considerably increased. Thus Germany could herself supply as much as 80 per cent of her alimentary needs. Darré's administration could congratulate itself upon having pretty well fulfilled its mission.

The produce of earth now regulated, those of the spirit were to be dealt with. Thanks to Goebbels, Germany was to know a single art, a single mode of state thinking, exclusively at the behest of National Socialism. Newspapers were immediately made to toe the line, impure elements were driven out of journalism, and Nazi commissioners first, then Nazi directors, appointed to take over. Press associations, including Wolff's, though it was loyalist by definition, were replaced by a single agency, the *Deutsches Nachrichten Bureau* (DNB), a government authority.

A first text in April 1933 and a second in October established "Press Statutes" creating a Press Federation and a Chamber of the Press. These bodies issued licenses to journalists, granting them only to persons who had served a period of apprenticeship and merited the confidence of the party. All newspapermen were compelled to join this organization and were held responsible to a corporative court which penalized any dereliction of duty.

For a while the press was subjected to a preliminary censorship, but this ruling was later modified; the Propaganda Ministry decided that it was preferable to indicate what themes newspapermen should stress or silence, and to lay down the general lines which they should follow. Within these limits they were free (at their own risk and peril) to say what they wished in such a way that their gazettes retained an individual distinctive character. Goebbels, who lacked neither wit nor cynicism, could boast that censorship was nonexistent in the Third Reich.

The radio, too, was taken over by a National Authority and a Chamber of Radio Activities, controlled by the Ministry of Propaganda and obedient to its orders. Twenty-five broadcasting stations, whose total power was gradually doubled, broadcast programs of strictly National Socialist inspiration and contributed assiduously to "popular education." The public, for whose benefit special low-priced sets were designed, doubtless enjoyed the new dispensation, for the number of listeners waxed apace.

Nazism handled the motion picture industry in the same way. A Chamber of Motion Pictures and a Credit Bank were created; production firms were reduced to a handful, and films favorably looked upon were financed by this bank. Historic films which fanned patriotic fervor by exalting the glorious national past and its heroes—especially Frederick II—were made all the rage and aroused immense applause.

Writers too were purged, brigaded, controlled, and brought to heel. Regardless of their talent or world-wide celebrity, Jewish writers or writers known simply for their liberalism were expelled from the academies, their seats reverting to authors who were generally mediocre but who redeemed their mediocrity by the ardor of their Nazi convictions. A "Professional Association" and a "Chamber of Writers" ruled the province of letters. To write and to publish, a man must perforce be a member, which he could do only at the price of sharing and expounding the ideas of the day. The Chamber of Writers kept the Minister of Propaganda informed of good and evil books, the former to be widely disseminated, the latter banned. The Booksellers' Guild, founded in 1933, contributed to the "education of the people." In every department of intellectual activity it bred a swarm of insipid works of tendentious vulgarization. Libraries were rigorously censored, any untoward work swept from their stacks.

This topsy-turvy housecleaning inspired Goebbels to loose a series of literary autos-da-fé. On May 10, 1933, in Berlin, a fleet of trucks made for University Place, the student chauffers singing to band music as they crossed the city; 20,000 volumes were heaped on a pyre, their titles proclaimed as fast as the books were tossed into the fire; firemen poured gasoline on the flames while Goebbels, presiding over the assembly, orated.

In the religious field, as in all others, Hitler's doctrine was applied the moment the Nazis came to power. By striking the Centrist party, it was Catholicism itself that Hitler had willed to destroy; he considered the conclusion of a concordat with the Vatican as no more than a respite and a ruse. The Protestant Church was treated no less roughly. Within this confession Hitler was not without allies; not a few pastors, especially eloquent and influential pastors, swayed by his propaganda, flew to his support. They founded an association, the "Christian-Germans," destined to serve as a fulcrum for him to reach his ends. Pastor Hossenfelder and Pastor Müller, a former army chaplain, headed the movement. At first the Protestants reacted exactly as the Catholics had done before them. The politicians and the prudent deemed it the better part of valor to offer no blunt resistance to a movement which called for unity and which obviously enjoyed government support. Forthwith Hitler, imagining that he had made his point, appointed Pastor Müller a bishop of the Unified Church. But the ideas professed by Müller and Hossenfelder met with rising protests among the orthodox, who feared that the Christian-Germans were interpreting the Gospel so as to make it compatible with racism, ridding Christianity of all its Jewish antecedents, adopting pro-Aryan despotism, breaking wholly away from the Old Testament—and indeed, partially from the New—and finally inaugurating a Christianity which they termed "positive" but which sacrificed the fundamental elements of Christian dogma. Orthodox Protestants arose, separated from the Unified Church, and rallied about Pastor Bodelschwing, whom they chose for bishop.

Rust, the Minister of Public Education and Worship, now stepped in to bring them to their senses. His ultimate solution allowed for the subsistence of the various Protestant groups, but under the jurisdiction of a Central Union, headed by Bishop Müller with the support of a Ministry of Church Affairs and a synod. Elections on July 23, 1933, were conducted under a constraint and a pressure that can be described only as shameless; they gave the German-Christians a two-thirds majority and endorsed Bishop Müller as head of the Unified Church. Müller, inspired by Nazi brutality, used dictatorial methods to sabotage Protestantism, dismissing recalcitrant pastors, whom he replaced with his adepts, and attempting to impose a hierarchy of prelates and bishops.

The dissidents did not yield ground. Under the auspices of a group called "Gospel and Church," they put up a stubborn, strictly religious fight, divorced of all politics. As for Hitler, he despised these sectarian squabbles but he realized how harmful they were to his rule; he was vexed by the complaints he kept receiving, many of them seconded personally by Hindenburg. He inveighed against the witlessness of Bishop Müller, a wan, starveling creature whom the Nazis themselves were the first to deride. Eventually, Rust having failed, Hitler instructed Kerrl, the Prussian Minister of Justice, to put an end to all these discussions. Kerrl, attempting strong-arm methods once again with even greater violence than previously, was up against the determination and courage of the dissident pastors, among whom Pastor Niemöller, a former submarine commander and hero of World War I, particularly distinguished himself. Niemöller and many others were arrested and thrown into prison. But resistance by the orthodox was not to slacken; and they were supported by the Catholics and their bishops, who at last awakened to the true character of Nazism and who, like the Protestants, were persecuted.

Thanks to this struggle with its multiple vicissitudes the Nazis were increasingly to expose their secret aims; no longer troubling to dissimulate their basic hostility to Christianity per se, they openly invoked the new purely Germanic religion, which acknowledged no gods save People, Race, State, Party, and Führer.

Achieving its objectives at the outset, the Reich suffered a setback in the spiritual domain, though Nazi arrogance prevented it from discerning the extent of this setback. To defy both Judaism and Christianity, not only in a Germany that was gagged but in the teeth of the whole world, required more heedlessness than audacity.

THE BREAK WITH THE LEAGUE OF NATIONS

Yet on assuming power, Hitler had nourished no intention of quarreling openly with the foreign powers. On the contrary he was determined to quiet any misgivings which his extremist nationalism could not fail to arouse. The more boldly he pressed forward at home without allowing scruples or an observance of gradual transitions to stop him, the more cautiously and circumspectly he acted abroad, at least in the early stages of his rule. The purpose of his revolution was to regain for Germany the strength she had lost. He counted on achieving it by submitting her to a total dictatorship which, having suppressed class and party struggles, would unify her and weld her into a coherent whole, animated by a veritable national fanaticism.

But once regained, this strength would not be content to enjoy its own resources; it was to be employed abroad too. The domestic rehabilitation of the Reich was but a means to further her rehabilitation abroad. Hitler's ultimate goal was to obtain his *revanche,* to wipe out the 1918 defeat, to cast off the shackles of Versailles, to restore Germany to her rank as a great power, and to win for her the position which was rightfully hers as a superior race, in other words the leading position in Europe. But since, on assuming power, he considered that a certain interval must elapse before Germany was capable of dictating her will, Hitler believed it opportune to avoid any clashes that might bring about foreign intervention, hobble his reconstruction program, or even overthrow his rule. Still he had vowed to break with the policy of meekness which had guided his predecessors and to put an end to the humiliations which Germany had suffered all too long. To rehabilitate German foreign policy enough to regain independence, without risking a premature war—such was the program he had in mind and would strive to carry out.

Probably in his early reign no word fell from Hitler's lips more frequently whenever he spoke in public than the word "peace." To be sure, he always added that that peace, to his way of thinking, should abolish distinctions between victors and vanquished; but it was in considerate and amiable terms that, in his program set forth on March 23, 1933, to the Reichstag, he expressed his desire to foster happier relations with Britain, France, Italy, and the Holy See.

At the same time he displayed a marked sympathy for Italy, to be quite naturally explained by the kinship of the twin regimes and by the admiration he professed for the Duce, whose example had charted his course. He entered into friendly conversation with Gombös, the Hungarian premier; he flirted with Japan, receiving her first emissaries with alacrity. These measures already indicated the blueprints for future combinations. He was no less conciliatory with the Soviet Union. On May 6 he extended the Russo-German Pact, which was about to expire.

He went further still. To the amazement of everyone and indeed to the indignation of some of his followers, he made advances to Poland, which had until then been considered by all Germans as a detested foe. To Wysocki, Polish minister in Berlin, he expressed his desire for improvement in Polish-German relations, while at Warsaw the German minister began unusual conversations with Colonel Beck. Finally, at Mussolini's instance but, to be frank, with scant enthusiasm, he was a party to the Four-Power Pact and on June 7 signed that document in the name of the Reich. Hitler hoped he had thus proved sufficiently that, despite the calumny of German refugees abroad, National Socialism had not isolated Germany and was in no sense a menace to Europe.

But peaceful though Hitler might pretend to be, the major problem in his eyes was that of German armament, still pending before the Disarmament Conference in Geneva. In this field he quickly realized that France represented the chief obstacle in his way. That obstacle he could neither clear nor directly and forcibly overturn. He recalled the occupation of the Ruhr, which could always be repeated, and he did not forget that the fate of the Saar remained uncertain. He must therefore get around or rather smooth out the French obstacle; he must compose his differences with France.

Unfortunately in *Mein Kampf* he had written pages bristling with fierce rancor and hatred toward my country. To settle accounts with France once and for all, to break her back forever, such, to the doctrinaire of *Mein Kampf,* was the first task incumbent upon a Germany regenerated by National Socialism. German nationalism was by definition anti-French; how much more so Nazism, which was simply an exasperated nationalism? One of the party's favorite songs had always been *"Siegreich wollen wir Frankreich schlagen*—Victorious, We Mean to Crush France!"

In the course of the year preceding Nazi accession to power none of their leaders ever once entered into direct or indirect relations with me or with any person in my embassy, and the National Socialist press never missed a chance to voice its deep-seated Francophobia. Requested after January 30 to re-

ceive the French journalists accredited to Berlin, Hitler roundly
refused. His feelings since writing *Mein Kampf*, in an atmosphere created by the presence of black troops in the Rhineland
and of a French army on Ruhr territory, may have subsided
somewhat, but he was still patently moved by hostile prejudice against us. Further, he must necessarily have known that
we were aware of it and that we for our part looked upon his
regime, his person, his ideas, and his acts with disapproval and
mistrust. Such being the case, it was not easy for him to adopt
the attitude which his opportunism counseled. Yet this was
the road he determined to follow.

On April 8 I had an interview with him at the Chancellery.
General von Blomberg's presence indicated that the disarmament question was uppermost in Hitler's mind. I was already
familiar with Hitler's countenance, voice, gestures, and ora-
tory, but I was now meeting him for the first time in diplomatic conversation. Viewing him at close range while he was
relaxed, I was struck, as I was to be struck whenever I approached him later, by the vulgarity of his features and the
insignificance of his face, though I realized that this very insignificance made him the representative of those masses which
acclaimed him and recognized themselves in his person. Nor
was I ever affected by his glance, which so many others considered magnetic but which always seemed to me to be vague,
dull, and opaque, save when some violent urge possessed him
and anger swept over him. Even at such moments, however,
I could not help feeling that his wrath was more comical than
frightening. During our conversation he behaved quite courteously, displayed no personal embarrassment, and was apparently quite at his ease, if fairly reserved and somewhat aloof.
He expressed himself in downright, clear terms which bore all
the earmarks of frankness.

I began our conversation by reminding him of that passage
in his Reichstag speech in which he had declared that good
relations between Germany and France seemed to him to be

desirable and possible. Next I expressed my fear that, in view of the regime's propaganda and the constantly aggressive anti-French tone of its press, this hoped-for improvement in relations between the two countries might prove impossible.

He replied with a long development of arguments. The propaganda I was complaining of did not imply that the Third Reich was war-minded. Franco-German relations depended more upon France than upon Germany. Why was France unwilling to accustom herself to the idea that a nation of sixty-five million inhabitants should rehabilitate itself? France was treating Germany much as the Reich authorities had treated National Socialism during the last few years. Yet the government Hitler headed was deeply and genuinely peace-loving. A war, even victorious, would cost more than it could yield. To suppress unemployment, to repair the economic crisis, to feed a hungry population, such were the problems with which he was coping. Their solution was to be found not in war but in an effort of pacification and European collaboration such as Mussolini had initiated with his plan for a Four-Power Pact. Hitler acknowledged that the revision of treaties was a complex and ticklish business which could not be settled overnight, but it had not occurred to him to consider resorting to warfare, even in order to change the present status of Germany's eastern frontiers. On this score German security was improperly assured. Why should not France, secure on her eastern border, allow Germany to become so on hers?

I objected that Reich rearmament, far from isolating storms, would on the contrary unleash them in all quarters. Peace in Europe and co-operation among European nations were also France's goal. At Geneva she had suggested a pact of arbitration and mutual assistance. The simplest and most efficient way to clear the atmosphere again and to permit a reduction of armaments would be to rally to France's plan.

Hitler confessed that he had never been aware of this plan. Blomberg confirmed its existence but took pains to add that most of the great nations had not seen fit to adopt it. Hitler then launched into sharp criticism of the Geneva organization; its worn-out machinery seemed to him incapable of leading to the agreements expected of it. In his opinion direct conversations between the powers concerned would prove infinitely preferable. Blomberg declared that, come what might, Germany would maintain her position, claiming the right to possess such weapons as were available to all nations. At that, such a dispensation would not constitute true rearmament; indeed, it was much to be regretted that this term had been injected into the discussion, for it served only to excite bitterness. Hitler and the General again insisted upon what a nightmare it was for Germany to know herself surrounded by neighbors against whom she must remain defenseless.

I replied that if they would only consider that none of these neighbors had displayed any intent of aggression against Germany, the ghastly nightmare they spoke of would be speedily dispelled. At all events I requested the Chancellor to temper the sensationalism of his press and to invite it to abstain from provoking the legitimate resentment and the mistrust of public opinion in France. Hitler nodded affirmatively and the conversation came to an end. It was clear that the Chancellor had been interested mainly in establishing contact, in presenting himself as a man of good will who was not by principle an enemy of France, and in feeling his way toward the direct conversations which Papen had failed to bring about. As for the bases of the problems discussed at Geneva, he was still but sketchily informed and he relied upon the competency of the Reichswehr Minister, who in this field directed German policy.

The Disarmament Conference at Geneva could scarcely be said to have made signal progress since the day when Germany, under Papen's rule, had walked out for want of obtaining "equality of rights." Still the Conference had at least resumed operations. Papen's tactics must be accounted as not too bad since, after the Reich withdrew from Geneva, the other powers strove earnestly to discover a formula that might prove acceptable to both France and Germany.

As a result, on December 11, 1932, the Conference declared textually that one of its objects was to be "Authorization for Germany and other disarmed powers to enjoy equality of rights within a scheme providing security for all nations." With Schleicher at the helm, Germany accepted this definition of her desired goal and resumed her place at the Conference. Alas! no sooner was this ideal solution to be applicable than everyone realized how nothing could come of it because it lent itself to various interpretations which each party advanced according to its own personal lights.

The accession and conduct of the National Socialist regime complicated and aggravated the debate. As early as the days when Papen and Schleicher ruled, it was apparent that the Reich was remiss in honest observance of the clauses of the Treaty of Versailles. Reichswehr soldiers were being mustered out before the accomplishment of their seven-year service in order that Germany might increase the number of its trained effectives and deliberately build up the authorized *Schutzpolizei* or *Schupo,* making the latter a kind of complementary army. Much suspicion and objection were also aroused by the Steel Helmet and the *Wehrsport* or War Games which this association and its numerous affiliates encouraged.

What, too, of the Storm Troopers and Shock Troopers, numbering over a million men, with a system, a hierarchy, equipment, and training that were frankly military and that needed only weapons to make of them out-and-out infantry effectives? What to say of the chauvinistic propaganda launched systematically by the Third Reich with an abundance and variety of resources hitherto unknown? What to say of how the existence of such groups, flatly contradicting the formal pacific assurances of the Führer, tended to encourage throughout Germany a spirit of *revanche* and a war mentality?

Was this a propitious time to disarm, thus yielding the margin of superiority which the French Army still enjoyed? Was it prudent to grant to this Germany the artillery, tanks, and planes which she lacked or which she was even now manufacturing secretly in small quantities? Would the Disarmament Conference be fulfilling its mission if it ended by effectually legalizing even limited rearmament by the Reich? Was the Conference to commit an act which belied its very name?

France thought not, but her partners within the Conference were not wholly in accord with her. The British especially and President Roosevelt were very eager that the Conference should achieve positive results. Arthur Henderson, the British representative, presided. He was close to believing that the discrimination imposed upon the Reich could not last indefinitely and that it was not unreasonable to accede to Germany's demands if they were moderate. London was as shocked and worried as Paris by the attitude of the Nazis. But the British Government seemed disinclined to contract any engagement which went beyond the stipulations of the Pact of Locarno and which, face to face with growing insecurity, would have enforced guarantees of security. Italy, for her part, was favorable to the German argument but carefully left a way open whereby she might play the arbiter and conciliator within the Four-Power Pact.

France was practically alone in opposing claims proffered by the Reich. Germany stubbornly denied that the Brown and Black militias were in any way military; they were, she argued, but political constabulary. Since France had brought up the question of paramilitary formations, Germany replied by raising the question of colonial armies, requesting that the French colonial forces be included among the total effectives of the French Army. Germany, the argument went on, would proceed only quite gradually to apply the principle of equality she was claiming; indeed, she would rest content with an equality purely relative. But she cited the promise implicit in the formula of December 11, 1932, and she called for its application.

Aware that France would not blithely consent to disarm, and basing her argument upon a dubious interpretation of the Treaty of Versailles, Germany clung steadfastly to the dilemma she had cited from the outset. She had disarmed, she said, according to her obligations. Either the other powers should disarm too as they had promised—in which case Germany sought nothing—or they should not disarm, in which case Germany should be granted the right to rearm under the same conditions, if not to the same extent. The German thesis, set forth by Ambassador Nadolny, was far from ineffectual.

On March 16 Ramsay MacDonald suggested a disarmament plan. It provided a uniform type for the armies of European nations, to be based on a short eight-month or one-year service and on limited effectives and matériel. The strong powers would progressively decrease their armaments until these matched the status imposed on the feebly armed powers. Equality was to be achieved within a period of five years. France would be allowed a continental army of 200,000 men of the type adopted and a colonial army of the same strength; Germany would transform her Reichswehr into an army of 200,000 men of the type adopted and would receive new weapons only when this change was effected.

The British plan gave no one full satisfaction. The French considered that control was not defined strictly enough and that security guarantees were not set forth with sufficient clarity. The Germans did not welcome an equality active only after an interval of five years yet entailing a radical change if not an enfeeblement of the Reichswehr. But as the British project had the advantage of being already in existence and of furnishing concrete matters for consideration, the powers unanimously adopted it as a basis for discussion. The debate did not follow the lines that the Reich had hoped for; Ambassador Nadolny put forward the German theses in new, more peremptory, categorical tones, better suited to the style of the Third Reich.

The British and French representatives, Eden and Massigli, replied forcefully. The conflict arose again, the majority proving itself unfavorable to Germany's pretensions. We were heading toward a new crisis. It was unloosed on May 11 by a ballot which decided that paramilitary organizations, that is to say the SA and SS, were to be classed as army effectives. From that moment on Hitler certainly considered breaking off relations with the Conference and with the League of Nations. But he judged that the propitious hour had not yet struck. His credit did not appear to him to be based solidly enough on public opinion in his own country; and abroad, too, people had not yet learned to see in him the qualified representative of the whole German realm. While gaining time he felt that he must furnish proof abroad that he had all Germany behind him; he must also display such moderation and pacifism as would discharge him in advance of all responsibility and assure him the moral advantage at least in the eyes of his compatriots. Only then could he carry out his long-premeditated plans of shaking free from Genevese protectorship once and for all.

When news was spread of the Conference's hostile vote Hitler assembled the Reichstag forthwith. The Goebbels press, warning the public of the importance of the forthcoming event, had created the required atmosphere of patriotic emotionalism and solemn gravity. Meanwhile secret pressure was exerted upon deputies whose attitude was uncertain, especially the socialists. Amid a greater curiosity because President Roosevelt was known to have sent a message to Marshal Hindenburg, Germany and the rest of the world, all agog, speculated on the outcome of these preparations. Hitler's speech, on May 17, was carefully calculated to depict him as a chief of government filled with moderate and lofty views, favoring conciliation but also firm and dignified. Side by side with the ritual condemnation of the Treaty of Versailles, he uttered sentences like:

"Germany does not want war. The love we bear our own people makes us respect the rights of other nations. . . . We are not dreaming of Germanizing peoples which are not German. . . . Any peace treaty should not revive old wounds but rather close them. . . . Germany," he continued, "is requesting only the application of common law. She has demonstrated her good will by disarming; let the other powers now demonstrate theirs by doing likewise. . . . People keep citing the SS and the SA, but these organizations have received neither financial support nor military instruction from the Reichswehr; their sole task is to maintain internal order against the Communists. . . . France invokes her anxiety as to her security, yet France it is who remains armed whereas Germany has disarmed. . . . It has been declared desirable that Germany's military status be modified; Germany is willing. She has concurred in the proposed MacDonald Plan, but on condition that it establish a strict parallelism and true equality among the powers involved. . . . If a decision were to be imposed upon Germany under pretext that it was a majority decision, then Germany would refuse to yield, preferring rather to resign from both the Disarmament Conference and the League of Nations. . . ."

The Reichstag unanimously applauded and approved the Chancellor's declaration. Even the Socialists, whom Hitler was five weeks later to banish from the assembly, voted in favor. At home, then, the session had exerted the desired effect: Hitler appeared to even the malcontent as a wise, reasonable man. Abroad Hitler's threatening conclusion was not properly appreciated, so that the speech left foreign opinion with the impression that an understanding was still possible. But such hopes were soon vitiated by the spectacle of a Reich continuing to indulge Nazi violence and vexation. Nor did the German delegates at the Disarmament Conference appear to possess that spirit of conciliation and concession which their Führer had proclaimed. After a brief lull the sessions resumed their stormy course, to be adjourned during October without visible progress.

On September 15 an incident brought me face to face with Hitler again. At the conclusion of the Nuremberg Congress, the Führer having distributed flags to the militia, the SA of the city of Kehl proceeded home bearing a banner which bore the word "*Strassburg*." I protested against this to Baron von Neurath but I also believed it advisable to request an explanation from the Führer in person.

Hitler readily expressed his regrets: the provocative inscription on the banner had escaped his notice, otherwise he would not have tolerated it. He had not the slightest intent of claiming the return of Alsace to the Reich. He knew Alsatians through personal experience; he knew that, whether attached to France or Germany, they would never be satisfied with their lot. It was therefore quite useless to go to war on this account.

Next the Führer, now far more cordial than at our interview on April 8, protested his sympathy for France; he even professed his esteem for French character, for French military power, and for the power of French national sentiment. He added, word for word: "If I nourish any ambition, it is that some day a monument may be raised to me as the man who brought about reconciliation between Germany and France. There is only one problem that divides us," he went on, "the problem of the Saar; but it should not be difficult to solve this problem without waiting for the results of the plebiscite."

As he spoke, his air was one of perfect sincerity. Yet how to reconcile such words with the frequent anti-French demonstrations going on in the Reich at that time—that at the Niederwald Monument, for instance, attended by Hitler himself and the most Francophobe citizens of the Saar? Actually Hitler was steadfastly pursuing his designs; foreseeing an early breach with Geneva, he meant to dispel our mistrust in order to win us over to the idea of the tête-à-tête negotiations he expected to inaugurate.

Late in September it was clear that clashes in the Disarmament Conference were fated to grow increasingly fiercer. The League of Nations was holding its annual assembly, and Goebbels caused himself to be included in the German delegation. The assembly applauded and cheered as Chancellor Dollfuss, who was then stoutly defending Austria's freedom against the Nazi menace, entered the hall. Goebbels' entrance met with hostile murmurs and derisive laughter; nor did the German Minister of Propaganda achieve greater success with the foreign journalists to whom he attempted to represent the Third Reich as an essentially pacific state. Undoubtedly Hitler felt the hostility shown his lieutenant to be an affront to himself.

That summer brought France, Britain, and the United States together in Paris where a project was agreed on to modify the MacDonald Plan, reinforcing it with further precautions. Hitler could have swallowed no pill more bitter than to be faced with a united front of the great powers, and worse, a front established by consultations in which he had not taken part. The system worked out by France, Britain, and America, with Italy's agreement, proposed that the five-year interval predicated in the MacDonald Plan be extended to eight years and divided into two periods.

The first period, of four years' duration, was to be a trial period, serving to set control in motion and leading gradually to the type of army outlined in the British plan. The Reichswehr, a professional army, was to become a militia, while the other powers prepared the reduction of their own armaments. If this initial period proved satisfactory, the nations would proceed to the second period, in which disarmament would progressively advance, equality to come into being by right and in fact at the end of the eighth year. This project was communicated to Neurath on September 28 during the League of Nations session. Neurath immediately rose in indignation, protesting that the Reich could be no party to it.

In general, whenever the Reich protested its desire for general disarmament it was uttering an untruth. What the Reich wished was not the disarmament of other nations but its own rearmament; it wished to be able to create a powerful army with tanks, 150-millimeter cannons and airplanes. Equality through disarmament at the end of eight years held no charms for Germany.

On October 6 the German Government announced that it could not second a project which left Germany discriminated against and placed her in a state of inferiority over a period of years. The institution of a trial period was offensive to German feeling, the note continued, and postponement of the second period might be too easily achieved under pretext that first-period control had proved unsuccessful. Despite German opposition the powers maintained their stand; it was set forth and defended by Sir John Simon before the committee of the Conference on September 14.

That very day a note from Neurath to Henderson stated that, given the Conference's persistent refusal to grant Germany the rights she was entitled to demand, given also the inability of the League of Nations to command respect of an essential article in the treaty, the Reich Government had decided to abandon both the Disarmanent Conference and the League of Nations.

The moment for which Hitler had lain in wait was now at hand; the Chancellor would have no trouble in rousing German public opinion by recalling the conditions other powers had sought to force upon him: the eight-year interval, the trial period, and the institution of an arbitrary control. Here was material aplenty to fire national feeling! The German public learned at one stroke that Hitler was breaking with the League of Nations, that he had dissolved the Reichstag, and that he was appealing to the people, which was invited to approve the policy of its government and to elect new deputies.

A double proclamation accompanied the publication of this news. The first, made by the government, set forth how, being forced by circumstances to choose between a breach with the League and dishonor, it had preferred the breach; the second, made by the Chancellor, announced that he would hold a plebiscite. Both documents were curious in that on almost every line they stressed good will, the determination for peace, and the desire for agreement, collaboration, and reconciliation that inspired the Reich Government and the Führer.

That evening, in a radio broadcast, Hitler renewed his pacific declarations, addressing particularly to France, whom he named "our old but also our glorious adversary," his assurances of esteem and congeniality. He thus inaugurated tactics which he was regularly to employ in the future. They consisted in drowning the act of violence which he had just accomplished under a flow of lenitive words, of cordial affirmations and of tempting propositions.

In the campaign preceding the plebiscite he presented himself with the most imperturbable aplomb under his most benign aspect. He posed as the surgeon who had used his lancet, aye, but in the patient's interest. Or, better, it was not he who had left the League of Nations of his own accord, he had been forced to abandon it when confronted with solutions incompatible with Germany's honor. He was also careful to indicate that in leaving Geneva he had not spoken his last word. It was not he who sabotaged the Conference; he merely opened the way to a more fruitful procedure, that of bilateral conversations; and he made it clearly understood that he wished to arrive at a ruling through a direct agreement with France.

One detail shed light upon Hitler's astuteness. The same decree which ordered the dissolution of the Reichstag suspended indefinitely the diets of the *Länder* and increased the powers of the *Statthalter*. Profiting by the fact that public attention was focused on the foreign problem, Hitler completed the abolition within his boundaries of all particularistic privileges. More, he bound the Geneva litigation to the body of his domestic policy, couching the question to be asked of the German people in the following terms:

"Men of Germany! Women of Germany! Do you approve the policy of your government? Are you prepared to declare that it expresses your own opinion and your own will and solemnly to make it your own?"

The Reichstag elections this time were held in conformity with the principles of the Third Reich. There were no rival lists, but a single list established by the government; all negative votes were considered null and void; so that it was the total of these null and void ballots that approximately reflected the opposition's opinion. The single electoral list won 39,500,-000 votes against 3,300,000 blanks. On November 12 Germany answered the plebiscite question by 40,500,000 affirmative votes against 2,100,000. The opposition in Germany did not constitute even 10 per cent! That demonstration established Hitler as the qualified chief of a people united under his aegis.

In Geneva, as soon as the first feelings of emotion had subsided, resignation followed. No one breathed a word about sanctions. Members were satisfied to refute German allegations and to adjourn the debates, hoping that normal diplomatic exchanges would in the interval allow the refloating of the shipwrecked Conference.

Thus Hitler reached his ends in the field of foreign politics just as he had in all others. He had achieved the resurgence of his own land. He had freed himself from the League of Nations without Germany's suffering any apparent damage. His cleverness and his audacity had borne their fruit.

It is astounding to consider what he had accomplished between January 30 and the autumn of 1933. He had overthrown the Weimar Republic and reared upon its ruins his total personal dictatorship and that of his party; he had swept away all his political adversaries and strangled all liberty; he had gagged the *Länder,* he had smashed their individualist tradition, and he had centralized the German Reich more than it had ever been centralized before; he had installed and set into motion a new regime with all its characteristic institutions; he had overturned the state; finally he had shaken Europe just as he had shaken his own country, and he had conjured up in international councils the picture of a Germany that was emancipated, awakened, and to be feared. In the years to follow, he was but to develop his work, adding nothing essential to it. As early as the close of 1933 National Socialist Germany was firmly established with its customs, its procedures, its vocabulary, its gestures in greeting, its slogans, its fashions, its art, its laws, and its festivals. Nothing was lacking. The Nuremberg Congress—the "Victory Congress"—proved this early in September in a finished, complete, triumphant ceremony. The party found itself flooded with applications for membership; it had to close its doors for fear of being overrun.

Is it exact to say that Hitler crushed opposition of every sort whatever? Closer inspection reveals that if there was no open opposition in a Germany which had suffered itself to be molded like clay, a masked opposition did exist. It came from among the former ruling classes which regretted that there was no chance now of a return to monarchy; they also worried about foreign reaction to German domestic events. And opposition also existed among the party's extremists, who reproached the Führer for not being radical enough, for bowing to the influence of the military chiefs and of the industrial bourgeoisie, for allowing the dynamism of the revolution to wane. To their way of thinking the revolution had not struck hard enough nor lasted long enough. They clamored for a second revolution.

Thus at the very moment when the plebiscite had assured Hitler of 90 per cent of the Reich's electorate, clouds were gathering on the horizon.

IV. 1934—THE CRUCIAL YEAR

INVITATION TO THE WALTZ

VERY shortly after his accession to power Hitler had attempted to establish contact with Poland. This was in truth cause for surprise, being clearly the very last initiative to be expected from the leader of an ultra-nationalist movement. The Germans had always looked down upon and detested the Poles, especially since Poland had formed an alliance with France, thus becoming the first among those nations which German opinion considered our vassals and which it accused of seeking to encircle the Reich. Moreover, the creation of the Corridor separating East Prussia from the body of Germany, and the granting to the city and territory of Danzig a statute isolating them from the Reich, were considered by every German without exception as monstrous and unbearable. The *Diktat* of Versailles had thrown an apple of discord between Germany and Poland, nullifying any attempt at conciliation.

Yet as early as May 1933 feelers which Hitler had put out were sufficient to enable him to announce in a press communiqué issued on May 4 that he had had an important conversation with Wysocki, the Polish Minister in Berlin, while similarly, in Warsaw, von Moltke, the German Minister, had had a talk with Colonel Beck, the Polish Foreign Minister. The Polish Government, in order to continue these exchanges of view, replaced Wysocki, too closely connected with the period of unfriendliness between the two countries, with Lipski, a younger man, better adapted to the atmosphere of relaxation and rapprochement which Poland sought to create. On November 16 a further step was taken. Hitler's reception of Lipski gave rise to a second communiqué: the two governments had decided to take up in direct negotiations all outstanding differences and to renounce all use of force in their mutual relations.

The reasons for the Führer's diplomatic action were easy to divine. He wished above all to allay the suspicions of Europe and to avoid foreign complications which might involve sanctions or a preventive war against Germany. Meanwhile he would find time to transform her along National Socialist lines and to restore her to her former strength. What more striking proof could he give of his peaceful intentions than to terminate a conflict which no one before him had been able to resolve and which was a cause of unending anxiety to all Europe? Indeed, subsequently, he never failed to invoke this magnificent alibi, claiming that no man had served the cause of peace with greater sincerity and liberality of spirit than himself.

Hitler needed this evidence at a time when he was about to break, or had just broken, with the League of Nations. Nor was he grieved to demonstrate that without going through

Geneva he could settle questions reputed impossible of settlement. On the other hand, determined as he was to shake off the shackles of Versailles, he found it useful to test the strength of the barriers with which the treaty had surrounded Germany; he would try to disjoint the system of states East of the Reich, solidary with France and more or less her clients. Finally, on the eve of celebrating the first anniversary of his revolution he wished to enrich his record with a diplomatic success which would lend him in the eyes of his own people and of the world the stature of a great statesman. On January 26, 1934, the press reported that a final interview between Hitler and Minister Lipski had permitted the conclusion of a German-Polish accord, to be signed that very day by Lipski and Baron von Neurath.

According to its terms the two parties announced their wish to inaugurate a new phase in their relations; with reservations as to observance of their international engagements and to respect of their internal affairs, each party undertook to consult the other upon all questions of mutual relations and to forgo the use of force as a means of settlement. In fine, they concluded a pact of consultation and nonaggression, valid for ten years.

This pact did not add much to the communiqué of November 16. It settled none of the moot points separating the two countries. It was rather the equivalent of a promise not to touch upon them for a period of ten years, and, in the interval, to adopt a friendly attitude in their mutual relations. None the less, at a time when National Socialism and its leader were sowing reprobation and alarm in Europe, this pact did constitute a strange manifestation.

The ministers plenipotentiary of the Little Entente, the Polish Minister, and I were in the habit, at this period, of dining once a month in a private room at Horcher's restaurant. The owner would light silver candelabra in our honor and adorn the table with Dresden china figurines representing

Napoleon's twelve marshals. Mastny the Czech, Balougdzic the Serb, Comnène the Rumanian, and Wysocki the Pole, differed in temperament, but they were intelligent, serious, and experienced men, excellent colleagues, entirely devoted to their duties, united by feelings of mutual esteem and sympathy, fully conscious of serving an identical cause and close common interests. The Belgian, Count de Kerchove, would often join us; always rushed and busy, he nevertheless loved laughter and talk and fun; full of life, he possessed a rich supply of varied anecdotes. His intelligent curiosity reached out in all directions.

We occasionally invited the British Ambassador, first Sir Horace Rumbold, then Sir Eric Phipps. The former was stiff, ruddy, tall, and phlegmatic, the latter of medium height, thin, supple, nervous—two opposite types of Englishmen, but both equally loyal, dependable in their relationships, perfectly upright and honest, and both equally revolted by the cynicism and cruel brutality of the Nazis.

I was bound by particular ties of friendship with Eric Phipps; he was my colleague for four years and ended his active career in Paris, where he left behind him the memory of a charming man and a great servant of the Entente Cordiale. I appreciated the delicacy of his feelings, his deep kindness, his playful humor, his unfailing amiability. He had lived much in France in his youth and showed a keen and indulgent understanding of our country. Possessed of a very steady and lucid judgment, he had seen through Hitler's real nature and had never been the dupe of the Third Reich. Events did not belie his keen insight. Before quitting this earth he was at least to know the satisfaction of seeing the collapse of that godless enterprise against which his brave soul rebelled.

My relations with his successor, Nevile Henderson, were equally good, though Henderson was one of those Englishmen who can never quite overcome the traditional anti-French prejudice with which they are born. A stubborn and stolid

Scotsman, a confirmed bachelor, an enthusiast of the chase, of dogdom and of golf, not very fond of society, of a simpler spirit but of a more difficult nature than his predecessor, he too was irreproachably loyal and honest. He had been sent to Germany to replace Sir Eric Phipps because it was felt in London that Phipps's hostility to Nazism was too marked.

Neville Chamberlain, the British Prime Minister, was determined to save the peace of the Continent at the price of even the greatest sacrifices. He deemed it possible, by friendly dealings, by marks of confidence, by careful treatment and by concessions, to contain Hitler's bellicose humor and ambitions. Henderson was to second this policy. "It is not I," I told him at our first meeting, "it is not I who will oppose you! So much the better if you succeed! But you will learn from experience!"

So instructive in fact did this experience turn out to be that he finally came to hold Hitler and the Third Reich in greater abhorrence than had even Eric Phipps.

At these dinners at Horcher's there reigned the most complete frankness. After Wysocki's departure we invited Lipski, his successor. He had arrived from Paris where for several years he had been welcomed as a friend. Now to our astonishment, Lipski was as silent, reticent, and reserved as Wysocki had been spontaneous and open. He listened without bringing any personal contribution to our little clearinghouse of information; it was as though he feared to compromise himself. We asked him about the negotiations announced in the communiqué of November 16. He answered evasively, giving us to believe that the conversations were making no headway.

It was precisely on January 25 that we dined together again and once more questioned him. He replied that German-Polish discussions were at present centered on economic problems and the establishment of an airline. Next morning we read in the papers that the German-Polish Pact had been concluded. We bitterly reproached Lipski. He claimed to have been ruled by formal instructions; his chief, Colonel Beck, had bound him to absolute secrecy. Of course we never invited him again; Poland's place at our board was thenceforth vacant.

The wider the scope of Hitler's actions, the less frequent—and frequented—did our dinners become. Melting away, or more exactly shrinking like shagreen leather, our dinners illustrated the growing process of disintegration produced in Europe by Hitlerian diplomacy.

The German-Polish agreement had nothing objectionable per se. The cause of peace seemingly had all to gain by this ten-year truce; and the understanding concluded between two peoples whose enmity was considered the most likely source of future conflicts should have given rise to real rejoicing. And such indeed would have been the case had the pact been concluded under normal conditions, namely in the broad light of day, within the framework of similar existing accords, under the aegis of the League of Nations, and more especially with the consent or participation of France, Poland's chief friend and ally. In that event the German-Polish Pact could have played a beneficent part and served as a starting-point in the elaboration of that "Eastern Locarno" which the diplomacy of the great powers was vainly seeking to establish. But Poland saw the matter in a different light. She had made a point of isolating herself in her tête-à-tête with Germany and of surprising even her friends by her signature to the pact.

Shortly thereafter I discussed the matter with Köpke, ministerial director of the Wilhelmstrasse. He was a man of sparkling vivacity and intelligence, with one of the best brains in the department from which he was soon to be expelled because one of his grandmothers was not of pure Aryan stock. I was telling Köpke that the German-Polish accord would have had a quite different and healthier import had Paris been a third party to it. "You are right," he replied. "We were of the same opinion. But the Poles refused!"

There was no mistaking it. France found herself confronted with the classical and characteristic change of partners for the next waltz! What promptings had Poland obeyed in deserting her regular partner?

France had most certainly offended Poland. Too many Frenchmen were in the habit of repeating that they were disinclined to get themselves killed off on the banks of the Vistula. Moreover the Four-Power Pact signed in June 1933 seemed to imply that only four, and not five, Western powers existed in Europe; this had deeply wounded the cabinet at Warsaw. And yet thanks to French effort this accord could not be interpreted as an all-European directorate; it was made in explicit conformance with the normal procedures of the League of Nations and carefully confined to its proper limits. Moreover France had been studious to allay Polish anxiety or Polish susceptibilities by a special démarche.

But most people had also forgotten a strange event which had happened on March 13, 1933. That day a Polish torpedo boat suddenly landed infantry units on the Westernplatte opposite Danzig. The various chancelleries and the Geneva authorities were much exercised about it. What did this gesture signify? The reasons inspiring it were not clear; the act looked like an act of provocation against Germany. Representations were made to Poland forthwith, calling upon her not to cause a conflict of unpredictable issue. After several days the detachment re-embarked and the torpedo boat disappeared. Many failed to realize the significance of the Polish gesture.

In point of fact Marshal Pilsudski was not slow to grasp the future dangers implicit in the coming to power of National Socialism and of the Hitler regime. He seems to have understood that these dangers must be crushed, broken in the yolk, as it were, before they became too formidable. Apparently then he wished to test the political spirit and resolve of the Allies by creating an incident out of whole cloth. Would they make the most of the occasion he offered them? The Allies merely heaped objurgations upon the Warsaw Government. Pilsudski, drawing the obvious conclusions, never doubted that some day the Third Reich and Russia must come to blows and that Poland must find herself caught between two fires. He preferred the Germans to the Russians. He therefore decided to orient his policy in that direction and to obtain guarantees from them. With all the ardor of one who had no love for either France or the states of the Little Entente, Colonel Beck gladly applied Pilsudski's directives. Out of all this rose the Polish-German Pact.

If the Four-Power Pact remained a dead letter, the same was not true of the accord between Berlin and Warsaw, which led to a series of supplementary accords, of conversations, of friendly exchanges and of mutual visits. Frontier incidents, hitherto so numerous, either ceased entirely or ceased to figure in press dispatches. Goering took to hunting lynxes and wild oxen in the forests of Poland; Beck took to sojourning in Berlin every time his travels brought him through the Reich capital. More, he never missed an opportunity to display a disagreeable or an hostile attitude toward France. Lipski remained courteous and affable, but kept steadfastly aloof. He dared not risk the charge of maintaining close relations with the French Embassy.

As for ourselves, we continued to treat Poland just as though nothing had happened. We displayed an extraordinary mansuetude. We scrupulously and fully observed every single pledge we had made to Poland—to the letter, just as we were to do in 1939.

THE NOTE OF APRIL 17, 1934

Withdrawing from the League of Nations, Hitler made it clear that he was not on that account abandoning his intention of solving the problem with which the Disarmament Conference was at grips. Repeatedly he pointed out that direct negotiations with France would accomplish this purpose more certainly than any other method. The notion of a dual debate of the sort was as unattractive to us as it had been when Herriot refused to countenance it. But it was difficult for France to evade the issue and, on principle, to neglect the last means by which the stalemate might be broken. The Allies themselves urged it upon us; Henderson, chairman of the Conference, was very insistent that we should accept the Führer's invitations. Moreover, discussions in conference having failed, it was but natural to resort to ordinary diplomatic channels and negotiation by ambassadors, as was usual in all other litigious questions.

The French Government finally accepted this viewpoint. But it took no step without informing the other parties interested and even the public. Britain and Italy were thus enabled to interpose in a controversy which, though transferred to chancellery levels, yet retained, from beginning to end, all the characteristics of a multilateral negotiation. The sole difference was that this negotiation, instead of being transacted in verbal debate, took the form of a laborious exchange of written notes, of questionnaires, of answers to questionnaires, and of memoranda and countermemoranda.

On November 24, 1933, on instructions from Paris, I called upon Hitler and, referring to his numerous previous declarations, I asked him to explain his statements and to specify how he proposed to solve the problem of disarmament.

In Neurath's presence, he proceeded to set forth his suggestions profusely and clearly. It was useless, in his opinion, to persist in the elaboration of a disarmament conference. In Europe's present situation, no nation could bring itself to disarm, France least of all; a convention for the limitations of armaments would therefore have to suffice. Germany would take part in it on condition that she did not have to remain in the humiliating state of inferiority and discrimination to which the Versailles Treaty had reduced her, and that she be authorized to rearm, on what, moreover, was a moderate scale. She therefore asked the right to raise an army of 300,000 men, based on conscription and short-term enlistment. This army was to possess armaments of like quality to those of other nations; their quantity would remain open to debate. Germany would furthermore accept the establishment of international control. Since she sought to attack no one, she was ready to conclude nonaggression pacts, valid for ten years, with all her neighbors. In addition she felt herself bound by the Treaty of Locarno which she had freely signed. Finally she desired prohibition of chemical and bacteriological warfare and of the bombardment of inhabited areas; she even hoped that total abolition of all bombing aircraft would be inserted in the new convention.

To these claims Hitler added an offer regarding the Saar basin. "The plebiscite to be held in this area," he stated, "will give us 90 to 95 per cent of the votes. Willy-nilly this result will be interpreted as a defeat for France, and the memory of this defeat will weigh upon Franco-German relations. Would it not be wiser jointly to abandon this plebiscite? In exchange for the return of the Saar to the Reich, the latter would agree to the extension of the present economic regime of the territory and to the exploitation of the mines by French companies and German companies or by mixed Franco-German companies."

The Führer's proposal concerning the Saar was immediately declined by the French Government. It was interesting at least in so far as it revealed its author's fears. Hitler was apprehensive lest, in case of conflict, we occupy the Saar basin permanently by way of sanctions or as a means of pressure. He judged us after himself. As a matter of fact France never thought of misusing the mandate entrusted to her and of violating her international engagements. She was even unwilling to accept the idea of any modification by mutual consent of the articles of the treaty which called for a consultation of the territory's inhabitants at the end of fifteen years.

As regards disarmament Hitler's suggestions proved that the German thesis had not varied one jot. It remained as originally put forth by the Reichswehr and it continued to chafe the

French thesis at the same sore spots. It still seemed to us just as unwise as ever to allow Germany to rearm, without gaining definite assurance from the experiment that eventual supervision could be satisfactorily exercised. And the Brown Shirt militia, numbering over a million men, still filled us with the same misgiving. Nor were the Führer's peaceful declarations, and the insistence with which he expressed his will to live on a basis of good understanding with us, sufficient to convince us of his good faith.*

We perceived on the other hand that his words were not without influence upon the governments of London and Rome. If Europe's efforts at disarmament were to come to naught, it was important that the blame should not be laid at our door, for this would give Hitler a moral advantage over us. Also the positions he had taken were not final and he might be persuaded to modify them, especially as some of them needed clarification. For these reasons the French Government considered it worth while to persevere in the discussions. Moreover the British Cabinet had shown marked interest in the declarations which the Chancellor had made to me; it had in turn instructed Sir Eric Phipps to question the Führer on this matter.

On December 11 I had a fresh interview with Hitler. I informed him that, while we declined his offer regarding the Saar plebiscite, we admitted that conversations looking to the economic future of the territory could usefully be undertaken. Furthermore, far from being convinced that disarmament was impossible, we remained determined to seek the solution of the problem by this means. At that, we did not refuse to examine the Chancellor's suggestions with a view to their elucidation.

* Although I had on several occasions suggested to Hitler that he soften the most violently anti-French passages of *Mein Kampf* in the form of a note to the effect that they had been written under the stress of emotions caused by the occupation of the Ruhr, he never, despite his declared willingness, could bring himself to do so.

For instance, under what conditions and within what lapse of time would the transformation of the Reichswehr be effected? Was the figure of 300,000 men, put forward by the Führer, unchangeable? If so, what would be the status of the Brown Shirt militia? Under what guise did the Chancellor envisage supervision? What was his interpretation of the pacts he had cited? How would they conform to the Treaty of Locarno?

Hitler expressed his deep regret at our rejection of his proposal concerning the Saar. Our agreement would have had a great symbolic significance and would have struck public opinion forcefully. But a conversation along economic lines, sundered from the plebiscite, would be meaningless; he gave up all thought of it. As for the remaining matters, he asked me to state my questions in writing.

Next day I sent him an aide-mémoire to which Germany replied on December 18 also in writing. This note gave rise to a second French memorandum followed by a reply from the Reich dated January 19.

Today it would be idle to treat these various documents in detail. They added nothing new to oft-repeated arguments, every aspect of which had been examined and discussed over and over again. Yet they were not altogether without value, for they brought Hitler to define more clearly the pledges of security which he would give in return for the equality which he claimed. The Chancellor expressed his willingness to subscribe to any supervising organization accepted by the other powers. He outlined rules applicable to paramilitary formations whereby these would be prevented from becoming disguised reserves capable of incorporation by the army. He consented to the SA and SS being obliged to observe these rules and to their being subject to supervision by the international control body. He defined the nature of the pacts which he offered to conclude with his neighbors; they would be pacts of nonaggression and consultation. He set forth the kind of armament to be used by the Reichswehr which was to be changed into a short-term army. He specified that he would be satisfied with defensive armament, consisting of cannons not exceeding 155-millimeter caliber, of tanks limited to six tons, and of pursuit planes numbering one half those of the French Air Force or one third of the combined total of the air forces of France and her allies.

But on the main point at issue, namely the immediate granting of this matériel to the Reichswehr, and on the figure of 300,000 men for the future effectives of his army, he did not yield an inch. In vain France specified at what periods and under what conditions she would disarm, cease heavy production, and stockpile or even destroy her existing matériel; in vain she suggested reducing her aviation by half or discarding it altogether in favor of an international air force which should constitute the only authorized military aviation: Hitler would not abandon his claims. Nor did we abandon our insistence that the proposed convention should provide for two periods, the first a trial period during which surveillance was to be developed, and a second period during which the Reichswehr was to receive its armaments. The gulf between the two arguments remained as great as ever.

Early in January 1934 Italy submitted a memorandum supporting the German argument on rearmament. Britain, after inquiries parallel to our own, attempted in a memorandum dated January 29 to reconcile the opposing viewpoints, or rather to combine them in a plan which favored granting of the matériel to Germany within four years and progressive suppression of French heavy armaments. The attempt was not a very happy one since it would have resulted in weakening the country which was least dangerous to peace and in strengthening the most threatening country; it could have proved valid only if it had also provided for extremely effective guarantees of security and execution. But it had at least this merit: it constituted an attempt to synthesize and draw together the conflicting views.

Matters stood thus when the storm of February 6 struck down the Daladier cabinet. The task of pursuing Franco-German negotiations fell to the Doumergue cabinet, that is to say to a cabinet which was bent upon repairing the tattered domestic unity by accentuating national feeling. Paul-Boncour, who had conducted the negotiations with much patience, tenacity, and presence of mind, was replaced by Louis Barthou. Immediately the change in atmosphere made itself felt.

On February 14 France replied to the German note of January 19. While this reply did not constitute a formal rejection, it was drawn up in colder and sharper terms than preceding ones; it indicated formal refusals where we had hitherto only made reservations; it stated bluntly that not to include the militarized police and the Brown Shirts among the 300,000 troops demanded by the Reich was unthinkable; and it rejected in absolute terms any idea that the German army could be granted additional equipment before having accomplished its transformation. Above all it formally, for the first time, accused Germany of having begun to rearm, exceeded her rights, and violated the stipulations of the Versailles Treaty. Decidedly the controversy was turning sharp to the point of acerbity.

Yet Hitler did not explode. He counted upon British and Italian support for his ultimate success. He replied a month later, on March 14, maintaining that the proposed disarmament could never reach a level low enough to relieve Germany of the necessity to rearm to some extent. As for the SA, he promised to submit them to an international regulation of paramilitary formations. But Germany would in no case accept any prolongation, to her detriment, of the unequal regime set up at Versailles.

The discussion thus turned in circles without being able to cross the deadline. The British were obviously eager to get it all over with. They sent us note upon note urging us to state what guarantees seemed to us to strengthen security sufficiently to gain our consent to a relative rearmament of the Reich. It was felt that a decision could no longer be postponed and that the hour for a clear-cut position, whether positive or negative, was about to strike.

For my part I felt that, after several months of parleying, the problem no longer presented itself in the same light as at the outset. Everything indicated that if a convention were not reached granting a limited and internationally controlled rearmament to the Reich, Hitler would rearm in any manner he saw fit, without limit and without control, but with the enthusiastic support of his people.

The crux of the problem lay in discovering whether the powers, particularly France, would leave Hitler free to rearm to any degree he might choose, or whether they would prevent him from doing so by force, punishing his flagrant disregard of treaty stipulations by the imposition of sanctions.

Every qualified person whom I sounded out upon the subject stated flatly that there was no possibility of any sanction being applied to the Reich in case of its rearming in violation of the treaty; England and Italy would not consent and France herself would merely denounce the offender to the League of Nations which in turn would assuredly be neither able nor willing to coerce him back to order.

In the face of such dereliction (alas! all too likely) it seemed to me that there was no use in clinging to the word "disarmament." Better a limited and controlled rearmament than unlimited, uncontrolled and unrepressed armament of the Reich! Any agreement, even a mediocre one, seemed to me better than none.

I left nothing undone to win over our leaders. It was a thankless task, for both public and parliamentary opinion steadfastly opposed any understanding with Hitler. Nevertheless the permanent officials of our Foreign Office recognized the validity of my argument. On April 9 I went to Paris in order to explain my point of view to the members of the government. That very day it was learned that the budget of the Reich, just published, included an increase of 50 million marks for the navy, 132 millions for the air force, and 175 millions for the army. Here was an open avowal that the Reich was beginning to rearm without further ado. From it, those opposed to a convention drew a further argument for insisting that, before all else, an international control should determine the real state of the Reich's armaments. But it was also proof that Hitler would rearm come what might, which contrariwise provided an additional argument in favor of circumscribing, or at least watching him, within the limits of a convention he might have accepted and signed.

Louis Barthou believed it best to conclude a convention linking and controlling a relative rearmament for the Reich. I saw him immediately upon my arrival in Paris and repeated in person what I had already written; as requested, I handed him a memorandum in which I had summed up in parallel columns the relative advantages and disadvantages of positive and negative solutions.

Barthou listened to me with the greatest attention, then said: "You have finished by persuading me!" But a moment after, with raised finger pointing to the ceiling, he added: "You must say all this up there! There is the man you must convince." Up there, overhead, was the room in which Gaston Doumergue, head of the government, had his private office.

I continued my visits, receiving the warmest welcome from the ministers with whom I spoke. They all assured me that they shared my views of the situation and that the government's decision would fulfill my hopes. But the scene changed when I called upon André Tardieu. I was bound by ties of friendship to him; I had been his fellow worker, I admired his outstanding intellectual gifts and his exceptional talents and, knowing his generous heart, I had a very real affection for him. There reigned between us a freedom of speech devoid of any oratorical niceties; we could speak as man to man.

That day he received me very badly. He spoke with brutal vehemence: "You are wasting your time! The convention which you favor will never be concluded for we shall never be a party to it! Hitler won't last much longer, his fate is sealed! Any convention with him would consolidate his power. Should war break out, not a week would elapse before he would be deposed and replaced by the Crown Prince. You have not sized up the situation properly; I advise you not to insist."

I asked him where he had obtained information that permitted him to indulge in such prophecies and I cast doubt upon their accuracy. To be sure, Hitler was encountering domestic difficulties, but he was very far indeed from the end of his tether. We would hear from him for a long time more. I believed that nothing could be worse than to allow him to rearm without exercising some kind of check and hold over him. Or else the first time he overstepped the mark we should set upon and destroy him. Would the government dare do this, I wondered?

Tardieu did not reply. He shook his head, drew wreaths of smoke from his exaggeratedly long cigarette holder, and refused to explain further.

The reception I received from Doumergue was quite different but equally disappointing. I spent a half hour with him. But throughout the audience I was not permitted to breathe one word. As soon as I attempted to broach the subject which inspired my visit, the Premier cut me short; he himself launched into an unending chatter, completely devoid of interest and punctuated by a little grunt peculiar to him. Had the object of my visit not been so serious, I would have laughed at this comedy. It was obvious that Doumergue knew but did not share my views. His mind was made up, he would listen to nothing that might shake it.

It was then that I grasped the full meaning of Louis Barthou's gesture in pointing with his finger to the ceiling. The
resolute hostility of the Premier, of André Tardieu, and of
certain other cabinet ministers, attenuated considerably the
value of the endorsement I received from Barthou, Minister
of Foreign Affairs. I understood that the chances of arriving
at an agreement were slim and I returned to Berlin without
any illusions.

On April 17 the French Government issued the awaited
note, addressed not directly to the Reich but in reply to
queries and pressure from London. This time our statement was
incautious and peremptory, as though to remove all possibility
of a reversal of opinion. It quoted the increase of Reich
military expenditure as proof of Reich rearmament, thus ruin-
ing the bases of any negotiation.

As the French Cabinet adjourned, it published the following
communiqué: "M. Louis Barthou submitted the text of the
reply he drew up in concert with the Premier in answer to
the latest British note. It was adopted unanimously. Having
read this text, M. Barthou developed its principal points, adding lucid and eloquent comments of his own. An exchange of
views ensued, several cabinet members voicing their respective
opinions. Whereupon, it was the unanimous sense of the
cabinet that the draft submitted by the Minister of Foreign
Affairs be adopted."

Later, Louis Barthou told me that he had been in conference
with Doumergue on the eve of the cabinet meeting. Just as
the Minister of Foreign Affairs was about to read the project
he had framed in favor of an agreement, the Premier, drawing
a paper from his pocket, said: "No, no, my friend, keep your
proposal to yourself and take this one. It is the proper one.
It was drawn up jointly by the two state ministers and by
myself. This is the text we are offering the cabinet."

Barthou was in the most delicate quandary. To persist in his
opinion against that of the chief of the government would

mark a step toward his own resignation and might easily entail the dislocation of the cabinet, formed only two months before, and revive a crisis from which the country was still recuperating. Could Barthou—a member of the French Academy, the author of the three-year-military-service law and a hardened patriot—provoke the fall of a National Union Government by striving at all costs to seek agreement with Germany?

France knew that the race for armaments was about to begin again; but her leaders were convinced at the time that we would retain an immense superiority in such a race. "You will see how long it will take Germany to catch up with the twenty billions we have spent on armament!" the Chief of the General Staff told me.

The Chief of the General Staff did not foresee that the Third Reich would cease to publish its budget, that it would suppress all quotation of the mark abroad, and that, having equalized its imports and exports, it would settle down within a closed and impenetrable circle containing all the funds it desired. What did twenty billion francs mean to a dictator who had the backing of an industry infinitely more potent than ours and who was later to confess that he had spent ninety-seven billion marks for the rearmament of his country?

Obviously Hitler's good faith in this debate was more than dubious. I did not believe that he would scrupulously observe limitations and rulings imposed by an international convention; I knew he would cheat. But I did believe that the existence of such a convention would embarrass him and slow him down; that the institution of a board of surveillance, to which complaints might certainly be addressed, would hamper the freedom of his movements; and that abuses cited by this board would place him in a poor position both before nations too readily inclined to trust him and before his own people. I also believed that publicity given to his acts of fraud, constituting a warning and an alarm more arresting than ambassadorial reports, would incite our government and the whole country to devote all their energies, all their labor, and all their ardor to increasing the strength of our military apparatus.

Now the moment Germany began to rearm freely, it was clear that one of the pillars of the European order had crumbled. The status of Europe as established at Versailles rested upon the fact that Germany was disarmed. If, ceasing to be so, she reappeared on the stage as a great military power, then everything was changed: a new phase was beginning, the edifice was tottering, and peace henceforth would be but war postponed; the defenders of peace would have to keep up in the race for armaments, and France in particular would have to assemble her forces, redouble her activity, correct her heedlessness and superficiality, remedy her increasingly frequent political crises, and operate a reform from top to bottom. Who would dare maintain that this is what she did?

At any rate the note of April 17 gave us the disadvantage of appearing as the perpetrators of the failure of the Disarmament Conference. In an interview to which he had summoned the foreign journalists on April 27 in Berlin, Neurath emphasized the Reich's good will, breadth of mind, and spirit of conciliation in contrast with a France which kept stubbornly refusing to grant Germany legitimate satisfaction. In the course of his argument, though, he made a slip. Explaining the increase of military expenditure which angered France, he described it as but a result of the Reichswehr transformation which France had recommended. Here was a confirmation that Germany had already reorganized her new army. At the same time Hitler sent Ribbentrop on a mission of information to London and Rome. It was the first public manifestation of the confidence Hitler had in this conceited and incapable man whom he was later to make his Minister of Foreign Affairs.

Was it still possible to save the Disarmament Conference? Efforts were made to do so, though everybody felt that the Conference had received a mortal blow. On June 8 after a stormy debate it adopted a formula which transferred to the ordinary League of Nations commissions the study of pending questions. In other words the Disarmament Conference was resigned to its burial.

France held that the best manner to check German ambitions was to face the Reich on its eastern border with a system of interlocking pacts of assistance offering a common front against a potential aggressor. Poland, the Soviet Republics, Czechoslovakia, and France herself were to form the links in this security chain which in its whole would represent an "Eastern pact" similar to the Western pact of Locarno. Germany would not be excluded at outset; on the contrary she would be invited to participate in this pact, thereby proving the sincerity of the peaceful intentions she advertised.

Here was a challenging plan in theory but difficult of realization in practice, and how fragile! Never were so many peace pacts concluded as in the years immediately preceding the war! Louis Barthou, who judged it useful to tighten our bonds with the Little Entente, saw clearly during his visits to friendly capitals in April and in June that the Little Entente lacked its former cohesion; if Czechoslovakian and Rumanian feelings toward us had not changed, it was obvious that in Warsaw those of Colonel Beck were anything but warm.

It was rash to believe that Hitler's Germany would be disposed to consult with the Communist republic which was the principal target of her propaganda. And, indeed, the Third Reich was never willing to take part in the scheme. Following Germany's negative attitude, Poland, too, hastened to abstain. The clearest part of the Eastern pact reduced itself to an agreement between France and the USSR signed in Paris on May 2, in Moscow on May 14. But Hitler pretended to see in this pact a return by France to the Russian alliance and to the policy of encirclement directed against himself. Despite the cautionary measures we had striven to put into the Locarno Treaty, Hitler considered our present move incompatible with the stipulations of that pact, a pretext he used in his attempt to justify his lightning reoccupation of the left bank of the Rhine in March 1936.

THE MASSACRES OF JUNE 30, 1934

Despite the speed and ease with which Hitler had installed his regime and his party in power, he was faced with many serious difficulties at home in the spring of 1934. Nazism was weathering a crisis. There was the open clash against the churches; there were the enormous Nazi expenditures which raised the ghost of inflation; the increase of arrests and deportations to concentration camps about which terrifying rumors ran rife; and a general mistrust and hostility throughout Europe. Hitler had also to fear lest a clumsy foreign policy expose Germany to the perils of isolation by adverse coalitions. All these factors stirred no apparent rebellion but they created a deep-seated uneasiness and they spread discontent and anxiety.

The opposition came especially from the high military command and from the Prussian nobility, from former Steel Helmet supporters and even from the tiny circle of Hindenburg's familiars. Papen, now Vice-Chancellor, was considered to be responsible for the Nazi rise to government; he was the daily object of bitter complaints and virulent reproach. There was talk of dissension within the party itself, but no one knew its cause or the persons involved. An iron curtain had been drawn down over reality. The Nazis themselves in their talk and in their newspapers uttered threats the exact sense and scope of which were obscure. The atmosphere was heavy, stifling, as before an imminent storm.

The first interview between Hitler and Mussolini took place in mid-June at Venice without producing the results awaited. The Führer was filled with admiration and respect for the Duce; he was deeply hurt by Mussolini's airy and patronizing manner. Mussolini judged his guest to be hotheaded, speechifying, confused and insufficiently attentive in accepting the advice tendered him. However he succeeded in making Hitler understand how ill-advised it would be for him, the Führer, to let himself be compromised by men useful in the hour of revolution but embarrassing in the future.

On June 17 Vice-Chancellor Papen made a sensational speech at Marburg. In extraordinarily free language he declared that the one-party system could be only a temporary measure. He recalled that Germany was Christian and deplored the fact that conservatives, who had always been good citizens and patriots, were being labeled reactionaries, and that anything connected with intellectual life was being discredited. Justice, he said, was the foundation of any state, and only a frank explanation to Germany as a whole could revive her certitude and her joy in action.

Such statements, coming from yesterday's chancellor and the Führer's official chief auxiliary, provoked intense excitement. What did this stern reprimand of the regime signify? Everybody knew that Papen was on the closest possible terms with Marshal Hindenburg; he would not have spoken thus without being certain of the approval of the Chief of State. How would his diatribe be received by those against whom it was directed? Of what augur was it and what was about to happen?

First, the press was forbidden to reproduce the Marburg speech and such newspapers as had already done so were seized. Rumor had it that Hitler, having roundly reprimanded Papen, went to Neudeck, where the Marshal resided, to give an account of his Italian journey. Less reserved, Goebbels in a meeting in Berlin on June 21 retorted angrily, threatening that the party would "ride roughshod" over the "gentlemen lolling in the armchairs of their tony clubs."

Two days later at Essen Goebbels renewed his threats. Hess on the Cologne radio and Goering in Franconia spoke in the same terms. On June 24, at the Hamburg Derby, Goebbels and

Papen met in the official grandstand. The crowd gave Papen an ovation as Goebbels sat by fuming with rage. On June 25 public attention was arrested by the announcement that the storm troopers of the SA were to be given furlough for the month of July and forbidden to wear uniform during that period. A further, even more striking announcement appeared in an article in the *Völkischer Beobachter* by General von Blomberg, Minister for the Reichswehr. Blomberg stated that since there was but a single party, identified with the state, the army would become the National Socialist Army, devoted exclusively to the Nazi regime.

In vain people wondered what this protestation of loyalty meant. Yet calm was restored. The press announced that Hitler had attended the wedding of one of his lieutenants at Essen on June 28 and had gone from there to inspect the work camps in the Rhineland. But suddenly on June 30 thunder broke loose.

In quick succession the following reports were made public. A certain Edgar Jung, an immediate collaborator of Papen's and presumably the writer of the Marburg speech, had been arrested in Munich where he was to be shot almost forthwith. Hitler had arrived in the Bavarian capital by plane from the Rhine and, having had some SA leaders imprisoned, had left for the spa of Wiessee, where Röhm, Chief of Staff of the SA and third ranking member in the party hierarchy, was staying. There in person in the middle of the night the Führer had arrested Röhm, who was sound asleep in bed, and had shot one of Röhm's colleagues, Heines, who was sleeping in the same hotel with a *Lustknabe*, a joyboy or professional catamite. Hitler had also sentenced a number of Nazi leaders to be shot for having planned rebellion and broken their oath of loyalty to the Führer.

In Berlin, late on the morning of June 30, the government security police surrounded a portion of the Tiergarten and occupied the SA headquarters. It made many arrests all over

Berlin. General von Schleicher, alleged to have attempted to resist, was shot down in his home; his wife, who sought to shield him, was murdered under the terrified glance of her daughter, a child of twelve. In the suburbs, in the region of the Lichterfelde Barracks, the firing of the execution squads was heard all day long Sunday. Berlin was rooted in stupefaction and terror.

Questions ran from lip to lip, bits of information were whispered here and there, and names quoted. Gregor Strasser, one of the most prominent Nazi leaders and the only one strong enough to figure as Hitler's rival and possible successor was among those executed, as was Ernst, SA chief of the Berlin Region, who had been caught at Bremen just as he was about to embark. Two close collaborators of Papen's were slain in their offices at the Vice-Chancellery. Papen himself was reported to be unhurt though assuredly under house arrest. News from Munich stated that Röhm, having lacked the courage to commit suicide, was shot down by a firing squad. In reality he was handed a revolver and invited to use it so that his voluntary death might appear as a confession of guilt. He refused and was shot in his cell.

Other persons who had played important parts not long ago, but whose existence had almost been forgotten, were also massacred; these included the aged von Kahr, head of the Bavarian Government at the time of the unsuccessful 1923 putsch, and Captain Ehrhardt, chief of the brigade that bore his name. Repressions and executions took place in a series of large cities. How many victims perished? Three hundred according to some, twelve hundred according to others; the latter figure would seem the more likely.

Seized with emotion and terror, public opinion was at a loss. People could not understand the reason for these summary executions. They knew of course that there were malcontents among the aristocrats and upper middle classes, in the *Herrenklub,* among former German Nationalists, among intellectuals and Catholics, and not only in Papen's circle but even in that of the old Marshal. But they did not know that there were conflicts sufficiently acute within the party itself to set up Röhm against Hitler. People could not perceive what connection could have linked Röhm with the discontented members of higher society. But the public was soon to be enlightened by Hitler himself in his speech to the Reichstag on July 30 at 8:00 P.M.

Pale, his features drawn, his voice hoarser than usual, the Führer stated that for some time previous Röhm's movements had been suspicious. Röhm had been playing personal politics; he had been steadily deviating from party lines. He had appointed men of ill repute to the highest ranks of the Brown Militia, homosexuals like himself, depraved, unscrupulous, and wicked. He had alienated the best elements of the party. Presently ambitious plans had sprung up in his mind; he had parleyed with General von Schleicher and Gregor Strasser with a view to preparing a bold coup, intended not to eliminate Hitler but to outwit him. Its objective was to persuade Hitler to dismiss Papen, putting Schleicher in his place, then to have the Führer dismiss General von Blomberg, Reichswehr minister. This done, the Brown Militia was to be amalgamated with the regular army and Röhm to be set in supreme command.

Hitler had declared himself completely opposed to this program. But instead of using his authority and adopting drastic measures, he had attempted to reason with the SA Chief of Staff and to put him back, in friendly fashion, on the right path. The nature of Röhm's plans had then changed, he was now flatly engaging in conspiracy. Röhm sought to make the Brown Militia believe that Hitler was betraying the National Socialist revolution, that he had fallen under the thumb of Blomberg and the old-style generals' clique, and that he was about to order the demobilization of the SA. It was therefore urgent, said Röhm, to forestall the Führer, to make a second revolution in order to save the first, and to seize the machinery of government.

Röhm, then, gathered money and arms, laid specific plans, and actually detailed a man to murder the Führer. Informed of Röhm's criminal intent, Hitler resolved to remove the SA leader from office; then, on June 29, he was suddenly warned that events had come to a head and that the conspirators were about to act. In point of fact on the morrow, June 30, at 4:30 P.M., the SA was to seize the ministries in Berlin; trucks had been alerted and that evening a similar operation was to be carried out in Munich.

Hitler, then resting at Godesberg on the Rhine, realized that he must precipitate matters. In the middle of the night he leaped into his plane with Goebbels and, while Goering was being commissioned to stifle the plot in Berlin, he personally, with his judicial hand, struck down the rebels at Munich and at Wiessee. "I punished the mutineers!" cried Hitler, claiming the right as representative of the German people to pass sovereign sentence without appeal. "I decimated the rebellious as has always been done at all periods of history! I ordered the leading plotters to be shot and this abscess to be cauterized."

So ran the official version of the drama of July 30 in its blend of truth and falsehood.

Certainly Röhm was a cynical adventurer. With his broken nose, his shaved head, and his air of brutality he was definitely repulsive. His homosexual habits were notorious. A fearless officer, wounded several times during World War I, Röhm possessed unquestionable military talents. In Bolivia, whither he had gone at the head of a German mission of military instruction, he had proved highly successful. Without Röhm, Hitler would never have been in a position to organize the Storm Sections, the Brown Militia. It is therefore not an exaggeration to state that the Führer owed his success in great part to Röhm.

When Röhm began to assemble and train the militiamen he

had been encouraged by the Reichswehr and had received its active aid, for the army saw in this corps a useful *ersatz*, a substitute for the military service abolished by the Versailles Treaty. But Röhm detested the Reichswehr. He was a front-line officer filled with animus against the titled squires who graced the staff. The Reichswehr could not forgive Röhm his emancipated ways, his contemptuous comments, and too, his pretentions to strategy, for he believed he had in him the stuff of a great military leader.

In this clash Röhm believed that he was not being supported by the Führer as firmly as he should have been. Embittered and sick at heart, he believed that Nazi access to power had not brought him the satisfactions he was justified in expecting. He wished the regime born of the revolution to be equipped with a new army, one of revolutionary inspiration formed about the nucleus of the Storm Sections, the Reichswehr to be incorporated with the militia, and he, Röhm, Minister of War. He certainly entertained thoughts of rebellion; he wished to raise himself and his SAS to independent status and, having begun to collect money, he was buying arms.

What credence are we to give that passage in the Chancellor's speech in which he declared that General von Schleicher was really associated with Röhm, for whom, fundamentally, Schleicher had nothing but contempt? There is nothing unacceptable in the allegation. Schleicher was none too fastidious about what means he chose; no excessive scruple would prevent him from exploiting such instruments as he believed might help him achieve his ends. He never hid the fact that he had vowed the downfall of the Nazi regime; he lavished loud sarcasm and unvarnished threats upon it and he was among the few men who could possibly upset it. Thus he might well have known of and supported Röhm's efforts, but nothing has so far been produced to prove such collusion.

It is much less probable that Röhm and his acolytes, with

or without the connivance of Schleicher, actually appointed June 30 as the date of their attempted *coup d'état*. When Ernst (chief of the SA for the Berlin Region) was arrested in Bremen, he had just boarded a liner on which he and his wife expected to take a three-week cruise to the Balearics. Röhm was nursing his rheumatism at Wiessee. He had taken no precautions, he was sleeping like a dormouse when Hitler surprised him. The very slumbers he and his comrades were enjoying seem to testify that the plotters were not about to strike. Further, a meeting of SA leaders had been called for June 30 at Wiessee, and Hitler had been informed of it. Even supposing it had determined to attempt rebellion, there could have been no question of carrying out such a resolution the same day.

Accordingly the information that Röhm and his comrades intended to act on June 30 was false. It had been trumped up in anticipation of events which were still only in the realm of possibility. It is doubtful whether Hitler was dupe or accomplice in these machinations. The haste with which he ordered the execution of the alleged rebels does not allow the latter hypothesis to be dismissed.

If the Chancellor spoke at length of Röhm in his speech to the Reichstag on July 13, he said almost nothing of a category of victims, numerous also, who did not belong to the Brown Militia and who had no close relations with the National Socialist party. Were Papen's intimates involved in the same plot as Röhm and his gang, for whom they professed the utmost repulsion? Hitler led his hearers so to believe, but it is incredible.

Truth to tell, these men were concerned not with Röhm's projects but with a vast intrigue of opposition which possessed far-flung ramifications. Apparently Edgar Jung was at its head, that young, ardent, bold intellectual, at once rash and candid, who had written the original draft of Papen's Marburg speech. Jung had made contact with malcontents among the aristocracy, the Catholic circles, and the intellectual classes throughout Germany; he used to write to them regardless of censorship and to telephone to them heedless of tapped wires. Yet it does not seem likely that Papen, his immediate chief, had been apprised of the secret. It also would appear that Jung never went beyond the preparatory phase.

The occasion offered by the maneuvers of Röhm and his acolytes was considered propitious by the leaders of the regime for the simultaneous destruction of two classes of opponents which were quite unrelated. A single liquidating operation would serve against both the Right and the Left; old scores like that against von Kahr in Bavaria would be wiped out as readily as newer ones; the carping critics among the higher classes would be recalled to order and, by means of a bloody example, one and all would be reminded that the Third Reich knew how to defend itself and refused to be undermined.

After interrogation and, doubtless, confession by duress of torture, Jung was killed at Munich; Gestapo bullets also accounted for the deaths of some hundreds of persons in Berlin and other cities. Certain people, victims of a similarity in names, were murdered by error; the Gestapo sent their ashes home to their families with a word of sympathy. Papen escaped the massacre, either because he was really innocent or because Goering, who directed the repressions, protected him through friendship, or finally, out of respect for Marshal Hindenburg, whose favorite he was. Was not the murder of his collaborators a warning eloquent enough for Papen and for the Marshal's circle, which was known to have approved if not directly inspired the Marburg speech?

In its earliest communiqués on the drama of June 30 the press had indicated more or less clearly that the culprits, Röhm and Schleicher, were dealing with foreign powers; it accused them of high treason. Hitler in his speech of July 13 had denounced them as traitors, citing General von Bredow, a former colleague of Schleicher's, as their agent in communications abroad; he had also alluded to a secret dinner during which they were alleged to have confided their criminal plans to a foreign "statesman." The press had hinted that I was the foreign statesman in question, adding that France was well aware of this plot, which explained the intransigent policy of Louis Barthou, French Minister of Foreign Affairs. The whole report was a pure falsehood.

I knew Schleicher tolerably well. I had seen him for the last time on Easter Monday when we spent the day together in the country. He was used to speaking freely to me and I never found cause to doubt his sincerity. That day he made no more of a mystery of his opposition to the regime than he had in previous conversations; but he at no time said anything indicating that he had subversive plans or was involved in any sort of plot; he at no time spoke the language of a traitor to his country, and whenever he uttered Röhm's name it was with contempt and disgust.

As for General von Bredow, his former deputy, the police had found among his files a few commonplace letters of introduction written to Belgian officers by Count de Kerchove, Belgian Ambassador in Berlin. These innocuous letters were six months old, written at a date when Bredow, newly retired, was planning a visit to Belgium which never materialized.

In a general way Louis Barthou was conversant with the domestic situation in Germany, but he had no more proof than I that a plot was being hatched. Unlike certain of his colleagues, he did not believe in the possible ousting of the Nazi regime. I was aware of Jung's secret activity but I had no idea of Röhm's maneuvers and I never suspected the acuity of his conflict with Hitler. Having always entertained the liveliest repugnance toward Röhm, I avoided him as much as possible despite the eminent role he played in the Third Reich. Von Bassewitz, chief of protocol, reproached me on this score; at his repeated entreaties I consented to meet Röhm at an evening reception. Our interview was scarcely cordial, our conversation without interest. Some time later, a banker prominent in Berlin society who enjoyed gathering at his board the most diverse personalities of the old and new regimes, begged me to dine at his house in order to make further acquaintance with Röhm. I accepted. Such was the famous dinner Hitler alluded to in his Reichstag speech. But Schleicher was not present.

Röhm came, flanked by six or seven youths striking in their smartness and good looks; the SA chief presented them to me as his aides-de-camp. There was nothing secret about the dinner, which took place at Horcher's, the smartest restaurant in Berlin; the guests were so uninterested in concealment that they parked their cars boldly on the lawn facing the banker's villa and close to the street. The meal was dismal, the conversation insignificant. I found Röhm sleepy and heavy; he woke up only to complain of his health and the rheumatism he expected to nurse at Wiessee. Returning home I cursed our host for the evening's boredom. But after June 30 he and I were the sole survivors, and he owed his safety only to the fact that he managed to escape to Britain. On this point too Hitler made use of totally false information.

It is surprising that the Reichswehr accepted Schleicher's murder so tamely. He was its true master for years and it owed him much; he had served it with passion. And yet he had no friends within its ranks. There were many to blame his taste for political intrigue, his ruses, his cynicism and his ambition; many of his colleagues considered his rapid advancement out of all proportion with his soldierly merits. There were many, also, to consider his collusion with Röhm an established fact, and to hold that by conniving with the leader of the Brown Shirts he had violated the *esprit de corps* of the Reichswehr and failed in his duty as an officer. Yet army leaders challenged the ignominious accusation of high treason publicly brought against Schleicher and von Bredow; they insisted on an investigation. Both generals were proved innocent; Nazidom had killed them but its efforts to besmirch their honor had failed.

In so far as I was concerned, I declared that I would not allow the insinuations of the press to disturb me. If I was suspected of plotting with Röhm, then let this be frankly stated, let the argument be produced and let the proofs of my alleged complicity be established. Naturally no such proof was ever found, let alone published. Through Koester, German Ambassador in Paris, the Wilhelmstrasse presented a note to the Quai d'Orsay stating that the suspicions leveled against me were wholly without foundation and that the Reich Government was happy that I was pursuing my mission in Berlin. One evening when I attended a performance of *Die Walküre* at the Opera, Hitler asked me to join him in his loge. During the intermission he was careful to let the public see us standing there, talking informally.

Such was the affair of June 1934. Many of its details are still shrouded in darkness, yet its importance in the history of National Socialism cannot be exaggerated, for it decisively presented the Hitler regime in its true light. It might have been followed by results dangerous to the regime. Since Röhm had ardent henchmen, the victims had relatives and friends, and public opinion was upset, it was permissible to believe that vengeance and reprisal would be indulged. But nothing of the sort occurred; everyone settled down in his corner and held his peace. The Chancellor's speech aroused no protest; the Reichstag unanimously approved the government and thanked Hitler for having through his energy preserved the country from civil war.

Better still for Hitler, Marshal Hindenburg sent the Chancellor a telegram widely published in the press to the following effect: "I note from the reports presented to me that by your resolute initiative and your courageous personal action you have nipped all the maneuvers of high treason in the bud. You have saved the German people from a great danger. I wish to express to you my deep gratitude."

Out of what pressure and trafficking and blackmail was this

text born? Certainly, given the feelings of the Marshal and his circle as voiced in the Marburg speech, and given the fact that Papen, compromised with certain victims of Gestapo firing squads, had himself escaped death by a hair, Hindenburg could not have drawn up or willingly accepted this document. Probably the aged man had been intimidated and outwitted, at once deceived by the reports presented to him and disturbed by threats against his son, his secretary, Meissner, his family, and his own person. Before a Hitler rampant, Hindenburg himself must have given way, baffled and contrite, thus removing the last scales of illusion from the eyes of those who had found in him their last resort.

The affair of June 30 shed light upon one of the Nazis' chief mainstays, the use of terror. The Gestapo demonstrated to what lengths it would go. Germany was no longer a *Rechtsstaat*, a country governed by law. The Führer claimed right of life and death over every German according to his own conscience.

The Reichswehr may have believed that it was emerging from the tragic episode to its advantage. As a matter of fact Blomberg proved to be a fatal leader. A dilettante, fascinated by Hitler's career and captivated by the charm of the tenebrous Führer, he lacked all perspicacity. To be sure, by striking Röhm down, Hitler had given Blomberg a pledge, but this did not mean that he intended to knuckle down to the regular army and to become the docile tool of the Reichswehr generals. Hitler knew that the General Staff was filled with adversaries who might use him in order to endow the Reich with an unequaled military power but who would never become serious converts to his regime. He felt that these conservative officers, this Junker clique, were a permanent danger to him and he firmly intended to eliminate them.

Antagonism between army and party continued, giving rise to many incidents, among which the most striking was the eviction of General von Fritsch. Hitler then assumed effective command of the armed forces through the assistance of

General Keitel, whom he had completely won over to his cause and who was devoted to him, heart and soul. Thenceforward, Hitler was supreme master.

THE MURDER OF CHANCELLOR DOLLFUSS

The stir caused by the drama of June 30 had scarcely subsided when a fresh Nazi crime once more sowed alarm and indignation over the earth. On July 25, 1934, Dollfuss, Chancellor of Austria, was assassinated.

He was slain by Austrian Nazis, but they were in close contact with the German National Socialist party and the conditions in which the crime had been perpetrated betrayed the same unforgettable Hitlerian trade mark as the Reichstag fire and the massacre of Röhm and his comrades. This act formed only one more tragic episode added to a long series of crimes of all sorts directed against the Vienna Government and its supporters. Yet one of Hitler's earliest gestures on assuming power had been to send a message of sympathy and friendship accompanied by greetings to a brother people and wishes for its prosperity.

In fact, Hitler did not intend to absorb Austria forthwith into the Third Reich; he was not going to effect an Anschluss whereby complications might arise abroad at a time when he did not judge himself capable of standing his ground. But he never doubted that events in Berlin must needs cause immediate repercussions in Vienna or that Austria, following Germany's lead, would herself unite in her turn to form a Nazi government. Thus there would be two distinct governments, with Vienna subservient to Berlin, until circumstances, seconded by appropriate propaganda, permitted the unification of the twin branches of the German family—a step which formed Article I of the program for Greater Germany.

In so thinking Hitler had not reckoned with the political, religious, patriotic, and moral scruples of many Austrians and precisely with those Austrians governing the sister people. These men had no desire to lose their independence or to mar the good relations they enjoyed with the Western powers, with the League of Nations, and especially with Mussolini's Italy, which had constituted herself protectress of Austria. More important, Hitler was reckoning without a man, small in build but great in heart, named Chancellor Dollfuss.

The resistance put up by the Vienna Government scandalized and exasperated Hitler and his Berlin Nazis; in their fanatical and sectarian mentality they could not conceive how a country of German race and language could be reluctant to leap into their arms. Dollfuss, refusing to bow to their rule, became for them a traitor to the German cause. That this little dissenter and pygmy should dare stand up to them seemed to them at once ridiculous and odious; they were filled with rage and scorn. From that moment onward they did not cease to excite their Austrian comrades against Dollfuss, to urge them to rebellion, to plot with them, and to furnish them with all necessary resources for an extraordinarily fierce, inventive, and diabolically relentless campaign of propaganda, agitation, assault, maltreatment of individuals, and ridicule of the authorities. The Bavarian frontier bordering the Tyrol became the scene of a constant exchange of German emissaries bearing instructions, arms, pamphlets, and money to Austrian Nazis and of Austrian Nazis seeking help or refuge in Germany. Munich was organized as the directing center of the revolutionary movement; there the threads of every plot originated or terminated.

In April 1933 a band of Hitlerites from Bavaria invaded Austrian soil and, in circumstances which have remained mysterious, assassinated a certain Dr. Bell, a former Nazi who, it was said, possessed important secrets. From then on rumor had it that a putsch was about to break in Vienna to set Nazism in the saddle. On May 4 the Austrian Government made the wearing of the brown uniform illegal and decreed that public offices be cleared of National Socialist elements.

This marked the beginning of a stubborn struggle fraught with vicissitudes, now underground and sly, now open and brutal. But what could Austria in the long run accomplish against a Third Reich steadily growing in power, especially when the Austrian Nazis, swept by the Hitlerian contagion, kept increasing numerically while their opponents were divided by inexpiable quarrels. Out of this unequal duel two episodes among many deserve to be cited because they recall the means employed by Nazi gangsters and in a sense illustrate before the act the crime by which Dollfuss was to perish.

In May 1933 Dr. Frank, recognized jurist of the Nazi party, made a lecture tour in Austria; these lectures were so violent and so indecent in regard to the established government of the realm that he was requested to leave Austrian soil. On May 28, seeking to avenge him and itself—for it believed itself personally insulted—the government of the Reich clapped a tax of one thousand marks on all exit visas to Austria, meaning thereby to deprive Austria of the profits gained from German tourists, whose visits were numerous and lucrative. But this masked closing of the border did not prevent the passage of seditious agents.

On June 12 men crossing the border from Germany made an attempt on the life of Steidle, the Commandant of the Tyrolean *Heimwehr* or Civic Guard. Their purpose achieved, they fled back to Germany, like the murderers of Dr. Bell. Investigation established the fact that the expedition had been organized in Germany and was to have set the signal for several like acts intended to start a general revolution. The coup was organized by the famous Habicht, a German subject appointed by the party to direct Austrian Nazism. The better to carry out his task and to enjoy diplomatic immunity, Habicht was listed on the personnel roster of the Reich Legation in Vienna as press attaché.

The Austrian Government arrested him and then, in view of his official status, released him and merely expelled him. Forthwith the Reich Government countered by arresting and expelling Dr. Wasserbäck, the press attaché at the Austrian Legation in Berlin, in spite of the fact that he had always been an official beyond reproach. And as if such base reprisal were not enough, Hitler insolently appointed Habicht inspector of the National Socialist formations in Austria, whereupon this personage, settling in Munich, proceeded to employ the Munich radio daily in order to incite the Austrian people against the Dollfuss cabinet.

The German Legation in Vienna was meanwhile acting in singular fashion. Overwhelming documents from authoritative sources revealed that German diplomats, headed by Dr. Rieth, were doing their utmost to favor insurgents, covering them with the protection of the legation and placing its diplomatic pouch at their disposal.

The sensation caused by the Steidle affair did not make Nazi agitators any more cautious. On August 30 three of them visited the prison at Innsbruck where Hofer, a Nazi leader in the Tyrol, was confined. Disguised as auxiliary policemen, they announced that they had been detailed to deliver a prisoner to the prison authorities. As the gates swung open they leaped upon the porter, bound him and chloroformed him, felled an inspector and a guard who had been attracted by the tumult, freed Hofer from his cell, and fled with him by automobile. Twenty-four hours later the said Hofer, the hero of this crime novel, could be seen proudly flanking Hitler in the ceremonies of the Nuremberg Congress!

Obviously Germany's flaunted protection of the worst revolutionary elements hindered the Austrian Government in its policy of repression. Austria needed a counterweight and that counterweight could be found only in the intervention of the great powers. France, Britain, and Italy, cognizant of the situation, determined to lodge a protest in Berlin, invoking

Article 80 of the Treaty of Versailles whereby Germany had agreed to respect Austrian independence. The time had now come to remind the Reich of its obligations.

To prove efficacious, the action of the three powers should have been discreet and accomplished firmly in common; exactly the opposite happened, admittedly through the fault of the Parisian press, which announced the decision of the powers ahead of time and with much fanfare, besides endowing it with a threatening character which it should not have had. Three days before I received my instructions from the Quai d'Orsay I had been able to read them in the press of the capital. This amounted to giving Hitler the time he needed to prepare his answer and especially obliging him to give a negative answer unless he were to lose face before his people and his party.

Britain and Italy, annoyed at the indiscretion of the French press, no longer consented that the step be taken simultaneously by the three representatives at Berlin. We therefore presented ourselves at the Wilhelmstrasse on August 7 in dispersed order, nor is it certain that the Italian diplomat did not break his word and remain aloof. As for the British chargé d'affaires, whose statement followed mine, he did his best to palliate the language I had used previously. The result was precisely what might have been expected under such conditions. The Reich Government replied haughtily that the démarche made by the powers was aimless; if the Four-Power Pact were to serve for interference of this sort, then Germany would take no further part in it, and, finally, the difficulties existing between Austria and the Reich were a purely German question, a domestic affair in which no one need mingle. The three powers accepted this rebuff without turning a hair, so that instead of intimidating Hitler they had encouraged him. Never until then had I been personally associated with so lamentable a move crowned by so flagrant a failure.

So the quarrel between pygmy and giant continued. Dollfuss increased radical measures against the Nazis, who nevertheless continued their acts of violence. On October 3 a man fired two shots at the Chancellor as the latter was leaving Parliament. On February 6, 1934, the Vienna cabinet authorized Dollfuss to bring the Austro-German conflict before the League of Nations and, at the same time, submitted an accusing memorandum to London, Paris, and Berlin.

For the second time the three powers deemed it opportune to make a gesture in Austria's favor. But experience, instead of making them more energetic, had made them more circumspect; this time they were content merely to publish a common declaration in which they expressed their attachment to the cause of Austrian independence. Naturally their platonic protestation had no more effect than their démarche of the previous August. However Mussolini was not at that time enchanted with the idea of seeing Hitler established in Vienna and he believed he might use Austria in his Danubian policy; he therefore gave proof of a more positive interest in that nation's fate and of greater inclination to protect Dollfuss, for whom he seemed to entertain friendly feelings.

Events in France, the Hitler-Mussolini interview in Venice, and the drama of June 30 served to divert general attention toward other problems, permitting Dollfuss to crush the uprising of the Viennese workers—an insurrection incomprehensible considering what times Austria was going through. In this new crisis the Austrian Nazis observed a neutral attitude; they loathed the Socialists as cordially as they did the Catholics and were unwilling to play into the hands of either.

But about July 20 their activity sprang up again and their terrorism indulged in new exploits. On precisely that date Dollfuss and his family were invited to spend a few days at Riccione as guests of the Duce; Frau Dollfuss was already there, her husband was to join her there on July 25.

On July 24 strange rumors spread through Berlin. The situation in Vienna was said to have suddenly turned critical, surprises were to be expected and serious events were imminent.

The rumors were so persistent and so disturbing that at eight o'clock in the evening I believed I should warn Paris by telegram.

On the morrow, July 25, in the course of the afternoon and evening the German capital was filled with sensational but still vague reports. Special editions of the newspapers announced that a revolt was said to have broken out in Vienna and that the rebels were in possession of the radio station and Chancellery Palace, in which the government was held incommunicado. Rintelen, Austrian minister in Rome, was reported to have assumed power. Who the rebels were—Socialists, Communists, Civic Guards, or units of the regular army—the German press did not state. But the Ministry of Propaganda felt the need of issuing a communiqué affirming its certainty that National Socialists had had no hand in the business.

At nine in the evening the official news agency DNB published an extraordinary dispatch which sounded for all the world like an anthem of triumph. The German conscience, it said, had at last expressed itself; a people whose most legitimate aspirations a small clique had vainly attempted to stifle had now arisen; Austria had freed herself and was entering the road that led to a common fatherland. But on July 26 all trace of this dispatch had vanished; it had been suppressed; no newspaper quoted it. On the other hand the morning papers gave a more substantial account of the events of the day before.

According to this version, on Wednesday, July 25, at 1:00 P.M., a body of insurgents seized the Radio Building in Vienna; it was these insurgents, allegedly, who broadcast the news that Dollfuss was wounded and had resigned and that Rintelen had replaced him. At the same hour another armed force was reported to have stormed the Chancellery, where Dollfuss, Major Fey, and Karwinski, Undersecretary of State for the Police, were meeting. In the course of a brawl, Dollfuss was mortally wounded and his colleagues arrested. The uprising had apparently been successful. But the regular army was alerted; it recaptured the Radio Building and surrounded the Chancellery Palace in which the rebels had locked and barricaded themselves together with their hostages. Fey was then reported to have parleyed with both the rebels who kept him prisoner and the military who were besieging him. Both sides agreed to call Dr. Rieth, the German minister in Vienna, who persuaded the insurgents to yield their hostages in return for a safe-conduct pass which would enable them to cross the German border without molestation.

Accurate in its main lines, the German press story nevertheless left some important details in abeyance. It still did not reveal who were these insurgents in Austrian military uniform, whether real soldiers or plotters disguised as such. At length the truth made itself known through reports from Vienna and the European capitals. The rebels were Austrian Nazis. About one hundred and fifty strong, led by a certain Holzweber, they had disguised themselves as militiamen of the Civic Guard just as Hofer's liberators had disguised themselves as policemen. Believing that they had come to relieve the troops on duty, the Chancellery guards admitted them and they easily seized the building. The government should have been in full force at a cabinet meeting but, warned over the telephone of suspicious movements observed in the city, the Ministers, including Schuschnigg and General Zehner, found time to return to their respective ministries, save Fey and Karwinski, who remained at Dollfuss' side. The part played in this tragedy by Major Fey has not been cleared up. Apparently he was in connivance with the rebels and, betraying Dollfuss as Seiss-Inquardt was later to betray Schuschnigg, he participated in the plot in order to bring about not the Chancellor's death but his disappearance from the political scene.

Miklas, President of the Austrian Republic, appointed Schuschnigg Chancellor at once and proclaimed a state of siege; at 7:30 P.M. the insurgents surrendered, and law and order were everywhere restored.

Germany's responsibility and guilt in this abortive putsch which cost Dollfuss his life are flagrant. Rumors gathered in Berlin on July 24, the eve of the assassination, furnish evidence that the ruling powers of the Third Reich knew that an uprising would be attempted on the morrow, July 25, against the Vienna Government. How could they have known this unless they were themselves involved in one way or another? The very haste with which, believing the operation fulfilled, they celebrated its success noisily and its consequences prematurely shows that they were informed of the nature of the coup. Equally significant were their initial efforts to keep National Socialism strictly aloof from the question and their subsequent efforts to conceal (or only to reveal much later) that Nazis were in reality the criminals. Would they have gone to such pains to mask the truth if the Austrian rebels had had no relations of any sort with Germany? And when the Austrian Nazis, knowing themselves done for, summoned the Minister of the Reich to their aid, were they not in a way confessing where their coup took its source?

When Hitler received the tragic tidings from Vienna he was attending the Wagner Festival at Bayreuth. With feverish hurry he piled up the measures destined to prove that he and his government were innocent. He canceled the safe-conduct papers granted the rebels and drove them back to Austrian soil where they were arrested. He immediately dismissed Rieth —that bungler who had intervened in favor of the insurgents without first consulting Berlin and who, above all, had not understood the compromising nature of his intervention and the avowal it represented.

Finally, still on the same day, Hitler appointed Papen in Rieth's place as Minister Plenipotentiary of the Reich to Vienna, accompanying this appointment with a letter immediately made public. In it he declared that the crime was judged in Germany with the utmost reprobation and deeply regretted by himself. Germany, he added, was in no measure responsible for it. Hitler assured Papen of his "absolute and unlimited" confidence and charged him to bring Austro-German relations, so long disturbed, back "to their normal friendly course." So much confidence seems surprising when placed in a man who one month before had narrowly escaped being a victim of the massacres of June 30! But Papen was a Catholic; he had made the Marburg speech; he was known to be no Nazi and to blame the excesses of the regime. These various considerations, Hitler believed, would win him the favor of Austria's rulers and present a valid guarantee of the desire for peace which the Führer had manifested. Accessorily the removal of Papen to Vienna would rid Hitler of a Vice-Chancellor who was disliked by the party and who had become more burdensome than useful. Even in the most critical hours Hitler never lost his gift of profiting by circumstance.

The same can scarcely be said of the allied powers. Hitler's abrupt decisions betrayed his uneasy conscience but they also betrayed his fright. The resentment aroused by the Dollfuss murder was so great that Hitler feared a fresh remonstrance by France, Britain, and Italy.

Mussolini had flown into a great rage and was violently indignant. His protégé and guest had been killed and he, the Duce, had had to break to Frau Dollfuss the news of her husband's death. To Prince Starhemberg, chief of the Civic Guards, Mussolini dispatched a threatening telegram in which he cited the "direct and remote responsibilities" for the crime and proclaimed: "The independence of Austria will be defended more doggedly than ever!" The Italian press raged and fumed. Mussolini was not content with words alone; he alerted his army and ordered Italian divisions to move up to the Brenner frontier.

But neither Britain nor France appeared disposed to support his military gesture. They believe that the events themselves had given Hitler a satisfactory lesson and that he would from now on leave Austria in peace. Looking on him as one

isolated and disgraced, they considered that he had lost ground
and that he must perforce turn cautious. Perhaps, too, they
judged that the extremists in his party had outstripped him
and that he was sincerely chagrined by what had happened.
Britain, furthermore, was reluctant to dabble in this Austrian
business; at bottom she was not far from believing that the
Anschluss would occur sooner or later and that it was boot-
less to struggle against a fatal current. France, for her part,
hesitated to take measures without being assured of British
collaboration. Also the Little Entente looked askance at the
Duce's intrusion into Danubian problems.

Hitler did not forget that his fears had been vain and that
the western democracies were less resolute, less realistic and
less energetic than he had supposed. In dealing with them, he
decided, much might be dared without running too many
risks. Nor did Mussolini forget that Britain and France had
not supported him at a critical juncture. He was often to
speak of this.

THE DEATH OF HINDENBURG

More than ten years have passed since Hindenburg died, yet
the mystery that surrounds his passing has not yet been cleared
up. There was nothing unnatural in his death itself: he was a
very old man of eighty-eight, he had been visibly declining for
some months, and when, in late spring, he left for his estate
at Neudeck, everyone knew that *"der alte Herr,"* as he was
called, "the old gentleman," would never return to Berlin.
Toward the end of July he himself asked Sauerbrach, the famous doctor, who had come to visit him: "Has Freund Heinz
come into the house yet?" (Freund Heinz is a popular designation for Death.) "No," the doctor told him. "He is not in the
house yet but he is prowling around the garden." On August
2, 1934, Freund Heinz came in to close the old man's eyes.

At least it was on August 2 that the decease of the President of the Reich was announced to Germany and to the world. The official communiqué specified that he had died that day at 9:00 A.M. But did he not really die earlier? Was not his death kept a secret for a day or two? Therein lies one part of the enigma.

When the news was published in Berlin at about midday, the public also learned that the Marshal's succession had been determined. A law immediately promulgated by the cabinet established the personal link between the functions of President of the Reich and its Chancellor. By virtue of this law Hitler was invested with the functions of President of the Reich. Next day he announced that he would forgo the title of President, unpleasantly redolent of democracy and doubtless disagreeable to Nazi nostrils, and assume instead the title of Führer and Chancellor of the Reich. That same morning, through Blomberg's good offices, the army and the navy had already sworn allegiance to the new Chief of State.

What speed in executing measures that tossed the Constitution of Weimar on the dunghill and constituted no more and no less than a *coup d'état*. Was it plausible to believe that a revolution on such a wide scale could have been effected between 9:00 A.M. and 12:00 noon?

True the Marshal's death was expected and provided for; it even offered a turning point for which adversaries of the Nazis were lying in wait. The country was still under the overwhelming impression caused by the massacres of June 30 and, more recently, by the assassination of Dollfuss. The government had many enemies, a good number of them among the Reichswehr generals, who dismissed Hitler as a dangerous adventurer and considered the Nazis as a rabble. To the malcontents the Marshal's death appeared as a ready-made occasion to submit Hitler to a higher authority more apt to keep him in hand than Hindenburg had been or to get rid of him altogether. Popular rumor stated that Wilhelm II might reascend the throne, or rather that he might delegate his son the

Crown Prince as *Reichsverweser* or Administrator of the Empire.

Hitler possessed sufficient political experience to understand that by allowing the highest office to remain vacant and by allowing an interval to elapse between the Marshal's death and the designation of his successor he would be incurring great dangers. We may therefore admit that he had made up his mind and prepared beforehand so that, the moment come, he had but to press a button to set in motion the machinery he had installed.

What I find astonishing in this hypothesis and what makes it seem rather unlikely is that the secret was so closely guarded that no one ever got wind of it. Given the political manners then reigning in Berlin, some hint of the tactics planned should have leaked out. Again, as the press recorded, Hitler did not arrive at Neudeck on August 2 but the day before. I conclude from this that the Marshal probably died the day before that, a fact which was kept hidden for twenty-four hours in order to allow for the redaction and printing of the law of succession and of the various proclamations to SA, SS and other Nazi organizations, and for the administration of the oath of loyalty to the armed forces. At any rate this forms but one part, and the least important part, of the enigma.

There is another signal circumstance. No sooner was the Marshal's death officially announced than Goebbels, Minister of Propaganda, experienced the need of publicly declaring that since no will of the deceased President had been found, he had made none. Then suddenly, a fortnight later, on August 15, Papen traveled to Berchtesgaden, bearing Hitler an envelope closed by five red seals. This was Hindenburg's last will and testament, he said, found by Colonel von Hindenburg, the Marshal's son, eleven days after the Marshal's demise. The text on the envelope was as follows:

"To the German people and to my Chancellor. Herewith is

my last will and testament. This letter is to be delivered by my son to the Chancellor of the Reich."

Yet it had taken eleven days to discover the document! And it was not Colonel von Hindenburg who delivered it to the Chancellor of the Reich in obedience to his father's injunctions, it was Papen. Why Papen? By a further curious coincidence the discovery of the will occurred on the eve of a referendum in which the German people were invited to state their approval or disapproval of the unification, in Hitler's person, of the twin functions of Chancellor and Chief of State. In all this are there not grounds for some astonishment?

The press, of course, republished lengthy extracts from the document, explaining that one half of it, the old part, had been written in Hanover in 1919, and the other, the recent part, was drawn up in Berlin and signed as of May 11, 1934. In the latter, Hindenburg waxed lyrical in praise of Hitler.

Now such feelings in no wise agree with those the old Marshal was known to have entertained shortly before his death. Before entrusting power to Hitler he must have overcome much hesitancy and much repugnance. He had noticed that, in spite of Hitler's promises, Hitler had established the dictatorship of a party over Germany and broken the barriers intended to confine him. To recommend Hitler to the German people as his successor could never have entered the Marshal's mind, for he was much too sincerely a monarchist and legitimist. In fact the secret drama in Hindenburg's existence was that Kaiser Wilhelm II, whom he considered his master and sovereign and to whom he had pledged his officer's oath, resented the fact that Hindenburg was occupying Wilhelm's position if not his throne. Can the clauses of the will, though couched in a full and lucid style, be ascribed to senility? Such was not the version current in Berlin in August 1934.

Talk in the capital had it that Hindenburg's will had been tampered with, that the entire second part was bogus and written by the man who had recently helped Hindenburg edit his memoirs. The whole operation suggested the complicity of several persons. It was made possible only with the connivance of Colonel von Hindenburg, of Meissner, the Marshal's Secretary of State, and of Papen. Well, shortly thereafter Colonel Hindenburg was appointed general; Meissner, a collaborator of the Socialist Ebert before becoming a collaborator of Hindenburg, remained at Hitler's side in the same post; and Papen, becoming a taboo personage, enjoyed the attentions and solicitude of the regime in his foreign missions. All of them then would seem to have received the just reward of their good offices.*

The Marshal's obsequies were magnificent and fraught with that romanticism which intoxicated the Nazis, criminals or not. The body, set on an artillery gun carriage drawn by six black horses, was transported by night to Neudeck, passing mile after mile between two rows of torches. Next day it was placed on a catafalque in the center of the Tannenberg monument—a monument whose eight square, massive towers, and battlemented wall connecting them, were reminiscent of a castle built by the Teutonic knights. Great lights burned at the top of each tower, soldiers formed a chain under the walls, oriflammes fluttered from the enceinte, but not a single swastika banner among them. To this extent at least the feelings of the deceased had been respected.

Following an embarrassed and banal pastor, Hitler made an address. He was more nervous than ever, excited, spasmodic, flushed, and in no sense in keeping with the rapt gravity of the spectators. By way of peroration, he shouted in aggres-

* I have never heard it said that the Allies after World War II apprehended Colonel von Hindenburg in Germany. But Meissner was arrested and Papen imprisoned in Nuremberg. It would have been worth while to question them about Hindenburg's will in order to settle this point for the benefit of history. It would be interesting to ascertain whether the Third Reich which burned down the Reichstag and murdered Dollfuss may be also considered guilty of forgery. Such a detail would complete the factors that contributed to give Nazidom its particular character.

sive tones: "And now, O dead General, take your place in Valhalla!"

After the ceremony, on my way back to Berlin by train, I thought of the old man whom we used to see in the course of our diplomatic duties four or five times a year. His tall stature was striking, he was almost a colossus. His face was divided into two parts by a heavy mustache that rose on either side like tusks over the corners of his lips; his hair cut short, stubble, like the hairs of a brush, was gray and close-set; his features were full and regular, suggestive of martial power and robust equilibrium, were it not for their sadness and weariness, accentuated by a waxen complexion and lusterless eyes overcast by leaden eyelids.

Yet there was a kindness in his glance and in his great, gruff voice which spoke in monosyllables and in military tones. He impressed one as an aged and weary leader of men, a kindly grandfather who was annoyed at having to leave his armchair. He remembered having been detailed as page to Marshal MacMahon in 1861 when Napoleon III had sent MacMahon to represent him at the coronation of Wilhelm I as King of Prussia. Whenever Hindenburg met me he would repeat the same anecdote. A huge African tent set up in the garden of the French Embassy had struck the young page's attention and the old Marshal never failed to allude to it. I would attempt to steer the conversation to MacMahon, whose destiny and Hindenburg's had much in common. But Hindenburg did not know or had forgotten the story of MacMahon.

He was a typical representative of the generation which grew up under Wilhelm I. He read the Bible every evening before going to sleep. He did not relish luxury, he lived stingily and was a miser. He wished to recoup the family fortunes, which had once been prosperous, and the Neudeck estate in East Prussia, a gift from the nation, turned him into a Junker.

THE MURDER OF KING ALEXANDER OF YUGOSLAVIA

The year 1934, so fertile in dramas of all kinds, ended with the most tragic of all, the assassination of King Alexander of Yugoslavia and of the French Foreign Minister, Louis Barthou, at Marseille on October 9 by two Croats belonging to the Ustachi gang. But it would be mistaken to believe that this event, while outside the National Socialist movement, was without connection with Nazism and failed directly to interest the German Government. In point of fact the crime of October 9 implicates Germany quite as much as the death of Dollfuss though less immediately and less evidently.

A few days after the murder some French newspapers, the *Journal des Débats, L'Œuvre,* and *Le Temps* among them, permitted themselves allusions to German complicity. The German press retaliated angrily against insinuations which it qualified as abominable. Goering himself at Belgrade on October 17 declared to the Yugoslav journalists that investigations conducted in Germany had proved that no terrorist within the limits of the Reich had had any connection whatsoever with the Marseille crime. "Germany," he added, "is not a country willing to tolerate within her boundaries the presence and activity of terrorist elements."

Despite these peremptory statements it is certain that, if the Ustachis who practiced marksmanship and the technique of assassination on a farm were chiefly Mussolini's hirelings, there were also close relations between them and a group of Croat agitators centered in Berlin. This group, which had founded a press bureau called *Croatia-Presse,* published pamphlets and other propaganda material. Its activities were downright revolutionary. Struck by this fact, I had not failed to apprise Paris of it long before the tragedy of October 9. True, Hitler's government had banned the group's publications in January 1934, but the group had survived this. Rosenberg was familiar with it; he encouraged and probably subsidized it. As chief of the party's Foreign Policy Section he considered it useful to have at his disposal men capable of provoking opposition or revolutionary movements in countries against which Germany nursed a grudge or in countries which she wished to force to become more docile.

Rosenberg's connivance with the Croats was actually confirmed to me on October 24 during a conversation I had with Baron von Neurath. Three days later Goering too admitted to me that Rosenberg had been "indiscreet." It is further averred that Ante Pavelic—the Ustachi leader who instigated and organized the Marseille crime (and who was later created chief of liberated Croatia by Italy and Germany)—was in Berlin on the eve of the crime and left hastily on that date for Milan.

After the crime an officer of the French National Criminal Investigation Department came to Berlin in order to investigate precisely the role and actions there of Pavelic and his gang. He was very well received. Goering in person promised to lend him all possible help and to open government files for his inspection. But on the morrow the departments with whom the French inspector had to deal showed a quite different attitude. They were chill, distant, embarrassed, and evasive; and they did not open their files. Our inspector returned home, his labor lost.

The scene of the King's arrival at Marseille, and of the murder committed so soon after, had been filmed. A copy of this film was brought to Berlin. Hitler and his companions studied it long and avidly. They were surprised at the mediocre, almost shabby reception granted the King; they were struck by the weak organization of the police; but, most of all, they were fascinated by the confusion, frenzy, and complete disarray that swept away both the crowd and the authorities. No detail of this disturbing spectacle but had been faithfully recorded by the camera. Hitler forbade the showing of this film in Germany because he feared it might encourage the spirit of emulation in some enemy of his regime. Goering spoke to me of this film repeatedly; he greatly wished to show it to me. I obstinately refused because I knew that the Führer's circle, including Goering—despite his lavish condolences—was overjoyed, if not at the misfortune that had struck us, at least at the insufficiencies and defects clearly revealed on this occasion. The Nazi leaders must have concluded from this that there were mechanisms, springs, and a framework in France which were obviously weakening.

Hitler and his colleagues had a fairly high opinion of France; they believed her a power to be feared. The murder of King Alexander and Barthou was one of the events which contributed to modify their opinion of us, bringing them gradually to consider us a less dangerous adversary than they had first supposed.

With consummate skill they turned to what might be termed the political exploitation of the episode. Yugoslavia was a terrain they had surveyed and marked out as seemingly propitious to their plans. They believed they could spread their influence there and, as in Poland, exert an action tending to dislocate the close-knit unity of adjoining nations, to shake up the Little Entente and finally to isolate Beneš and Czechoslovakia. Further, they considered that their efforts to approach Yugoslavia held a threat and a retaliation against Italy, whose attitude toward Chancellor Dollfuss' murder had violently irritated them.

Fundamentally the King's death favored their designs because it suppressed a vigorous personality, a man who would not have been gulled by their game into abandoning his alliances. Affecting a sincere grief and a noble commiseration, they multiplied signs of their most cordial sympathy. The Reich press was filled with pompous and unreserved eulogies of the sovereign, backed up by insistent protestations of friendship for the Yugoslav people. It went so far as to stigmatize the Croatian autonomists, whom after all Berlin had sheltered and helped, and to reproach them with having failed to comprehend the dead monarch's vast Balkan ideal.

A mission, headed by a diplomat, was designated to attend the obsequies; just as it was about to leave Hitler wished to raise its prestige and Goering was appointed to lead it, as special representative of the German Army. One of the wreaths he laid on the royal bier bore for inscription: "To her heroic adversary of yore—the German Army, in heartfelt grief." To the press, he affirmed that Germany, in her own interests and in those of peace, wished Yugoslavia to be as powerful a state as possible. In this Slavic land, where France possessed many friends, he openly sought contact with Marshal Pétain and took pleasure in appearing in public at his side. This in no wise prevented the German press from relating that the Yugoslav people felt highly resentful toward the French authorities who had proved unable to protect King Alexander's life; nor did this same German press fail to note with pleasure that France's popularity in Yugoslavia had suffered a lasting setback.

The Third Reich hoped to profit by the decline of French influence which it believed evident. Subsequently the Germans worked perseveringly to that end, and neither their hope nor their efforts proved absolutely futile. Thus King Alexander's death broke one more link in the chain that had been forged in Versailles and that Hitler had sworn to smash.

V. THE REBIRTH OF
GERMANY'S ARMED FORCES

DESPITE its troubled course the year 1934 ended favorably for Hitler. The crisis of June 30, the death of Marshal Hindenburg, and the murder of Dollfuss gave him some difficult moments; but, having emerged unscathed and indeed the gainer, he was able to appreciate the truth of the adage that fortune smiles on the bold. The beginning of 1935 was to bring him two events, one agreeable, the other not.

The disagreeable event was the signature of agreements between Italy and France on January 4 at Rome, a proof that after the murder of Dollfuss, Mussolini bore him a grudge. Hitler had always desired an alliance of the two governments which had so many affinities. His disappointment and bitterness were great as he saw the man whom he persisted in regarding as his forerunner separating from him and turning toward France. He was the more hurt and worried because the Rome agreements showed the intention of defending the integrity and independence of Austria and of surrounding that country with a network of protective pacts.

The agreeable event was the Saar plebiscite, about which he had long been anxious. Not that he had any doubts about the result; he had told me that he was sure of winning 90 or 95 per cent of the votes. But he was afraid lest, in order to restrain him, we exercise reprisals either by taking possession of the Saar or by postponing the date appointed for the plebiscite. These fears proved to be groundless. The plebiscite took place on January 13, 1935. By a vote of 90.36 per cent the Sarrois favored the return of their territory to Germany.

The French had failed to realize the force of attraction wielded by a regime which pleased Germans for precisely the reasons that it displeased and repelled us. Nor had they realized that the Sarrois knew perfectly well that by voting against a return to Germany they would receive more blows and suffer more persecutions from that quarter than they would gain benefits and win rewards from the other. The operations of the election were quite normal, and the Germans were surprised at this; they had expected disputes and incidents. The League of Nations accepted the decision of the Sarrois with exemplary propriety and fairness. Far from trying to put off the moment when the Reich was to re-establish its sovereignty in the Saar, the League set the date for March first. Seven thousand SA and SS men entered the Saar together with all the Nazi leaders. The bells tolled, the swastika was hoisted over all the buildings, and armed hosts paraded in cadenced step for long hours. "We hope," Hitler declared in his speech, "that the return of the Saar to the German Reich will finally improve relations between France and Germany.

Just as we wish for peace, so we think that our great neighbor nation is also ready to seek to effect peace. We hope that we may clasp hands in this common task which will bring about the salvation of Europe!"

Following these words, a gust of optimism rose and spread for a moment over Europe. But these illusions were short-lived. Freed from his anxieties over the Saar, which had been like a ball and chain around his ankle, Hitler wasted no time over sentimental effusions. He was impatient to use his new-won liberty of action and to pass to the next chapter of his program, a fundamental chapter concerning the official reorganization of the German Army.

It would have required much candor to believe that Hitler, having failed to win the powers' agreement to limited German rearmament and having failed in direct negotiations with France, was going to fold his arms until some solution approved by all was forthcoming. In truth, he had begun to rearm from the moment he became Chancellor. That was why the Reichswehr, urged by Blomberg, overcame the repugnance many of its officers felt for the Third Reich, and lent it their confidence and their support. For a while Hitler's problem had been to legalize the rearmament in which he was secretly engaged, on the high level which he proposed to reach.

Now his problem was different. It was no longer a question of soliciting the powers to accept a formula discussed and negotiated with them, but to apprise them of the military organization which he had decided, on his own sovereignty, to set up. The very progress of the work in hand forced him to do so. The manpower of existing Reichswehr divisions could not be raised, nor tanks and cannons accumulated in factory yards, nor military planes camouflaged as civilian craft indefinitely. But public revelation of the real state of Reich rearmament and of the blueprints for future developments would arouse a sensation in Europe and cause a shock which might have dangerous consequences.

How to soften the blow? How to present the matter so that, appearing natural and legitimate, it created the least possible emotion and scandal? Hitler was perplexed. Should he justify his conduct by denouncing Soviet Russia's military plans? Should he take advantage of France's plans whereby the duration of military service was to be extended? Should he put his trust in the British, who had always been the most inclined to admit and to persuade others to admit his claims? No one, probably not even the Führer himself, knew what decision he would make.

On February 3, 1935, Flandin and Laval, the French ministers, met the members of the British Cabinet. The two governments were unwilling to give the master of the Third Reich a free hand; they wished to catch him again, as it were, to bring him back into the framework of the powers and to bind him by pledges which would render him more or less inoffensive. They therefore published a declaration setting forth a plan for the strengthening of peace.

This declaration, condemning unilateral acts, voiced an unshakable loyalty to the League of Nations. But it also expressed the hope that co-operation with Germany would remain possible. It recommended the conclusion of an Eastern pact of non-aggression and mutual assistance and of a similar Danubian pact, thanks to which an armaments convention, replacing Part V of the Versailles Treaty, might give Germany the satisfaction she desired. Further, in order to implement the conditions whereby the Pact of Locarno was to be applied and to strengthen security in the West as well as in the East, the Franco-British plan proposed a regional agreement of assistance by aircraft in case of aggression. Italy, Germany, Belgium, Britain, and France were to participate in this agreement.

Sir Eric Phipps, the British Ambassador, and I personally delivered this document to Hitler; following our instructions, we urged on him the necessity of examining it in a spirit of sympathy. The Reich replied on February 14, in a brief, somewhat dry note, embarrassed in tone but not negative. The Reich promised to associate itself with the two powers to prevent Europe from plunging into a frenzied race for armaments. But it remained evasive on the question of the Eastern pact and of the Danubian pact; it accepted the idea of air assistance as a complement to the Pact of Locarno, adding, however, that it remained skeptical as to the efficacy of multilateral discussion. It preferred, it said, to proceed by means of private conversations and wished to begin by an exchange of views with Britain.

Hitler had retained the impression that Britain, more conciliatory than France, regretted the failure of the Geneva Conference and would give a great deal in order to come to terms. The appeal he made to Britain in the German reply of February 14 gave the British to suppose that he intended to inform them of his plan for military organization and to attempt to convert them to it.

London hastened to accept the invitation contained in the German note. It was agreed that Sir John Simon visit Berlin on March 6. Preparations were made to welcome him. The Reich press seemed mightily pleased and expectant of great results. But an unforeseen incident was to upset the whole scheme.

On March 4, two days before Sir John's scheduled journey, a White Book appeared in London signed by Ramsay MacDonald. A debate on increasing the budget for military expenditure was imminent in the House of Commons; the White Book explained that this increase of £4,000,000 was due to German rearmament, to the spirit prevailing in Germany, to the education its youth was receiving, and to the resultant insecurity in Europe. Publication of the White Book loosed a tempest of vociferations in Berlin. The newspapers foamed with rage, vying with one another in indignation that in a foreign official document anyone dared represent Germany as a peril to peace and pretend that her youth was subjected to warmongering propaganda. "Never," said the newspapers, "has Britain increased its war budget to such proportions. Britain is rearming, she is setting the example for rearmament; we are therefore free to do likewise. Since she accuses us of rearming, we would be very wrong to give up doing so. Besides, the rearmament of our neighbors is a threat to our security. Our security, jeopardized, compels us to rearm."

Next day, March 6, through his Minister of Foreign Affairs, Adolf Hitler informed the British Ambassador that he had caught cold during his visit to Saarbrücken and, having lost his voice, found himself obliged to forgo the pleasure of receiving Sir John Simon. Everybody understood that this was a diplomatic illness, the expression of an irritation which did not attack the vocal cords alone. At any rate Neurath confirmed this by telling me that Hitler was beside himself. Furious that the pacifism he advertised on all occasions was not taken seriously, he was more furious still that Britain, whose favorable disposition he had counted on and through whose mediation he had hoped to put through his rearmament program, judged him exactly as France did.

At this time he was certainly thinking of countering the White Book by notifying Britain of the measures he had decided to take for the reorganization of the German Army. Yet a remnant of caution held him back. Unwilling to deliver the entire confession—or challenge—at one fell swoop, he would move twice.

On March 10 Goering informed Ward Price of the *Daily Mail,* whom Hitler and he frequently used when they had an important communication to make to foreign public opinion, that thenceforward the Reich was to have a military air force, distinct from civil aviation. It had been proposed that Germany participate in an international aviation pact. How could she, when she had no air force? The same day, the air attachés, or, where there were none, the military attachés of the diplomatic missions of the great powers, were invited to repair to the Ministry of the Reichswehr.

There Commodore Wenninger informed them not without embarrassment that a German Air Force was born. It would consist of a certain number of wings, groups, and squadrons, with three groups of three squadrons of nine to twelve planes per flight, allotted to six different air regions. He was speaking of the future. But it was quite clear that everything in this program that could be accomplished without attracting too much notice already existed. So soon as the Nazis came to power Goering had declared his will to endow the Reich with a military air force despite the prohibitions of the Versailles dictate. If he had caused himself to be appointed Minister of Aviation, it was not in order to preside over the destinies of commercial lines. Besides, everyone knew that the Junkers plants at Dessau, Heinkel, and Warnemünde had been working at capacity for months.

In his conversation with the attachés Commodore Wenninger quoted no figures. What was the size of the German Air Force to be? He did not say. He never mentioned the limitation to 50 per cent of the French and Allied air forces which Hitler had cited when he was negotiating with us. What had held good a year before was no longer valid. There was no longer any question of allowing France a margin of superiority; the point was to claim at least equality with her.

Britain furnished the occasion whereby Germany divulged the existence of a German Air Force in violation of the Versailles Treaty. Now France was to offer the pretext whereby Germany announced the existence of a new army. On March 15, in the Chamber of Deputies, Flandin introduced a bill tending to make up the shortage in the incomplete annual contingents by temporarily prolonging the duration of military service. Arguments supporting the bill revealed the already alarming state of German rearmament.

The next day, at 5:00 P.M., Hitler sent for me unexpectedly. I found him in his study at the Chancellery, flanked by Neurath, who was present throughout the interview. Hitler's voice betrayed no sign of hoarseness. He was sure of himself, intense, solemn, conscious of the gravity of the moment. He declared that he wished to inform me that he had just decreed a law re-establishing conscription and compulsory military service in Germany. The German Army would consist of twelve corps and thirty-six divisions. He likewise informed the British and Italian ambassadors. During my interview with him he handed me the text of the law, which was set forth in but a few articles. It was preceded by a statement of his motives which actually amounted to a manifesto for the use of Germany and world opinion.

This manifesto recalled the successive events after Versailles. Germany had disarmed according to the stipulations of the treaty. The disarmament promised by the other nations had not followed; all efforts to accomplish it had failed. The chief powers had increased and were continuing to increase their armaments. Russia had created a hundred and one divisions. Had not Mr. Stanley Baldwin declared that a great state must rely only upon itself for its security? And here was France returning to two-year military service. In these circumstances the Reich could not remain disarmed or equipped with an army of ridiculous size. Thenceforth the nation would through her own strength assure her honor and look to her security. Germany had no intention of attacking anybody; her dearest wish was to live at peace with one and all.

I immediately informed Hitler that, as the representative of a country signatory of the Treaty of Versailles, I protested against this notification as a flagrant violation of the treaty. It was inexact that France had increased her army effectives; she had simply maintained them at their usual level, making up the shortage in her incomplete annual contingents by merely temporary measures. I expressed regret that by decreeing this law, without previous contact or discussion, the Führer believed that a decision he was not free to take unilaterally would face us with a *fait accompli*.

Hitler retorted that he was always ready for any conversation. In our discussion he indicated some highly interesting facts. As I emphasized how excessive the figure of thirty-six divisions was, he opposed the forty-one divisions which, according to him, France possessed, adding that Germany asked for no more than equality of effectives. He launched into a vehement diatribe against Soviet Russia: he would never consent to guarantee the frontiers of this land, which did not border upon the Reich and which was a menace to it.

With these significant declarations Hitler sang the customary song of his feelings toward France. In his eyes the Franco-German frontier was fixed once and for all; he would never lift a finger to bring up the question again. If our relations were not better, it was not his fault. He regretted that our ministers had not been willing to deal directly with the German ministers.

The exact information I obtained on the conditions in which the Führer made his decision furnished proof that the military law of March 16 was by no means the result of the measures taken by France. The Führer had been waiting for an opportune circumstance. During the week preceding March 16 Hitler was at Berchtesgaden, supposedly nursing his sore throat. In reality he was meditating. From Berlin he had brought with him the text of the military law and a memorandum drawn up by the Wilhelmstrasse. From this memorandum he elaborated the manifesto which was to accompany publication of the law. He wrote and rewrote it as many as three times. Then he suddenly returned to Berlin on the afternoon of Friday, March 15, called his confidants together and read them his statement. At that hour the vote in the French Chamber was not yet known. Next day the Cabinet of the Reich was summoned for 1:00 P.M. Hitler informed his ministers of the law and of the manifesto he had drawn up. A wave of enthu-

siam spread among them. They rose to their feet and, at Blomberg's command, gave three cheers for Hitler before shaking
his hand, thanking him and assuring him of their unfailing
devotion.

Why were Hitler's movements so hurried? He could have
allowed a few days to elapse after the vote in the French
Chamber, since he meant to justify his resolution by that vote.
In truth, he was concerned with his role in history. Yielding
to the naturally romantic bent of his imagination, he wished
the proclamation of Germany's return to conscription and
compulsory military service to coincide, on March 17, with
the anniversary of the manifesto addressed to his people by
Frederick William III of Prussia in 1813—a manifesto which
set the signal for the "War of Liberation" against Napoleon.

The Führer's decision produced a considerable effect in the
Reich. Crowds formed in front of the Chancellery to give
Hitler delirious ovations. "Henceforth the ignominy of the
Versailles Treaty is blotted out," wrote the gazettes. Certain
of them confessed ingenuously: "We were arming secretly;
now the world knows what we are doing and whither we are
going. It is healthier so."

The day of the glorious seventeenth was celebrated by the
most brilliant ceremonies. Blomberg, in a speech at the Opera,
exalted the German military tradition from Frederick the
Great to Ludendorff. Hitler decorated the colors and reviewed
a parade of detachments from every arm, including the air
force and the navy. He appeared flanked on the right by old
Mackensen, on the left by Blomberg, the one symbolizing the
ancient army, the other the new.

Many people abroad reasoned like the German press when
it said: "Better to know where we stand!" Nevertheless Hitler's
attitude was a veritable slap in the face, a provocation and a
challenge to the powers. They understood that they could not
accept the outcome and that a *riposte* on their part was imperative. Yet the idea that the Reich had created a *casus belli* never

entered anyone's head. No one contemplated the possibility of reducing Germany to obedience by force of arms. The matter was generally considered to fall within the competence of the League at Geneva; political and diplomatic agents must be employed to render it impossible for Germany to do harm.

As early as March 17 I for my part suggested that the powers immediately recall their ambassadors and, by hastening the conclusion of the Eastern and Danubian pacts, quickly form a defensive association against Germany. Naturally Britain should signify that all negotiations were useless now and Sir John Simon should definitely abandon all plans for a visit to Berlin. My suggestion, doubtless considered to be too radical, failed of adoption. The powers reacted, but by paper and procedure.

The British Government dispatched a note to Berlin in which it protested the Führer's behavior as contrary to his previous assurances and as settling on his own authority matters actually in litigation. After which the note expressed the amazing desire to know whether Berlin was ready to receive Sir John Simon and to confer with him on the basis of the Franco-British note of February 3 and the German reply of February 14. Hitler hastened to reply that he would be happy to converse with Sir John. How could this man, who was after all utterly simple, fail to believe that the British protest was purely formal, that Britain was favorably disposed toward him, and that she would raise no serious obstacle in his path?

The French displayed a little more energy. Britain and Italy were immediately summoned to a meeting in Paris on March 23. It was decided to lay the question before the League of Nations. It was proposed that after March 23, after Sir John Simon had had his interview with Hitler, the three powers meet at Stresa or Milan. On March 21 Flandin delivered a very firm speech in the Senate, without, however, mentioning the hypothesis of war. Hitler could not have hoped for anything better. The same day I handed the official French protest to Neurath. It cited the violation of the treaty and the breach in the procedure of discussion which the communiqué of February 3 had reopened. It recalled that no one had the right to abrogate a pledge without the agreement of the other parties to the contract. It expressed the most explicit reservations as to the consequences of Germany's attitude. But the conclusion of the note robbed its beginning of all effect. In it France declared herself prepared to continue to seek means of conciliation and to make every effort to dissipate the present discomfort. The Italian note was couched in similar terms. Thus at that moment Hitler could be certain that he had weathered the worst of the storm. On March 23 Eden and Suvich conferred with the French Government; the solidarity of the three powers was affirmed. It was agreed that Sir John Simon's visit would be a strictly informational one and that he would not go beyond the plan formulated on February 3. Eden was to accompany Sir John to Berlin, then to proceed to Moscow, Warsaw, and Prague. And the three powers were to meet at Stresa on April 11.

It might be supposed that Hitler, faced with Simon and Eden, would strive to lull their mistrust and to set their fears at rest. But since there they were, he felt that they could not have any very serious grievances against him; he need therefore not stand on ceremony. Casting caution to the winds, quite roughly and crudely and with the utmost assurance, Hitler cited his claims, informing his interlocutors of the various positions which he was determined to adopt and from which nothing could divert him. He was willing to conclude nonaggression pacts in the East but he rejected any clause of mutual aid. He would not contract an engagement of noninterference in Austria so long as what constituted interference had not been defined. And he would not return to Geneva before the settlement of the problems still in suspense and before a sweeping reform of the institution had been effected.

As for Reich rearmament it was imposed upon him by the development of the Russian forces. His own army would number 550,000 men; he would lower this figure only if the European political situation permitted. This army would be equipped with heavy artillery and matériel if the armies of the other powers possessed them. Hitler was not opposed to the elaboration of a Western European aviation pact to complete Locarno; in such an event he would claim air equality with either Britain or France, i.e., with the stronger of the two. He went on to renew the expression of his attachment to the Treaty of Locarno, which had been freely discussed and signed by his country. Finally he tackled a subject upon which he had not previously insisted, the naval question. He informed his visitors that he intended to build a war fleet equal in tonnage to 35 per cent of the British Navy's; he was further prepared to pledge himself not to exceed this proportion.

Hitler did not treat his interlocutors as statesmen with mandates, come to open a discussion, but rather as delegates, appointed to record his will. Privately Sir John Simon was astounded, but he gave no sign of it. He listened very politely and seemed much interested in what the Führer was saying; he did not interrupt and he made no objections. Later it was said that Hitler had asked him: "When Wellington saw Blücher coming to his help, did he think of inquiring by what right the Prussian Army may have exceeded the effectives imposed upon it?" It is reported that Sir John enjoyed this sally very much. He did not dislike the man. And the prospect of a German naval war tonnage that did not exceed 35 per cent of Britain's gave him food for thought.

As for Hitler he was certain that he had charmed Sir John and convinced him of the justice of the German thesis; he could from now on count on Britain's support.

When on April 11 the Stresa Conference met, with Mac-Donald and Mussolini present, the German press was not at all disturbed as to what might ensue. It prophesied that the French suggestions would not win the support of the other powers. Soon news came to shake its serenity. But when it read the final communiqué it could not believe its eyes; it was overwhelmed. For, impressed by the report Sir John made of his interview with Hitler and by Eden's reports on his visits to Moscow, Warsaw, and Prague, the Conference had unanimously asserted its loyalty to the League, approved the Eastern and Danubian pacts, censured Germany, and proclaimed its determination to oppose strongly any repudiation that might be unilateral and dangerous for the peace guaranteed by the treaties. Two days later, on April 16, the same scene was repeated in Geneva in the Council of the League of Nations. France won all along the line. The memorandum she filed met with no objection and the resolution she drew up was carried unanimously.

On April 18 the Italian and British ambassadors reminded the Wilhelmstrasse that their governments maintained all the guarantees subscribed to in the Pact of Locarno. Finally, on May 2 and May 14, a Franco-Soviet agreement for consultation and mutual aid in case of aggression was signed in Paris and Moscow.

All this procedure was belated since it occurred a whole long month after the Hitlerian challenge. It made the best of the past since it did not exact the abolition of the German military law. Its value was hypothetical only, since it referred to an uncertain future; it was characteristic of the attitude of the powers, which, at each successive *coup de force* carried off by the Third Reich, were less anxious to repress the violence committed than to prevent the next future violence. Hitler, on the contrary, saw in every gain accomplished a reason to pursue a further gain. Be that as it may, the powers had succeeded in forming an anti-German league of defense; Britain and Italy belonged to it; and France had renewed its former ties with Russia.

German public opinion was deeply affected. The press launched into protestations and imprecations that betrayed its resentment and fury. Never, to me at least, had Germany's leaders, diplomats, and semiofficial journalists appeared more at a loss and more discouraged. It seemed as if the horizon had closed before their eyes, as if the dreams of grandeur they caressed had slipped between their fingers. In fact, April 1935 marks the climax of European unity against the ambitions of the Reich. There can be no doubt that if the powers had been able to maintain their cohesion against the Third Reich, they in the first place and the world in general would have been spared many misfortunes.

But scarcely two months passed before this cohesion began to waver. Hitler employed his usual recipe; he played the hermit. In the Reichstag on May 21 he made a speech which, without repudiating the past, conjured up vistas of a future of agreement and concord; in conciliatory terms he showed himself desirous of participating in the organization of general security. He proposed setting a ceiling on the armaments of the various countries, offering particularly, as he had before, to limit his own fleet to one third the size of Britain's. He suggested the suppression of heavy offensive arms while leaving France the benefit of her Maginot Line. He proposed to define interference so that he might advisedly enter into pacts of noninterference, and to conclude agreements on nonaggression with his neighbors.

Britain leaped at the bait. Baldwin, hailing the gleam of light Hitler had kindled, moved wide-eyed toward it. Whereas France in April 1934 had been unwilling to conclude an agreement on limitation of Germany's land armament, the British Government, negotiating quietly and on its own, concluded a bilateral treaty with Germany authorizing the Reich to build a navy limited in tonnage to 35 per cent of Britain's.

So far there had been but a breach in the wall of anti-Hitlerian solidarity. But at the same time the Ethiopian question was worsening apace. All attempts at mediation failed. Mussolini plunged into an attempted conquest which was to make him quarrel with the League of Nations, Britain, and France. Soon Stresa was but a distant memory. Italy's defection, exploited by the Reich, was to bring the two dictatorships together and reopen for Hitler ways that were thought to have been sealed against him.

VI. THE END OF LOCARNO

IN *Mein Kampf*, Hitler wrote that the worst of crimes was to leave things unfinished; he harshly condemned *die Halbheit* or half measures. What he called half measures others would term moderation.

In this he represented an outstanding trait in the German character. Germans go to extremes. They want everything immediately; like spoiled brats they are annoyed, and they feel wronged, if they are not given forthwith what they crave. No sooner have they made one gain than they are obsessed by the lust to make another. Not knowing when and where to stop has ever been the cause of Germany's successive defeats.

After the Stresa Conference, Hitler, blocked and paralyzed by the unison of the three powers, suffered a temporary discouragement. But his luck soon turned. The Italo-Ethiopian war revived his hopes. Italy was in conflict with the League, with Britain, and even with France. The coalition was broken up; the barrier raised against him was lowered. Now he could pursue the execution of his methodical plan and free Germany from her last remaining fetters.

There remained the obligation not to garrison the Rhine and the demilitarization of the Rhenish provinces. The German nationalists considered this clause a painful curtailment of German independence. Hitler shared their opinion. But in this case neither he nor they could say that they were faced with an exigency imposed by force or with the stipulation of the dictate of Versailles. Germany had freely discussed and signed the Treaty of Locarno, negotiation of which she herself had originated. By its terms she was pledged to respect the statute concerning the Franco-German frontier on the Rhine, as established at Versailles; demilitarization of the Rhineland was specifically stated. Germany had profited thereby, as she had by the arbitration pacts with Belgium, Poland, and Czechoslovakia, all of which accompanied the Rhenish pact. At the time she was still living under the impression caused by the occupation of the Ruhr; she wished to avoid repetition of such a sanction and to be safe from such coercive measures as the French and their allies might be tempted, once again, to take. For this the pledges of Britain and Italy, who had guaranteed observation of the pact, were very precious to her.

But as time passed the situation was reversed. Now Germany was no longer at the mercy of her neighbors; she believed herself strong enough or her neighbors weak enough for her to shake off the trammels that hindered her. But by violating the Locarno Treaty she would be putting herself even more seriously in the wrong than she had by re-establishing conscription. For this breach could well be defined as an act of aggression; it might well call down reprisals not only by France but by the guarantor powers or by Britain, at any rate, if not by Italy. Germany must therefore find some trick or pretext to allow her to avoid being accused of repudiating her signature and of considering her promises as so many scraps of paper.

Hitler went to no great pains to reach his ends. On March 16, 1935, he had said that France's return to two-year military service, plus the increase of the Russian divisions, forced him to assure the security of the Reich on his own. A year later he was to pretend that conclusion of a pact between France and Soviet Russia, incompatible with Locarno, voided this treaty and therefore relieved Germany of her pledges.

It is true that from the beginning Germany fought the efforts made by French diplomacy to organize an Eastern pact of which the Franco-Soviet Pact was but a component part. France sought to give shape to a collective security which the League of Nations had never been able to translate from the realm of theory and principles into that of reality. She believed that regional pacts, specific and effectual, could practically and durably organize partial securities. The Locarno Pact offered a valid example of a regional agreement. It recorded the solemn pledge whereby Germany, Belgium, and France would respect their common borders and the Treaty of Versailles which had set them. Britain and Italy, as co-signatories of the pact, had guaranteed its execution; if it were broken they were bound to lend immediate aid to the injured party, and, amid cases of possible violation, the text expressly cited the mustering of troops in the demilitarized Rhine zone.

It was upon this model that French policy after the failure of the Disarmament Conference attempted to establish an Eastern pact which would group Poland, the Baltic States, Czechoslovakia, France, and Germany. All these countries would be bound to one another by obligations of nonaggression, of respect of the status quo, of consultation, and of mutual aid. Were any one country attacked, it would receive support from the others. Louis Barthou presented this conception of a "Locarno of the East" at Geneva on June 6, 1934; he won approval of it in London in July. But on September 10 the Reich addressed us a note of criticism and formal refusal.

What reasons did it advance against the regional pacts? Very often I discussed the matter with the Secretary of State, Bülow, for it was obviously he who had been entrusted with establishing Reich doctrine, supplying it with appropriate arguments and assuming its defense. He did so with much gentleness and vast politeness but with an obstinacy that withstood all attacks.

Bülow was a man of charm, of unfailingly even temper, of excellent manners. A solitary, old, somewhat eccentric bachelor, he lived in a modest apartment, aloof from Berlin society. He was very representative of that old Prussian aristocracy which had retained very simple habits of life and which, steeped in a quasi-religious patriotism, considered it a natural vocation to devote itself, either in the army or in diplomacy, to the service of the state. His pink complexion, his full and rather babyish face, contrasted with his prematurely white hair. His eyes, blue as forget-me-nots, lent his delicate and refined features an expression of melancholy. Whenever he could escape from the capital his greatest pleasures were to ramble the countryside lost in the contemplation of nature, or to row down its rivers in a canoe. A tall man, stooping forward, his head to one side, he had been wounded in battle and could not fully open his right hand. This slight infirmity emphasized his reserve. Evidently he lacked the brilliant qualities of his uncle, the former Chancellor, for whom he was named. But he was earnest, precise, punctual, and thoroughly familiar with every aspect of the matters he dealt with. A colleague of Stresemann and of Brüning, he seemed particularly attached to the latter. By the same token Neurath doubtless inspired him with scant regard. The violences and audacities of Nazism

were assuredly not to his taste, but he deemed it his duty to
help with all his might in the work of national regeneration
which it had undertaken. A specialist in problems involving
the League of Nations, he had no liking for it. Though he
attributed to the League a prejudice of hostility toward Germany and an excess of docility toward France and Britain,
his sympathies went out to Britain more than to France, which
in his heart of hearts he considered Germany's chief adversary.
Yet his relations with me were always most courteous and he
could remain agreeable even in the fiercest debate. He was a re-
doubtable debater. An excellent jurist and a fine dialectician,
he never grew excited and never lost the thread of his argument.

When we first discussed the organization of security through
regional pacts, Germany evaded the issue; she did not enjoy
the same rights as the other nations, she said, she had no real
army and therefore was in no position to pledge her aid on an
equal footing with the others. We attempted to persuade her
that, once the security problem was resolved, that of equality
of armaments would raise no difficulties. Germany remained indifferent to this bait.

But when after March 16, 1935, her army was officially reorganized, she was obliged to change her stand. Nor was she
lacking in arguments. The following was Bülow's favorite:
multilateral pacts and regional agreements destroyed the basic
principle of the League of Nations; they were its very negation; where there were particular friendships, general friendship ceased to exist; such combinations reintroduced into an
institution founded to abolish them the system of hostile
groups and they threatened the very peace they pretended to
consolidate.

If I objected that the pacts in question referred to the
stipulations of the League Covenant, were subordinate to them,
and merely sought to put them into practice, that they were
essentially defensive and intended solely to eliminate any one

country's desire to trouble the peace, he would reply: "They
arouse mistrust. Imagine a meeting where one group huddles
in a corner consulting in whispers. These peoples' cabals per-
plex and worry the outsiders, who at once seek support for
themselves, and there we are, back to antagonist blocs! Regional
pacts inevitably create antagonist blocs; they result in a generalization of war, where wisdom teaches us to restrict war.
Their incidences cause a country to go to war by ricochet
though it be quite unwilling; they expose it to serve as a battle-
ground or a passage for foreign armies, both equally deplor-
able eventualities. Pacts come into play when acts of aggression are committed but the definition of aggression opens the
door to the most arbitrary interpretations. Regional pacts
should be concluded only between neighbor states. Why is
France interfering in regions which do not concern her? In
Eastern Europe where she has no business to be, in Russia,
in Czechoslovakia, where her interests are not involved? The
only sensible procedure is that of agreements between neighbors, dual pacts whose signatories agree not to attack each
other and to consult each other in difficult times. Without
promising mutual aid, they should merely pledge themselves
not to aid the aggressor."

I stoutly refuted him. Regional agreements, I countered, did
not invite suspicion; they were open and clear as day. The
pacts that recorded them were made public; the League of
Nations controlled them and supervised their enforcement. In
what respect were dual pacts any less suspicious than multiple
pacts? Germany was not excluded from our arrangements, she
was deliberately excluding herself. Why was she rejecting a
system she had considered proper at Locarno? Regional pacts
did not generalize war, they neutralized it because the instigator risked a concerted action by the signatories in support of
his victim. As for "aggression" the invasion of foreign soil
was a perfectly valid interpretation of the term. Finally, it
was both natural and legitimate that countries remote from

such and such a region governed by such and such a pact should nevertheless be associated with this pact because their interests were general, European and world-wide. All nations were, in a sense, the trustees of peace.

The Franco-German controversy followed this pattern for months. Like the disarmament question it gave rise to an abundant exchange of notes which served no purpose save that of allowing the Reich to gain time and to develop its military forces. The system of regional pacts was manifestly conceived to defend the European status quo. How could the Third Reich possibly have concurred? It dreamed only of upsetting, to its own profit, the order born of Germany's defeat in 1918; it had quitted the League of Nations precisely in order to escape the precautions that League members were taking to ensure peace.

If Germany seemed to make the best of the Locarno Pact, it was because modification of her western frontier was not the first point on the program of her resurgence. Nazidom's plans for conquest looked to the East; to carry them out it needed to maintain peace in the West. But it understood clearly that its plans for the future would be compromised if it suffered the Locarno idea to spread to Eastern and Central Europe. Therefore it threw its whole political and diplomatic weight into the balance in order to foil the French undertaking. It found valuable support at Warsaw and thus managed to prevent Poland and the Baltic States from joining in the pact. In the end the Eastern pact was reduced to a proposed agreement between France and Soviet Russia. From then on Hitler's irritability waxed apace as prospects of a new crisis loomed in the offing.

Never indeed would the Führer believe in the sincerity of our repeated proposals that he join in a triple pact with ourselves and Russia. Forgetting that his first act on becoming Chancellor had been to extend the Treaty of Rapallo, he declared that we suggested this only because we well knew he would never accept it. Could we seriously suppose him capable of concluding a political agreement with the most dangerous enemy of Europe? If we the French did so, it was because we were returning to the old policy of encirclement, the true cause of the war of 1914.

On that point Hitler's language and Bülow's never varied a jot. It is only fair to acknowledge that at the same time in order to intimidate us they indicated that in their opinion our possible pact with the Russians would deal a mortal blow to the Pact of Locarno. They argued that through some Soviet machination our obligation to assist Russia might lead us to attack Germany, whereas the nonaggression clause in the Treaty of Locarno forbade us to do so. The Locarno dispensation had admitted of exceptions in favor of Poland and Czechoslovakia. If a third was now to be added in favor of the USSR, nothing was left and Locarno made no sense.

It was easy to reply that the obligation to bear aid was not automatic; that the League of Nations would first have to determine the aggressor and, were there machination, the League would not be duped; that the Covenant took precedence over the pacts; that the guarantor powers at Locarno had made no objection to the proposed France-Russian Pact, and lastly, that they would be consulted in any case. But we were no more successful in making Germany understand us on this score than we had been on the regional pacts question.

If only the general attitude of the Third Reich had tended toward peace, we might have been tempted to take its opposition into account. But its every word and gesture were alarming. The official proclamation of the Reich's rearmament removed our last scruple. No check was superfluous against the increasing encroachments and audacities of Nazism. On May 2 and May 14 France, taking no notice of Germany's representations, signed the Franco-Soviet Pact at Paris and at Moscow respectively.

A week later, on May 21, Hitler made a great speech in the

Reichstag in answer to the decisions of the Stresa Conference and of the League of Nations Council. He boasted of his peaceful intentions, in order to shake the coalition formed against him, and he commented on the recent Franco-Soviet Pact. Persisting in terming it a military alliance, he declared that it resembled the old alliances and presented the same dangers they had; he added that among other drawbacks it injected an element of confusion and uncertainty into the Locarno Treaty. However Germany would respect the commitments it had made freely, even those made before the advent of the Third Reich; the Treaty of Locarno would therefore be honored. But this public assurance of his was followed by a significant restriction: *Germany would respect the treaty so long as the other signatories themselves respected it.* By these words he kept a door open and reserved himself the means, when he judged the time opportune, to maintain that, the other signatories (i.e., France) having violated the treaty, it was null and void.

On June 1 the Wilhelmstrasse submitted a memorandum to us in which it declared that the Franco-Soviet Pact was incompatible with Locarno. On June 25, in a countermemorandum, we refuted the German allegations. Then the debate was suspended. Germany did not insist: Hitler appeared to be resigned. Truth to tell, he was nothing of the kind. But he knew that the conclusion of the Franco-Soviet Pact had to be ratified by the French parliament; he was not unaware that stiff opposition to the pact had risen in our country and he reckoned that this might defeat its ratification. He had also learned that Britain looked none too favorably on the rapprochement between France and Bolshevist Russia; help might be forthcoming to him from this direction too. Besides he must allow the war in Ethiopia to unsettle the Stresa coalition and detach Italy. Finally the reorganization of the Reich's army, though feverishly pursued, had not progressed enough. For these reasons he was satisfied at having laid the mines; when the time was ripe he would set them off. Meanwhile he repeated that, despite serious objections aroused by the Franco-Russian Pact, he would for his part continue faithfully to observe the Locarno agreement.

I myself did not trust these would-be appeasing declarations. Too many signs warned me that Hitler's state of mind remained alarming. On September 10 at Nuremberg he had himself presented with a replica of Charlemagne's sword, symbolic of the might of the German Reich. The Party Congress concluded with a great military parade. On October 15 the building of the War Academy, which had been revived, was solemnly dedicated. But most significant, the tenth anniversary of the signature of the Treaty of Locarno, which fell the very next day, was completely ignored by the press.

On November 21 I paid Hitler a visit in the middle of the afternoon. I had been charged to inform him that the debate on the ratification of the Franco-Soviet Pact would shortly be held in the French Chambers and to remind him once again that the pact in question was in no sense directed against Germany, that its nature was purely defensive, that it was but one fragment of a whole, inspired by the desire to organize security with the Reich's co-operation, and finally, that no notion of excluding or encircling Germany figured in its clauses.

Hitler appreciated the attention our government had charged me to pay him, but this did not prevent him from launching into a long tirade against a pact he considered criminal. There could be no doubt, he asserted, that this was a military alliance directed against him. Russia was a permanent menace to Europe; she did not belong to Europe and thought only of overturning Europe. The present Italo-Abyssinian conflict served to emphasize the absurdities of the system of collective security. Would not France find herself drawn into a position hostile to Italy with whom she had bound herself in friendship only a few months ago? Would not Britain be driven to set up a blockade and go to war? Who could tell what stratagems the

Soviets would resort to in order to embroil matters between France and Germany? Today France interpreted the Franco-Soviet Pact in a given manner. But tomorrow a different government would interpret it differently. Hitler also expressed indignation at sanctions because they upset the economic life not only of the country against which they were taken but also of all other countries. Sanctions would lead to the development of substitute products. "I can assure you," he told me, "that we are going to apply ourselves to the ersatz industry more than ever before."

Obviously the case of Mussolini worried him; but it was chiefly his violence in criticizing the Franco-Soviet Pact that left me with no doubt as to his future intentions. If he uttered such an indictment, then he must already have decided to retaliate, and his retaliation could be only the denunciation of Locarno and the occupation of the demilitarized zone.

I had already instructed the Quai d'Orsay to this effect; I had advised it that Hitler's sole hesitancy now concerned the appropriate moment to act. After my conversation with the Führer I renewed my recommendations. In a long dispatch on November 26 I requested the government to consult upon what conduct it should fittingly adopt on the day when Hitler passed from words to action. Personally I suggested that we should not wait for this to happen; we should forestall it by openly asking the question, thus forcing Hitler to lay his cards on the table. Such a policy might perhaps persuade Hitler to pledge himself to raise no fortification in the Rhine zone in return for our approving the establishment of a few garrisons, limited in number and in effectives. Or else, I urged, let us threaten to oppose with armed force the realization of his aims.

My suggestion was disapproved. It was objected that if we appeared to admit any possibility of revising the Locarno Pact there was reason to believe that the whole pact might crumble, with Britain regaining freedom of action and Italy, absorbed in the Ethiopian war, losing all interest in the problems of the Rhineland frontier.

Our military high command, which knew of my dispatch, asked in its turn what attitude the government would adopt if the possibility I indicated were to become a fact. The answer was that in such an event we would depend upon the regular procedure of the League of Nations. Past experience, it would appear, had still left us with illusions about the efficacy of the Geneva system.

I continued to be so deeply preoccupied by the situation which might face us shortly that I made it the subject of my last telegram in 1935. On December 31 I insisted on the striking recrudescence of the campaign by the German press against the Franco-Soviet Pact and the Locarno agreement. "In 1936," I wrote, "the efforts of Reich diplomacy will clearly tend to free Germany of a servitude she judges to be too harsh. Invoking the demands of national security, Germany will strive to make possible the establishment of garrisons and fortifications on her western frontier. The means to be employed by the Reich's leaders will depend upon circumstances, the course of events, the dispensations of the League of Nations, the state of our relations with our friends, especially Britain, and the firmness of our attitude."

On January 1, 1936, having to offer to the Chancellor the condolences of the French Government on the occasion of the death of Herr Koester, German Ambassador in Paris, I complained of the articles that were still being published in the Berlin press. Hitler assured me that he had no intention of again bringing up the Locarno question. On January 10 and January 13, in the course of two conversations, I reproached Bülow sharply. "You are behaving," I said, "as though you wished to establish juridical justification for a future act already planned. This act is, of course, the occupation of the demilitarized zone. . . . You doubtless realize that in such an event the situation would become very serious!"

Bülow remained evasive and, like his master, protested that Germany had no intentions of denouncing Locarno.

On February 11 the debate on ratification of the Franco-Soviet Pact opened in the Chamber of Deputies. On February 25 the Minister for Foreign Affairs, P. E. Flandin, established clearly that this pact was perfectly in keeping with that of Locarno. But since Germany was of contrary opinion, he offered to carry the problem to the World Court at The Hague. The German press, ignoring this proposal, found ever more furious terms in which to accuse France of preparing the encirclement of the Reich.

The signature of a similar pact between the USSR and Czechoslovakia at just that time supplied Hitler with an additional argument. On February 27 the Chamber of Deputies ratified the Franco-Soviet agreement by 353 votes to 165. "An act fraught with consequences!" wrote the Reich gazettes. But next day, February 28, to the amazement of everyone, the Paris daily *Le Matin* published an interview which Hitler had granted Bertrand de Jouvenel. In it Hitler evinced the warmest feelings and the most conciliating disposition toward France. With remarkable insistence he expressed a desire for amity and a will for agreement and rapprochement. People rubbed their eyes: had they read aright? On February 29 the government invited me to inform the Chancellor that it was not indifferent to the declarations the French journalist had received; it asked him how he conceived this rapprochement which he appeared so devoutly to wish for.

Hitler received me on March 2 in Neurath's presence. His color had risen, his eyes were brighter than usual; he was nervous, excited, and disturbed; he looked very impatient and very much annoyed. He at once discussed the interview which was the motive of my visit. The thing was a piece of trickery! We had made a fool of him! He did not deny the accuracy of his statements as published by Jouvenel, but they had been made a week before; they were to be published before the vote in the Chamber: their publication was deliberately delayed by what was doubtless an expedient of the French Government or of its embassy in Berlin. At present they had been overtaken by the event. But Hitler was willing to answer the question I had come to ask him. The matter was being studied: he would give me exact and detailed proposals in the near future.

I protested that neither my embassy nor the French Government had had a hand in delaying publication of an interview of which they had had no knowledge. But the Chancellor remained incredulous; he imagined that the French press, like that of the Reich, took government orders. His aspect and tone of voice were not reassuring; I foresaw no good in the forthcoming proposals.

On March 6 it was announced in Berlin that the Reichstag would meet next day at noon. This signified that something serious was afoot. Sure enough, on the morning of March 7 Baron von Neurath summoned me to the Wilhelmstrasse in order to give me, as well as the British and Italian ambassadors and the Belgian chargé, a note denouncing the Treaty of Locarno. I asked whether I was to consider this note as constituting the awaited proposals. He replied in the affirmative, warning me that some military units "symbolic in character" had already begun to enter the demilitarized zone. Soon after, this news was confirmed by our consuls, who reported to me that the Reichswehr was parading down the boulevards of the principal Rhenish towns amid great popular enthusiasm. But the "symbolic" units mentioned by the wily Neurath were already nineteen infantry battalions and thirteen artillery sections strong.

Hitler's behavior proved that he was resolved some months earlier to denounce Locarno if the Franco-Soviet Pact was ratified. On the strength of inaccurate information he believed that ratification would fail; hoping to dissuade parliamentarians from ratifying and to influence French public opinion, he had given Bertrand de Jouvenel statements calculated to dis-

turb them. When the interview had no effect and his hopes
proved fruitless, he carried out the plan he had kept back.
Now was the opportune moment. Italy's victory in Africa was
assured; the League of Nations had been powerless to save
Abyssinia, and Mussolini's resentment made it improbable that
he would care to intervene, in the name of the League, in a
conflict over Locarno. Intelligences received from England did
not give Hitler cause to believe that the British Government
was in a mood for war. Nor had he the impression that France
would go to extremes either; the country was rife with political struggles, and parliamentary elections, scheduled for April,
held the attention of government and public. By now the rearmament of the Reich had progressed considerably; already
the Wehrmacht constituted an important force. He could well
try his luck. . . . Again the tactics inspiring him all along
the line were the same he had employed previously with happy
results. He struck his adversary in the face and as he did so
declared: "I bring you proposals for peace!"

The denunciation of the treaty was accompanied by a memorandum whose contents permitted Neurath to pretend that
it embodied the answer Hitler had promised to my question
of March 2 and the detailed proposals he had announced. The
document was twofold. Part I repeated the thesis so often
upheld by Bülow and the Wilhelmstrasse on the incompati-
bility of the Franco-Soviet Pact with the stipulations of Locarno. But Part II tendered offers of rather far-reaching import. The Reich, it stated, was prepared to open immediate
negotiations in view of creating a new demilitarized zone, this
time on both sides of the frontier and in conditions of equality
for France and for Germany. It was prepared to conclude a
pact of nonaggression with France and Belgium, valid for
twenty-five years, and complemented by an air pact, with
Britain and Italy as guarantor powers, and Holland included,
if she so desired. With Germany's neighbors to the East it proposed the conclusion of pacts similar to the existent German-

Polish Pact. Finally it implied that, equality of rights having now been restored, Germany might discuss the colonial problem and the reforms to be introduced in the statutes of the League of Nations.

In the Reichstag Hitler, excited, fierce, and deeply moved, merely paraphrased the memorandum. Goering announced that the elections, to be held on March 29, amounted to a referendum which would ask the nation's opinion on the policy which had been seeking "equality of rights and the reconciliation of the peoples" for the last three years.

In Paris the denunciation of Locarno and the entrance of troops into the demilitarized zone fell like a thunderbolt. Yet France had foreseen them at considerable distance and had had ample leisure to prepare for them! All the same the event caught our leaders unawares. A government communiqué related the facts preceding the Führer's action; it emphasized the scandalous nature of this unilateral act which its author sought vainly to justify by an arbitrary and false interpretation of the Franco-Soviet Pact and which, one week after protestations of friendship for France, shamelessly tore up a treaty freely concluded with her.

As early as the morning of March 7 the ministers sat in council; a second session was called that evening with the three chiefs of staff present. On March 8 they met again at the Elysée. It was announced that the Locarno signatories would meet in Paris on March 10 and that immediate security measures were to be taken on our eastern frontier. That evening Premier Albert Sarraut broadcast to the nation. In a grave, solemn voice he gave a picture of the situation, declaring that he refused to entertain Hitler's offers. How could Germany ever be expected to keep her word? Besides France would not consent to negotiate when faced with a *fait accompli* and outright threats. "We are not inclined," he added, "to leave Strasbourg exposed to the fire of German guns."

It might be supposed, thereafter, that France would dispatch

troops into the Rhineland zone to expel the Germans without waiting for the guarantor powers and the states interested
to decide upon the question. The Reich could denounce Locarno but it had no right to reap the consequences of this
brutal act forthwith by occupying the Rhenish towns. Germany's infringement and defiance were flagrant, Hitler's attitude amounted to an aggression and created a *casus belli*. Was
war about to break out? Many people thought so.

But it was not to be. The French troops did no more than
man the Maginot Line. On March 10 the government explained to the Chamber that it entertained no fundamental
enmity toward the German people but that to negotiate today
was senseless. It would negotiate when respect for international
law was assured. Meanwhile, within the framework of the
League of Nations, it was determined to add all its efforts to
those of other League members in order to oppose a veritable
outrage to international trust. For all the vigor of its tone, this
condemnation showed that we were singing small. France
would not act alone but in concert with the powers of Locarno
and the League of Nations just as she had done the year before
in a less acute conflict. The hour for war was past.

The government of the period has been taxed with weakness. It has been reproached with missing its chance to give
Nazism a lesson which might perhaps have spelled its ruin.
Yet somewhat later it was learned that the government weighed
with utmost earnestness the hypothesis of a military demonstration. A force of a few army corps would have marched into
the Saar and occupied Saarbrück. The civilian ministers favored the operation but the three military ministers were
unanimously opposed. General Gamelin advised that a war
operation, however limited, entailed unpredictable risks and
could not be undertaken without decreeing a general mobilization.

The government, unsure of itself, withdrew before this
possibility. It was not unanimous. It was not certain that it

could depend upon the full enthusiastic endorsement of public opinion despite general aversion to the Hitler regime. It was not certain of the approval of the Chambers, whose votes should have been solicited. Pacifism at that time was still very powerful; the notion of war ran counter to prevailing sentiment. People persisted in expecting the League of Nations to bring the recalcitrants and rebels to heel by virtue of its mere weight. The experiences of March 1935 and of the Ethiopian war had not availed to modify the current attitude. People remained attached to the principle of collective security based on a policy of solidarity and co-operation. France was averse to the prospect of acting on her own initiative without the guarantee and assistance of all the others and especially without being assured of Britain's full agreement and close co-operation.

Britain in March 1936 happened to be in exactly the same position as in March 1935. The Foreign Secretary confessed in Commons on March 9: "Occupation of the Rhineland by the Reichswehr deals a heavy blow to the principle of the sanctity of treaties. Fortunately," he added, "we have no reason to suppose that Germany's present action threatens hostilities." Truly Hitler's trick was proving effective once again. British diplomacy pinned its hopes and effort upon Hitler's offers of negotiation; it saw in them the means of retreating from a critical situation which it was resolved to prevent from degenerating into a war because it feared being dragged into a war or because it did not judge Britain in a position to fight. By sacrificing the past, British diplomacy was no doubt preserving the present; but far from safeguarding the future, it was busy making it more terrible and more ineluctable. The illusions under which British policy labored were to prove tough, resisting a long time against test after test: Simon was their dupe and, after him, Eden shared them, and when Eden was at length disabused, they were to rise again in Neville Chamberlain.

After the occupation of the demilitarized zone Britain not only failed to encourage us to resort to arms against the Reich but she gave us to understand that she would not second us in a coercive undertaking. Yet she attempted to ease our resentment and apprehensions for the future by agreeing to define her obligations toward us in case of a fresh crisis and, specifically, to join us in consultations between the general staffs. At the same time she was attempting to persuade Germany to furnish appeasements, after which complete negotiations on the basis of the Chancellor's offers might permit us all to restore harmony and concord in Europe.

For forty-eight hours, while German troops were settling in Rhenish towns, Hitler with beating heart awaited the turn of events. Subsequently Goebbels acknowledged the anxiety endured at the time by Hitler and his lieutenants. Had French troops entered the Rhineland, the Reichswehr would probably have withdrawn across the Rhine, leaving weak contingents to defend the outskirts of inhabited places in a delaying action. On the other hand it is much less certain that the failure of Germany's attempt would have caused the downfall of the regime. Nazism already had too strong a hold on the country. More likely the Reich, seized with fever and rage, would have organized some counteraction making war inevitable. It remains to ascertain whether war at this time would have broken out under conditions more favorable to us than those of September 1939 and whether Britain and our other allies would have come to our aid. Be that as it may, when after two days Hitler noted that France, far from mobilizing, was headed in the direction of League conferences and procedures, he heaved a deep sigh of relief. Instantly he recovered his composure and arrogance, just as he had done at the time of the interview with Sir John Simon. For he felt that he had won.

First at Paris on March 10, then at London on March 12 and March 13, the Locarno signatory powers expressed their indignation. Eden requested that Germany diminish the

strength of the effectives she had sent into the Rhineland.
Hitler replied that the Reich would not suffer any limitation
of its just rights. It was unwilling to diminish its effectives
but would agree not to increase them provided that France and
Belgium did likewise. Obviously Hitler was once again sure
of himself. On March 14 and in the days following, the council of the League of Nations met. It invited Germany to send
its representative; Hitler delegated Ribbentrop. In spite of
Ribbentrop's protestations that France, not Germany, had violated the Treaty of Locarno, Germany was charged with the
violation. The Locarno powers then announced their decision.
For them the 1925 agreement was still valid. The World
Court at The Hague would be consulted on the compatibility
of the Franco-Soviet Pact with the Pact of Locarno. A neutral
zone, fifteen miles wide, would be established in the Rhineland,
to be controlled by international forces until a new system
of security was adopted. Britain, France, and Belgium were
to conclude general staff agreements. Germany was to pledge
herself not to build permanent fortifications in the Rhineland.

Unfortunately the Locarno powers mistook their desires for
verdicts and their verdicts for realities. They were deceived
both as to themselves and as to Hitler's Germany. On March
20, in the Chamber, P. E. Flandin was overhasty when he
boasted of the results obtained in London as a brilliant success.
On March 24 Hitler declared through Ribbentrop that his
understanding was quite different. He would not bow to decisions that were virtual dictates; he would suffer no discrimination to his detriment; if he had re-established German sovereignty in the Rhineland, it was not in order to brook its curtailment or suppression. He would gladly offer suggestions
intended to consolidate peace but would reject any humiliating
stipulations that might be appended.

British opinion was stirred by this haughty rebuff which
threatened to revive the problem in its most acute form. It
feared lest its government had gone too far in the military

guarantees promised to France. On March 26, in the House of Commons, Eden beat a hasty retreat. The Locarno powers, he said, had handed down no dictate but had merely offered proposals; the general staff conferences between Britain and France lacked the importance ascribed to them; Britain's plea for moderation applied to France as well as to Germany. And Stanley Baldwin invited Ribbentrop to luncheon.

Italy had attended the London meetings as a silent witness; this silence had been interpreted as agreement with the decisions made. Now she announced that it was impossible for her to participate in the program established by the Locarno powers. The Ethiopian war had put her on bad terms with the League, with Britain, and with France; it had oriented her toward Germany.

Meanwhile the referendum ordered by the Reich was held on March 19. Ninety-eight per cent of the voters approved the Chancellor's foreign policy: the opposition totaled only 543,000 out of 44,950,000 votes.

On April 1, primed by the en masse assent of his people, Hitler addressed a "peace plan" to the powers, preceded by a long and virulent indictment of the policy practiced by France. He took exception to the competence of the Hague Court and protested against military conversations between France and Britain. Germany proposed that the future be divided into three periods. The first, lasting four months, would serve as a cooling-off period, during which the Reich would not increase its effectives in the Rhineland, on conditions of reciprocity. During the second stage Germany, Belgium, and France would conclude a nonaggression pact for twenty-five years, complemented if necessary by an air pact; Germany would also sign nonaggression pacts with her neighbors to the east and southeast. During the third period the Reich would arrange to return to Geneva in the hope that her colonial claims would be examined and the statutes of the League of

Nations be modified so that the text of the Covenant would be finally separated from the text of the Treaty of Versailles.

There was nothing new in all this; in effect Hitler was simply repeating the terms of his memorandum. Did he honestly believe that his "peace plan" offered a basis for serious negotiations which might lead to a general agreement? What lay at the depths of this strange, troublous man's soul? The question was put to me on April 3 by P. E. Flandin and Albert Sarraut, who had summoned to Paris the French ambassadors in Britain, Italy, Poland, and Germany (Corbin, Chambrun, Noël, and me). It was incidentally the only meeting of the sort that I was ever called upon to attend.

I told the Minister for Foreign Affairs and the Premier that Hitler must not be considered as a chief of state or chief of government of the current type: he was a pirate who observed neither the manners nor the morality of the regular navy. He had a plan of action in mind. He was determined to shake off the consequences of the defeat of 1918, to establish his domination in Central Europe, and to enlarge the Reich at Russia's expense. This program concerned regions with which he considered that France and Britain had no business; he preferred and would do his best to carry it out without going to war. But if France and Britain attempted to stand in the way of his ambitions, and if war were required to sweep away the obstacles they reared, then he would go to war. When Hitler spoke of peace, it was German peace, *pax germanica.*

For the time being, his chief care was to feed the conversation, for, while it was going on, his troops remained in the Rhineland and the world was growing accustomed to their presence there.

France answered the Chancellor's plan in a memorandum addressed to the British Government and filed with Brussels and Rome. Things were being done as though the lawyers of two parties to a suit were exchanging briefs before an imaginary jury.

The French document consisted, for the first part, in a sharp rejoinder to Hitler's indictment, accompanied by direct and precise counterquestions. Germany had stated that she signed the Pact of Locarno under duress. Did she mean to state the same for all the clauses of the Treaty of Versailles, especially for those relative to Memel, Danzig, and Austria? Was she prepared to recognize unreservedly the existing territorial and political status of Europe? Did she acknowledge that peace was to be assured by the collaboration of all, respectful of the rights of each and every one, or did she maintain that each state was free to settle its differences in a duel with some other state whose good faith it had abused?

In the second place Paris opposed a French peace plan to the German. Our plan in turn was but a repetition of the thesis that we had constantly upheld and that the Reich had obstinately rejected. We recommended collective security, organized through regional agreements, themselves based on pacts of nonaggression and mutual aid within the framework of the League and of a European Commission and implemented by an international police force to repress violations and failure to fulfill engagements contracted.

As in the case of the disarmament controversy the respective positions were the same. The debate continued with no progress and no prospect of any means of solution.

In this impasse Britain's chief concern was to avoid the breaking-off of discussions. Under the pretext of clarifying certain points in Hitler's proposals the British Cabinet drew up a questionnaire, inspired by the questions contained in the French memorandum; it submitted them for discussion as one might toss wood on a fire to prevent it from going out.

Yet the fire did go out. Hitler simply never replied to the British questionnaire, which he considered offensive. Efforts intended to substitute some agreement in place of the pact torn up by Germany dragged on fruitlessly until July. Other preoccupations cast it little by little into the shadow, then into oblivion. *Un clou chasse l'autre* says the proverb, one nail drives out another. The French elections, held on April 26 and May 2, returned a new majority, placed a Popular Front government in power, and caused a series of domestic difficulties which absorbed France's attention. In December the League of Nations, attempting to liquidate the Ethiopian affair, emerged defeated; Italy's victory contributed to the building of the Rome-Berlin Axis. And the Spanish Civil War, especially, presented a danger of general war conspicuously more pressing than was any settlement of the problem of the Rhine frontier. In August, celebration of the Olympic Games in Berlin sealed the triumph of Adolf Hitler.

VII. GAMES, FESTIVALS, VISITS AND VIGIL OF ARMS

I N THE history of the Nazi regime, the celebration of the Olympic Games in Berlin
in August 1936 illustrated a great mo-
ment, a climax of sorts, if not the apotheosis of Hitler and his
Third Reich. Hitler had impressed himself upon the consciousness of Europe as an extraordinary personage. His prestige was enormously increased; his powers of attraction spread
far beyond the borders of the Reich. Crowned heads, princes,
and illustrious guests thronged to Berlin, eager to meet this
prophetic being who apparently held the fate of Europe in
his hand and to observe the Germany which he had transformed and galvanized in his irresistible grip. Beholding a flaw-

less organization, an impeccable order, a perfect discipline, and a limitless prodigality, everyone went into ecstasy.

The picture was magnificent indeed. From the moment the Nazis came into power they began preparing for this great day. At the gates of Berlin, in the suburbs to the west, strewn with lakes and forests, they built a mammoth stadium holding one hundred thousand spectators. From outside the edifice was disappointing; it lacked the imposing eminence of the Colosseum at Rome, for it nestled in the earth. But within it was strikingly noble. Wide ramps permitted the crowd to enter and leave in a few moments without the least jostling. It was fitted with all the appointments and improvements suited to its purpose: the athletes' dressing rooms, the press quarters, the restaurants, and the stands for the authorities left nothing to be desired.

But Hitler was dissatisfied, objecting, as he told me later, to its being built in concrete, a material he did not fancy. How, he asked me, could concrete ever possess the austerity of stone? Besides, who could tell of its resistance to time?

In February the Winter Events, held in Garmisch-Partenkirchen, were both colorful and brilliant; but they were as nothing against the real Games on August 1, 1936.

At the appointed hour a breathless crowd burst into cheers as the last runner appeared, brandishing the symbolic torch borne, stage by stage, from Olympus. From a basin set on a tripod at the entrance of the stadium it kindled a flame which was to burn for the duration of the Games. Slowly the Olympic banner rose, unfurling its twined circles at the top of the flagstaff. The slow, deep tolling of a bell emphasized the solemnity of the moment.

In the official stand Hitler and his lieutenants sat with the King of Bulgaria, the Prince of Piedmont, Princess Maria of Savoy, the crown princes of Sweden and Greece, and the sons of Mussolini. Facing them the members of the International Committee, magistrates of an ideal republic made material for but an instant, proclaimed the opening of the Games and heard the athletes' oath. A choir sang the occasional hymn composed by Richard Strauss as thousands of doves flew into the blue sky amid a great whirring of wings. Then the competing teams filed by. The Austrians aroused warm applause, but the French were greeted with even greater enthusiasm. After the breach of the Treaty of Locarno it had been feared that they would not participate. But Leon Blum knew how paltry it would be to inflict a pinprick when the energy to wield the sword was lacking. So the French were here, headed by a giant waving a huge tricolor flag. They cut a good figure as they marched smartly by. As they neared the stand, on a given order, they gave the Olympic salute, raising their right arms horizontally on a line with their shoulders. The crowd mistook this gesture for the Hitlerian salute. Believing it a chivalrous homage to the Third Reich and its leader, they gave vent to a wholly mistaken enthusiasm.

During the days that followed, the Games illustrated the elemental forces of national sentiment rather than the existence of any vigorous international solidarity. Everyone applauded chiefly his own compatriots, gloried in their victories, and bemoaned their defeats. Hitler, his face contorted, observed the performances of his athletes with a passionate interest. When they won he beamed, slapping his thighs loudly and laughing as he looked at Goebbels; when they lost his expression hardened and he scowled.

In conjunction with the Games, splendid festivities roused the surprise and admiration of the guests of honor. Hitler received majesties and royal highnesses at his board. Goebbels entertained about one thousand people for supper and a reception on the lawns of the Pfaueninsel. As it had rained during the day, airplanes were dispatched in all directions to collect new material. The trees were turned into flaming chandeliers. Reichswehr engineers set up a pontoon bridge linking the island to the shore; they formed twin lines across the river, their oars raised in salute, as a bevy of girls, dressed as Renaissance pages, led the guests to their places. At midnight the dazzling and thundering display of fireworks suggested nothing so much as a bombardment.

Ribbentrop, newly appointed Ambassador to Britain, invited seven hundred persons to his sumptous villa at Dahlem where under a giant marquee they celebrated both the Olympic Games and his rise to the highest diplomatic post in the gift of the Reich. Champagne flowed like water; it was the best Pommery, a brand for which he had long been salesman and agent. Meanwhile he strolled from group to group under the admiring glances of a family marveling at his brilliant fortune, his expression the picture of assurance and self-content.

As for Goering, in the gardens of his ministry he reproduced a miniature eighteenth-century village, complete with inn, post office, bakery, shops for the various crafts, and the rest. He himself rode a merry-go-round until he was breathless. He also gave a sumptous dinner, followed by a ball, at the Berlin Opera. The whole building had been newly done over in creamy satin; a floor linked stage and house. A profusion of lackeys in powdered wigs and red livery lined the aisles between tables aswarm with dazzling uniforms, beribboned and bemedaled dress suits, and gala evening gowns. The regime's general staff was there to a man, rutilant, radiant, showering attentions upon one and all; the orchestra filled the vast nave with its peerless harmonies. How, one wondered, could these men, so obviously pleased with this fashionable and exquisite entertainment, be the persecutors of Jews and the torturers of the concentration camps?

The Third Reich always had a taste for festivals and a sense of their importance; it attributed a high social and civic value to them, emphasizing their virtue as propaganda. Germany now enjoyed a splendor of ceremonies such as it had never previously known. The calendar of these events was strictly appointed, the diplomatic corps regularly invited; the Chancellor considered it important that chiefs of missions attend, both in order to dazzle them and to give his own people the notion that foreigners were dazzled by Hitlerian Germany. The German people, like their master, combined an inferiority complex with a sense of pride.

During the early years of their reign the Nazi leaders, like Hitler himself, had treated diplomats somewhat distantly and haughtily. They would have invited suspicion had they frequented the foreign embassies and legations, especially the French. But about 1936 this prohibition was modified, and they were allowed, indeed advised, to mingle in Berlin society. In the interval most of them had grown rich and become sociable; they learned to enjoy comfort and luxury.

For a long time Goering had set an example. He loved publicity, decorum, etiquette. He enjoyed society. He liked to appear in his glory, his pomp, and his bulk and to observe what interest and curiosity greeted his resplendent uniforms, his wide ribbons, his medals and his jewels. Goebbels lacked Goering's abandon; he was reserved and reticent. Although infinitely more cultured, he was more shy. Besides he belonged to the xenophobe clan of chauvinists and he found it difficult to conceal his special abomination of France. Himmler, who was crude, sullen, curt, and gloomy, rarely emerged from his own circle. Ley, a drunkard and debauchee, and Baldur von Schirach, elegant and enigmatical, were no more assiduous in the drawing rooms of Berlin than Himmler. On the other hand one constantly met Neurath, Papen, Schacht, Ribbentrop, Tschammer-Osten, Frick, Keitel, Schwerin-Krosigck, Funk, Gürtner, Blomberg, and the secretaries, later ministers of state, Meissner, Lammers, Bouhler, and their families.

Early in March, it was *Heldentag*, the Festival of the Heroes, commemorating and exalting the heroes killed in World War I or in party combat. It consisted in a ceremony at the Kroll or Charlottenburg Opera, with speeches by Goebbels and the

Reichswehr Minister; a second ceremony at the shrine of the Unknown Soldier (where Hitler, flanked by aged Marshal von Mackensen, laid a wreath); and a final short military parade.

On April 20 Germany celebrated the Führer's birthday, as it used to celebrate the Kaiser's in pre-1918 days, but with more pomp, banners, and speeches. Delegates arrived from all parts of the country, bearing sumptuous gifts which the press described in touching terms. A vast Reichswehr parade took place at noon along the rectilinear thoroughfare that passed through the Tiergarten and Charlottenburg.

Labor Day was celebrated on May 1 in honor of workers, employees, and artisans. The ceremonies followed the pattern of 1933, attempting each year to surpass the record previously established.

In early September the Nuremberg Congress—the party festival—lasted a whole week.

A month later the hill of Bückeberg, near Hanover, served as setting for the Harvest Festival, honoring the peasantry. Clad in local costumes, the countrymen from the various provinces produced the various fruits of their soil and indulged in song and dance. Hitler would make a speech and the day would end with a Reichswehr parade.

The most spectacular of these festivals was the Nuremberg Congress, one of the Third Reich's most original institutions. Nuremberg was not selected by chance; several excellent reasons governed Hitler's choice. In the first place Nuremberg had had the merit of welcoming the Hitlerians at an early and painful period in their existence. More important, Nuremberg illustrated one of the supreme periods in the history of ancient Germany. For several centuries the crown insignia of the Holy Roman Empire were stored there, then some were transferred to Vienna; so soon as Hitler brought Austria into the German fold, he made a point of restoring these treasures to their original repository. The shadow of Richard Wagner, the prophet of the Third Reich, lay heavy over the city; its narrow streets, lined with carved gables, and its flamboyant churches were as the permanent echo of the Meistersinger. Here was the predestined site for a sect of fanatics who boasted of reawakening Germany, of leading her back to her most glorious traditions, and of restoring to her the eminent position she once occupied in Europe. Munich would always be considered the capital where Nazism took shape and whence it advanced to the conquest of the Reich, Berlin as the governmental and administrative center; between the two, Nuremberg figured as the pilgrim shrine at which thought and sentiment met to reverence great memories of bygone days and great ambitions for the future.

Each year the Nuremberg Congress bore a distinctive title: there were the Congress of Victory, the Congress of Honor, the Congress of the Triumph of Will, the Congress of Faith. For one week throngs filled the city, doubling its population. A remarkably efficient organization managed to orient, house, and feed this human flood without the least confusion. Stranger still and difficult to describe was the atmosphere of collective enthusiasm that permeated the ancient city, the singular exaltation that seized hundreds of thousands of men and women, the romantic fever and the mystic ecstasy and the sacred delirium, as it were, that possessed them!

Seven days yearly Nuremberg was a city devoted to revelry and madness, almost a city of convulsionaries, Holy Rollers, and the like. The surroundings, the beauty of the spectacles presented, and the luxury of the hospitality offered exerted a strong influence upon the foreigners whom the Nazi Government was careful to invite annually. Many visitors, dazzled by Nazi display, were infected by the virus of Nazism. They returned home convinced by the doctrine and filled with admiration for the performance. Heedless of the sinister realities lurking beneath the deceptive pomp of these prodigious shows, they were ripe for collaboration.

At Nuremberg, Hitler erected a group of forums of various size, surrounded by high and wide bleachers of stone. Here he would utter his harangues, himself carried away by the waves of passion which emanated from his own being, which spread to the far ends of the arena he occupied, and which returned to him, boomerang-fashion, in a clamor of applause. A flagstone track, up which one hundred men could walk abreast, linked the central forum to the stadiums where open-air demonstrations took place; there was also the "Hall of Congress" where reports were submitted by the Führer's lieutenants—Goebbels, Rosenberg, Hierl, Darré, Todt and Frank—on the year's achievement in their respective fields. But Hitler considered this hall too small. He laid down the plans and began the construction of a mammoth hall which was to be the largest roofed auditorium in the world. Doubtless he dreamed of it as the background against which he was to receive the tribute of the universe—once he had conquered it.

Nuremberg week followed an immutable ritual, one day assigned to each rite. There was Inaugural Day, marked by the reading of the Führer's proclamation. There was Workers' Day, when 40,000 youths went through intricate maneuvers, drilling flawlessly as they bawled songs composed for and by them to celebrate their labors, and wielding spades and shovels that sparkled like artillery. There was Hitler Youth Day, when Nazi boys and Nazi girls had their innings. There was the day devoted to the political bosses and ranking party officers, assembling as many as 150,000 men, links in the close network of Third Reich security and surveillance. There was Brown Shirt Day, when the militia paraded for three, four, and five hours in the market place before a Hitler arm-outstretched and frozen in a hieratic attitude. There was Reichswehr Day with extensive mock combat. And there was Closing Day, with its fireworks, as hundreds of army searchlights in a circle flashed an immense blue dome over the city.

The excessive eloquence with which both Hitler and his deputies attacked democracy, parliamentary institutions, and western liberalism, and the undisguised threats he uttered against such states as Soviet Russia and Czechoslovakia, dictated my refusal to attend the Nuremberg Congress until 1937. Naturally, diplomats were among the preferred guests. As the city lacked sufficient hotel space to lodge them they usually stayed in the Pullman cars that had brought them, which were supplemented by a barber shop and bathrooms. Hitler would visit the diplomats here. And he always gave a tea in their honor at the Deutscher Hof, where he stayed. In the course of the reception speeches were exchanged.

Such was the protocol, which my British and American colleagues and I ignored for four years. Our common absence reflected a sense of disapproval which the Chancellor noted with vexation. But in 1937 the British Ambassador, Sir Eric Phipps, was replaced by Nevile Henderson, who left no stone unturned to please the Nazis and to win their confidence. He decided to go to Nuremberg. In order to avoid the impression that Franco-British solidarity was impaired I resolved to spend one day there, but I made it clear that if offensive remarks were made in my presence about the government I represented, I would leave forthwith.

As I arrived I learned that among the exhibits, one, celebrating anti-Communism, included huge panels depicting the most tragic scenes of the French Revolution. Protesting forthwith, I was able to have these removed. As senior ambassador it was my task to make the occasional address to Hitler. I used it to advantage by picking up a statement which, I was told, Goebbels had made. The day before he had compared democratic peoples with the most stupid calves who, according to a German proverb, choose spontaneously their own butchers. I thanked the Führer for having given his propaganda minister the lie, since I did not suppose he would have invited us if he had considered us to be representatives of the most stupid calves. Hitler joined the audience in laughter: Goebbels, blushing, cast a furious glance in my direction.

Dodd, the American Ambassador, persisted in his attitude of aloofness; nothing could possibly persuade him to set foot in Nuremberg. Scarcely equipped for a career which sometimes requires the diplomat to hide his thoughts and feelings, this old professor, all of a piece, a specialist in the domestic history of his country, a rugged and uncompromising liberal, entertained an aversion for National Socialism which he made no effort to conceal. He discerned and he denounced clearly the ambitions and warlike projects of the Third Reich. But as he had long prophesied world war for the end of the current week, people smiled at his predictions. All the same here was an excellent man of strong character, fundamentally upright and true, a singularly honorable exemplar of that American idealism which managed to remain so fervent despite the rising tide of realism. Had the Nazis studied his reactions more carefully they would have spared themselves many a disagreeable surprise in store for them.

Since 1934 a team of French cavalry officers had taken part in the Berlin Horse Show, meeting with a warm welcome. In May 1937 German officers, greeted as cordially, competed for the first time in the international events of the Paris Horse Show.

All summer the Paris Exposition of Arts and Crafts attracted a number of German tourists, including many less prominent Nazi leaders, most of whom had never been in France. They discovered Paris with manifest pleasure and, at their return, Hitler sought to obtain minute information about all they had observed. Moreover the Third Reich made it a point of honor to appear to advantage.

Its pavilion stood next to the Soviet pavilion, one of the most interesting and best designed exhibits, whose pediment was adorned by two figures, brandishing hammer and sickle, and looking for all the world as though they meant to leap upon their German neighbors. Schacht came to Paris to inaugurate the German pavilion. In his speech he expressed the desire for mutual comprehension that the Reich allegedly entertained. During a week of artistic events the Berlin Opera gave performances from its Wagnerian repertory.

In June an exhibition of French painting was organized in Berlin by the Prussian Academy of Fine Arts. Hitler's taste in this field did not go beyond the 1850s; for him, impressionism and cubism were one and the same thing, both products of the Jewish mind. Nevertheless he took the trouble to visit the exhibition and to purchase a statuette.

In June the training ship *Jeanne d'Arc* put into port at Kiel; its staff was received by Chief Admiral Raeder.

In July foreign diplomats were invited to the opening of a German Art Museum founded in Munich by Hitler; they witnessed a historic and allegorical procession through the city with floats and thousands of actors illustrating the great periods of German history.

Finally, in November, an international exhibition of hunting took place in Berlin, under the patronage of Goering as Reich Grand Master of the Hunt. He made of it his personal enterprise and assured its success.

Goering was, by origin, more bourgeois than most of his fellows. His father had been a colonial governor; he himself had attended the Cadet School and in 1914 was a career officer. His position in the hierarchy of the Third Reich was above the rest; he exerted a prerogative of which he was very jealous and which he defended vigorously against rivals he suspected of designs to supplant him. One day, he asked me point-blank: "Do you know what would happen if the Führer disappeared?" I afforded him vast pleasure by replying as though the issue were automatic and indubitable: "Why, of course. Goering would succeed him."

Indeed he was the heir designate, the *Kronprinz* of the regime. He possessed all the classic features of this position. He was devoted body and soul to Hitler, he proclaimed himself the Führer's "first peer," and nothing on earth could make him betray the Führer's cause. But he did criticize and find fault and, deep in his heart, he considered that Hitler had been reigning somewhat too long. The two often quarreled. Goering, sensitive and easily hurt, would withdraw to his tent like Achilles: but Hitler would soon call him back and pat him on the shoulder, saying, "Good old Goering!" At which Goering flushed with pleasure, and everything was all right again.

The heir apparent to the Third Reich had a noble head, regular features, an open brow, light and cold eyes with a hard, disquieting expression. Unfortunately for him he was obese and tortured by his obesity. From time to time he would undergo a strict cure, and soon take off seventy pounds, then, a month later, put on eighty. He had a more serious infirmity, namely his addiction to morphine. He tried periodically to cure himself and would succeed, but here, too, he suffered relapses.

His war record was brilliant. On his own initiative he transferred from the infantry to the air force. Here he proved himself an ace and, at Richthofen's death, assumed command of the famous squadron. After the war, forced to earn a living, he became a commercial pilot. His flight was Germany-Sweden and return. One evening he made a forced landing on the grounds of a Swedish castle. Welcomed by the lord of the manor, at dinner he met the lady, a young woman of great beauty. Like the hero of the Phantom Vessel he fell in love with her. She divorced her husband and married him, in memory of which he called the palace he was later to build Karin Hall.

In Munich he happened to hear Hitler speak at a public meeting. He was fascinated and won over on the spot. Joining the National Socialist movement, he participated in the abortive 1923 putsch, fell wounded at the Führer's side, escaped from prison and, thanks to his wife's loyalty, found refuge in Italy. Pardoned by amnesty, a widower now, he became one of Hitler's chief henchmen and advisers.

He was not a man of wide culture but his intelligence was prompt and elastic. Clearsighted, he appreciated the mediocrity of certain of the Führer's collaborators. He did not hesitate to tell me that Rosenberg was a blunderer, Bishop Müller a starveling, and Prince August Wilhelm a puppet. Yet first time we ever conversed he spent two hours explaining the fundamental principles of racism to me with the most profound conviction.

Goering was shrewd, skillful, tricky, cool, and collected. His audacity knew no bounds; he had a will of iron. No scruple stopped him; a cynic, not without moments of chivalry, he could be implacably cruel. He was the real inventor of the Gestapo and the concentration camps.

Hitler valued him and made no decision without him. The accomplishment of tasks Hitler considered most important he placed in Goering's hands. Thus Goering went on missions to Poland, Italy, Yugoslavia, and Greece. It was Goering who gave the Reich a powerful air force. It was to Goering that the Führer entrusted the direction of the second Four-Year Plan, in other words the economic preparation for World War II.

Yet there were weaknesses, enormous weaknesses in his make-up. He was not only ambitious but vain, and beyond vanity, greedy for money. He could never collect enough decorations or titles. He gathered the most diverse offices into his lap: he was Premier of Prussia, Reich Minister of Aviation, President of the Reichstag, Director of National Economy, President of the Hermann Goering Factories, and Reich Grand Master of the Hunt. He had been a captain; he was promoted general, then field marshal, but as there were other field marshals, he asked for unique ranking: he would be a supermarshal, a Reich marshal, subordinate to Hitler alone.

He never had money enough. Salaries allotted to his various positions did not suffice; he collected percentages and dividends from the businesses he controlled or created as part of the Four-Year Plan. This money helped him to enjoy life. With never a qualm he seized possessions confiscated from the Jews or grabbed such objects in national museums as pleased him.

Some fifty miles from Berlin he built himself a sumptuous lakeside residence in a wood of pines and birches. Originally the place was a hunting lodge, a rustic building of rough-hewn logs. There in 1934 he gave a garden party to the diplomatic corps, on which occasion he was dressed as the Siegfried of Wagner's opera. Subsequently the log building was transformed into a vast palace to house the immense treasures Goering acquired. It was equipped with every refinement of comfort, including a Finnish bathhouse and a gymnasium where, thanks to special apparatus, he could go through the motions of any sport he wished. He was fond of showing his friends over the splendors of his residence. The Hall of Honor, lofty as a church, was much admired. Here, clad in a white uniform, a wide cordon over his breast, his hands laden with rings, the satrap welcomed his guests nobly. He led them from room to room. "This is where I receive visitors," he would say. "This is where I meditate." "This is where I work!"

A vast estate surrounded the palace, with woods, heaths, and ponds. A flock of reindeer and a herd of bisons could be observed grazing; the Reich Grand Master of the Hunt had vowed to acclimate them. On a slope inclining toward the lake he had set up an ancient Germanic cemetery. Tall menhirs formed a circle, a red granite slab in the center; under it, in a crypt divided into two parallel galleries, was Karin's coffin, the empty gallery being reserved for the master of the house.

Against this amazing background Goering usually led a bourgeois, family existence beside his wife and small daughter. For after Karin's death he married Emmy Sonnemann, an actress no longer young, who had played queen's parts in the

Weimar Theatre, a preparation for her future career. She was blonde, simple, and of agreeable manners. The whole diplomatic corps attended her wedding, which was celebrated with great pomp in the Cathedral of Berlin. The ceremony over, friends released a great flight of storks. The gesture proved of happy augury, for despite contrary insinuations disagreeable to Goering, he soon became a father.

In the bosom of his family Goering was kindly, affectionate, and attentive. This cynic and adventurer, who in earliest youth ran away from school to seek his fortune afar, this *condottiere* and pirate chief, fierce in action, had but to return from his expeditions to meet his family in the shelter which housed his treasures, and forthwith he became a candid, goodhearted soul. Such contrasts make one shudder, but they exist in the natures of thousands upon thousands of Germans.

In the huge attic of his palace Goering set up a small electric railway. It was operated from a keyboard like a harmonium and rolled through a painted countryside. There was a whole system of signals and disks, of junctions and branch lines, of switches and stations, and finally a yard with trains of various types. The Reich's Marshal spent hours at a time playing at this game with his nephews. One day he showed it to me and made it work for me. But suddenly, forgetting my presence perhaps, one of the nephews cried: "Uncle Hermann! send out the French train!" The train in question emerged from the yard. Then over the wires dominating the countryside Goering's nephew sped a tiny airplane out of which fell bombs equipped with caps that exploded as the small boy tried to hit the French train. . . .

To us diplomats Goering offered a valuable advantage. Far from seeking to avoid us he actually sought to establish contacts with us. He accepted and returned our invitations. Appreciating the arrangement and brilliance, the rich fare and the fine wines of these soirees, he would converse familiarly and reply to indiscreet questions. Disdaining precautions and circumlocutions, he spoke out bluntly and freely, raising for us one corner of the veil which the Wilhelmstrasse and the Goebbels press had cast over reality. We were grateful to him for it and we cheerfully obtained for him satisfactions of vanity to which he was susceptible.

Conceived by Goering and carried out with the co-operation of numerous foreign countries, the Exposition of the Hunt, over which he presided, achieved unprecedented success. Never had such collections been assembled. But more than the trophies and weapons, the horners and the hunts they assembled; more than the Finnish riders in their fur caps, astride small bristling horses, lance in hand, mounting guard before the doors of the exposition; more than the fêtes on its program; more than all these, it was the visit of Lord Halifax, a member of the British Cabinet, which lent the exposition exceptional interest.

The noble lord was not satisfied with spending several days in Berlin and lunching there with Neurath. He went to Berchtesgaden as Hitler's guest and conferred at length with him. This atmosphere, just as that of the Olympic Games, suggested that peace was solidly established and war forever banished. The more since early that year (January 31, 1937) Hitler had declared in a speech to the Reichstag: "The period of surprises is over. Peace is our supreme blessing."

Yet behind this setting and these demonstrations many disquieting facts and symptoms were to be observed.

The Spanish Civil War threatened at any moment to set off a generalized fire in Europe; all the patience and pacifism of Britain and France were required to keep it within bounds. Germany and Italy vied with each other in impudence and hypocrisy as they supported Franco. In September 1937 Mussolini came personally to Berlin on an official journey. His visit set a seal upon the understanding between the two dictators; thenceforward Nazism and Fascism set up their Axis athwart Europe and, while loudly proclaiming their devotion to the cause of peace, developed their armaments more actively than ever.

On the morrow of the violation of the Locarno Treaty—on April 20, 1936, Hitler's birthday—for the first time an armored division paraded publicly through the streets of Berlin. It was the Third Division; there were therefore already two others at the time. The whole organization was brand-new, remarkably homogeneous and amazingly flexible. The men seemed thoroughly familiar with their equipment and the equipment in perfect shape. That evening, as I drew up my report on the striking spectacle I had witnessed, I voiced the hope that our experts would not fail to apprise the French high command of this exhibition which perhaps marked a date in the art of warfare.

The progress made by German aviation was no less evident. At all hours of the day, wherever one might be, the skies were furrowed with planes. On the outskirts of every city of the Reich were airfields filled with planes. In the immediate vicinity of Berlin huge barracks rose overnight, as if by magic, to house aviators. In Berlin itself Goering built a Ministry of Air whose mere dimensions revealed the scope of his enterprises. In 1937 German factories were already in a position to produce five hundred planes per month.

Throughout my mission in Germany I remained in close touch with our General Staff. I practically never went to Paris without stopping in the Boulevard des Invalides to report my observations and impressions to the military. In addition to the officers regularly attached to the French Embassy in Berlin, I always had a special agent at my side whose duty it was to cull from my daily reports—telegrams, documents, précis, and other information—anything of military interest and to transmit it directly to our generals. The latter, of course, had other sources of information. But in so far as my own work was concerned they were regularly advised of the devel-

opment of the war effort in the Reich and of the various forms
it assumed.

From 1936 on the Nazis did not trouble to disguise it. At
all moments one fell upon families whose father or sons were
absent, having been called up for a training period. In August
1936 Hitler added one year to the duration of military service,
thus raising the number of effectives permanently with the
colors to one million. In 1937, in spite of the organic law setting the number of army corps at twelve, he created two supplementary corps. Each year the Berlin Automobile Show
proved that manufacturers were working chiefly to fulfill
army needs; for every touring car, they exhibited five trucks
of various models.

The Chancellor decreed the elaboration and application of
a new Four-Year Plan, execution of which was entrusted to
Goering. People said its avowed aim was to prepare the Reich
to withstand a war, but they implied it was to undertake a
war. Germany began piling up stocks of all indispensable materials. Germans gave up butter, to quote Goering's famous
mot, for guns; scientists were urged to study and to perfect
all ersatz products, the necessity for which had been proved
by the sanctions imposed on Italy during the war in Abyssinia.
In May 1937 an exposition called "Give Me Four Years!" proposed to stimulate public interest in the work in progress; the
stands showed nothing but military planes, submarines, and
tanks.

Nor were these the only indications of the thoughts and
plans Hitler was pondering. His speeches never ceased to rise
in tone, especially when he mentioned Soviet Russia. Never had
a chief of government, let alone a chief of state, expressed himself with such violence about a foreign government with which
his country maintained normal diplomatic and economic relations. His lieutenants and his press echoed his sentiments; all
Germany resounded with a campaign of systematic excitation
against the USSR. Thus Hitler may be said to have armed

Russia himself and forged the instrument which, by a just reversal, was to cause his downfall. Czechoslovakia was treated no better. Despite the most official denials the Nazis persisted in considering her as an accomplice of the Russians, accusing her of being a platform whence Soviet aircraft would take off on bombing flights over luckless Germany. Even in Austria the calm following the murder of Dollfuss and the agreement of July 11, 1936, gradually gave way to a renewal of agitation fomented by agents of the Reich. It was not hard to guess that this agreement had been but an expedient to reassure Mussolini and to facilitate the forging of the Rome-Berlin Axis.

Finally the removal of Schacht, who abandoned the Ministry of Economy on November 26, 1937, offered a warning impossible to disregard.

Schacht, too, was a cynic, a frantic blusterer, a person possessed of unbridled ambitions. A tall, dry, spare devil of a man, his features might have been hacked out by a bill hook, and his long wrinkled neck was like the neck of a bird of prey. His receding chin and his ridiculously high collar reminded one of some caricature of old in *Simplicissimus*, the traditional German comic magazine. Schacht threw his lot in with National Socialism; he foresaw its rise to power, contributed to it, and was rewarded accordingly. Yet he did not consider that the advantages he gained were proportionate to his merits, for he had hoped at one time to succeed Hindenburg and even Hitler, should things go ill with the Führer.

It was Schacht who organized the monetary and financial system by which the Nazi regime disposed of enormous resources without immediate risks of inflation. Nor did he hesitate to support rearmament expenses with the resources of the Reichsbank and discreetly to print banknotes to this end.

However Schacht was an intelligent man, much more intelligent than the Nazis whom he judged and gauged. Neither his ambition nor his covetousness destroyed his lucidity and perspicacity. He was perfectly aware of Hitler's blunder in persecuting the Jews and rousing Anglo-Saxon opinion against the Nazi regime, for, contrary to the leaders of the Third Reich, Schacht had had experience abroad. He was a friend of Sir Montague Norman; he knew his way about in financial circles in London and New York, where, indeed, he was much esteemed. He never possessed enough courage or influence to prevent excesses which he blamed, but the consequences which these excesses involved did not escape him. So long as the expenditures of the Reich did not rise above a certain figure, so long as a European war seemed improbable to him, he fell in with the way of things, though at times he did attack the government fiercely. As of 1936 his attitude changed. He must at this time have been informed of the Führer's secret intent. The speeding of rearmament and of warlike preparations caused him discomfort; he was disturbed and worried about the future.

Late in August 1936, before going to Paris to return the visit he had received from Labeyrie, Governor of the Bank of France, he took a significant step. Calling on me at the French Embassy, he disclosed his qualms about the perilous direction Hitler's thoughts were taking. Haunted by the Czechoslovak question, the Führer, it would seem, was entertaining the notion of solving it by force, if necessary. Schacht declared that Hitler should be diverted from this at all costs in order to avoid the bloodshed of general war in Europe.

One means of so doing might lie in opening up other prospects that might tempt him, such as, for example, colonial prospects. For a long time Hitler had rebelled against any idea of claiming colonies, but his most recent demonstrations proved that his opinion had changed. It was not, said Schacht, a question of giving Germany full title to colonial property. But without infringing upon established sovereignty, could not Britain, France, and Belgium concede to the Reich a territory in Central Africa which might be exploited by a German tenant company? Schacht believed that a gesture of this sort might prove successful. In any case, desirous during his forth-coming visit to broach the subject to the French Premier, he requested me to procure him an interview with Leon Blum. Schacht's journey caused a considerable stir in Paris, arousing a lively dispute between French Socialists and Communists.

Nevertheless the interview requested took place on August 28. Leon Blum did not receive Schacht's suggestion unfavor-ably; its counterpart was to be Hitler's pledge to observe the European status quo, which might thus safeguard peace. But resolute opposition on the part of Britain soon quashed the plan before it had even taken shape.

The Führer, assenting reluctantly to his minister's scheme, had prophesied that it would come to nothing. Did Schacht's failure prejudice Hitler's mind against him? Did Schacht then emphasize his attitude of disapproval and opposition? The fact remains that relations between Schacht on one hand and the Führer and party on the other turned increasingly sour. In view of Schacht's proposal in Paris and the apprehension he expressed at that time, his resignation as Reich Minister of Economy was a bad sign.

From all this it may be gathered that the games, fêtes, visits, exchanges of cordiality, personal contacts established at expositions, demonstrations, and effusions, from mid-1936 to the end of 1937, fell very short of justifying an optimistic view of the situation. At best the period was a pause between acts, while refreshments and sweetmeats were served, after which the tragedy was resumed.

Possibly Hitler's tactics duped certain people. We were not of their number. In mid-December 1937 P. E. Flandin spent three days in Berlin on a private errand. He breathed the air of the capital, he conferred with some members of the Reich Government, particularly with Neurath and Goebbels. From these conversations he emerged convinced that Germany would invade Austria within three months. Sir Nevile Henderson, the British Ambassador, disagreed.

"We are moving toward peace," said the Briton.

"What we are living through at this moment," replied the Frenchman, "is a vigil of arms."

In my presence, the two made a wager.

On March 12, 1938, at 5:30 A.M., the German troops entered Austria.

VIII. THE FALL
OF VON FRITSCH

ARLY in 1938 several of my colleagues and
I had been invited to dine on February 3
at General von Fritsch's. We were some-
what surprised since the Commander in Chief of the Reichswehr had never mingled in the social life of Berlin. An incor-
rigible bachelor, he appeared rarely at official ceremonies and
never in the salons of the capital. Of medium height, tightly
encased in his uniform, with his crimson complexion, his
monocle screwed into his eye, and his husky voice, he was representative of the classic Prussian officer type. Meeting him
several times at the races, which he frequented assiduously, I
had occasion to observe that his haughty and surly exterior

covered a keener wit and a more amiable nature than appeared.
I had also learned that he was blamed in higher places for
failing to live up to the social obligations of his office. And so
when I received his invitation I thought: "Well, the bear is
softening up!"

But on February 2, the eve of the appointed date, the dinner was canceled. Here were further grounds for surprise, the
keener because it was rumored that Fritsch had just been arrested and was held prisoner at his home. Nobody knew anything save that there had been unusual goings-on. On January 27 Kaiser Wilhelm II's birthday had inspired more numerous and less discreet demonstrations than ordinarily, in particular in officers' messes in eastern and western Prussia. On January 30, the anniversary of his taking over the government,
Hitler, contrary to habit, had made no speech. Great changes,
people whispered, were imminent. A nervousness was in the
air, a sort of muffled anguish. The atmosphere in the capital
recalled that which had reigned during the massacres of sinister memory on June 30, 1934.

A communiqué appeared at 9:00 P.M. on February 4 announcing a series of extremely important measures. Hitler, who
had previously been but the theoretical commander, now decided personally to assume command of all the armed forces
of the Reich. The Ministry of the Reichswehr, headed for the
past five years by Marshal von Blomberg, was abolished. In
compensation Hitler created an *Oberkommando der Wehrmacht* or Higher Command of the Armed Forces, which was
to constitute the Führer's military staff, headed by General
Keitel, who was to have ministerial rank and to enjoy all the
prerogatives previously vested in the Minister of War. Marshal
von Blomberg and General von Fritsch, both admitted to retired rank, were rewarded with letters of thanks from Hitler;
the tone of that to Blomberg was most cordial, of that to
Fritsch, icy. Goering became Field Marshal. Sixteen high-rank-

ing generals were relieved of their duties; forty-four others and a host of senior officers were transferred.

This large-scale shift did not strike the army alone; diplomacy paid its tribute too. Baron von Neurath, ceasing to be Minister of Foreign Affairs, became head of a "Secret Cabinet Council" which was destined never to know a real existence; Joachim von Ribbentrop succeeded him at the Wilhelmstrasse; Hassel, ambassador at Rome, von Dircksen, ambassador at Tokyo, and von Papen, ambassador at Vienna, were recalled. Finally, the Ministry of Economy was combined with the agencies of the Four-Year Plan and reorganized under the direction of Funk.

Far from seeking to play down the wide range of these decisions, Goebbels' press emphasized it, declaring that February 4 would remain a memorable date in the annals of the Third Reich. But the press denied quite as stoutly that these reforms resulted from a political crisis. The Führer, it said, wished to concentrate the powers of government in order to lend Germany more weight in the competition among nations, to set new blood flowing in the veins of the Reich, to call younger men to high executive positions, and to simplify the essential works of administrative machinery.

Actually the measures enacted on February 4 marked the epilogue of an acute conflict between party and army. And the strangest part of it was its origin. If so radical a reform of the military was undertaken, if so many eminent personalities who seemed so firmly established were evicted, it was solely because Marshal von Blomberg had expressed, around the New Year, the intention of remarrying. Here is a rich subject of meditation for anybody interested in the role of intangible factors in history.

With his small worn face perched on the end of a tall thin body, Blomberg, a sexagenarian, was gay, cultivated, alert, and still brisk. He had long been a widower, his children were grown; it was not astonishing then that he should seek the companionship of a woman. He wished to marry a woman he knew well and trusted thoroughly, his own secretary-typist. Hitler was under heavier obligations to Blomberg, Minister of the Reichswehr, than to almost any other man. He had always been perfectly loyal to the Führer. Blomberg had prevented the Reichswehr from launching a systematic opposition against Hitler; he had kept the army disciplined and obedient; and on June 30, 1934, he had urged and helped the Führer to liquidate Röhm. When Hindenburg died Blomberg had been a confederate in the juggling act which enabled Hitler to proclaim himself Chief of State; at the earliest hour he had brought Hitler the oath of loyalty sworn by officers and soldiers.

As a reward for all this he received his marshal's baton. Hitler considered him a friend. More, Hitler liked his collaborators and ministers to have an establishment and to participate in the social life of Berlin. He therefore sent Blomberg his cordial congratulations and grasped both his hands, gazing long at him with his reputedly fascinating, irresistible glance.

Suddenly, a few days later, Blomberg returned, shamefaced, begging the Führer to accept his resignation. He had been wrong, he declared, in believing that a minister of the Reichswehr was free to marry as his fancy willed. Certainly the Führer's approval was precious, but it was insufficient; Blomberg also required that of the Reichswehr. And the Reichswehr, through General von Fritsch, Commander in Chief, and General Beck, Chief of Staff, had stated that it considered his marriage "*untragbar,*" "intolerable." Consequently Blomberg must choose between his matrimonial plans and his position as minister.

The reasons of this decision were doubtless peremptory, since Blomberg bowed to them and was preparing to resign. He had not time to finish his report: Hitler flew into one of those customary mad rages that made his followers tremble. His vociferations may be readily imagined. What! these gentlemen had the audacity to oppose a marriage which he had approved! He would not tolerate such insubordination! What they would not admit, said Hitler, was the fact that Blomberg was marrying a girl of modest condition, a woman risen from the people. These idiotic reactionaries, these Junkers rotten with prejudice, these mummies of Potsdam still believed they were living in a state divided into classes! They had understood nothing of what the Third Reich had accomplished. Since they did not know that all Germans formed but a single people, he, the Führer, would teach them. He would lick them into shape, sweep them away, crush them!

As a first step he refused Blomberg's resignation and promised to be a witness at his marriage. On January 17 Blomberg was married, with Hitler on his right, Goering on his left.

But General von Fritsch was in no wise intimidated; he did not mean to withdraw his objections. In an audience with the Führer he declared that Blomberg, now married, could not remain Minister of the Reichswehr. This was not, he added, because he had married a daughter of the people but because he had married a woman whose past could not be considered as honorable. How could young officers be held to the conduct and dignity exacted of them when the Minister of War himself lay open to criticism?

Hitler, angry, showered insults and reproaches upon the General; Fritsch, sanguine by nature and bad-tempered, gave tit for tat. In turn, he unburdened himself of all that had weighed upon his chest, of all the grievances welling up in him against the regime. He denounced its brutality, its blunders, its dilapidations, its corruption, the introduction of politics into the barracks, the antireligious propaganda which demoralized the soldier, and even the conduct of foreign affairs, which, rash and provoking, risked drawing Germany into a European war before she was of a stature to confront it. Hitler foamed with rage, the more so because all the General's allegations about Blomberg's marriage were confirmed by Himmler's police. His fury turned upon Blomberg, who had involved him in a piece of nonsense and made him play a ludicrous role. But he did not forgive Fritsch either, for the General had not only been lacking in respect but had also revealed a disturbing state of mind, symptomatic of how at least one part of the army leaders felt.

At just the right moment Himmler offered the Führer a chance for revenge, claiming that the General was a homosexual and he, Himmler, could prove it. Fritsch, choking with indigation, demanded trial before a Court of Honor, resigned as generalissimo, and remained under house arrest until such time as his case was decided. This was why his dinner was canceled and rumors of his arrest ran through Berlin.

But Fritsch's personal case did not settle the question. Blomberg must be replaced, the High Command must be weeded out. The party took up the question, for it had its case, too, against the army leaders, who represented the main obstacle in the way of nazification of the troops. Blomberg's successor at the Reichswehr Ministry, it said, should be an authentic Nazi, a man with an iron hand. Himmler, chief of the SS and of the Gestapo, offered his candidacy; Goering too. Hitler would have to decide between them.

Discussions dragged on and on. Not only the military were incriminated; other essential government posts, especially in diplomacy, were held by too many of the old guard. The Führer had attained power with the support and connivance of Hugenberg and the German Nationalists, in other words of a squire and a bourgeois clique with which Nazism had nothing in common. He had eliminated a certain number of the clique but still too many remained; there was no point in dealing tactfully with them, the time was come to dismiss Neurath and ambassadors of his stamp. Also, Hitler had been much impressed by the French law on the wartime organization of the nation and by the changes France had made in the machinery of the High Command.

During the year 1937 Hitler was relatively calm; he executed no new coups. He was plotting how to pass on to the second phase of his program, which called for the absorption of Austria and the annexation of Sudetenland. To accomplish these he must hold solidly in hand the two chief instruments of future action, which Hindenburg had preserved under his own control when he had called Hitler to the Chancellery. These were, of course, the army and the diplomatic service.

Thus the idea of recasting the whole system occurred to Hitler. He would have done so in any case at some other time and under another form, for it corresponded to his inmost concerns and to his calculations for the future. But the incident created by Blomberg and Fritsch hastened its birth by offering him a chance to carry it out at once. One of the Führer's great talents was to seize opportunity on the wing; he did so now.

Blomberg and Fritsch would be retired, but neither Himmler nor Goering was to succeed Blomberg. The Reichswehr would be spared this humiliation. What was the use of embittering it further? The War Ministry would be suppressed, or rather it would become the Führer's military cabinet; Hitler, self-promoted, was to be the real commander of land, sea, and air forces, assisted, in this office, by a dependable man like Keitel, who was known to favor the democratization of the High Command. Goering, the most tumultuous of Hitler's lieutenants, would be consoled in his disappointment by the award of a marshal's baton. Generals and officers suspected of being lukewarm, or guilty of having too clearly displayed their monarchist sympathies, were to be transferred or dismissed.

As for the Ministry of Foreign Affairs, Neurath, a remnant of the "Barons' Cabinet," was too old to continue at its head. Besides, Neurath was too courteous to foreign ambassadors, he was pusillanimous, he was "soft"; Ribbentrop, a young man in the prime of life, would replace Neurath to advantage. Ribbentrop held high rank in the SS, he was "tough," he could be counted upon to clean out that other nest of reactionaries, the Wilhelmstrasse, and to bring in young Nazis. In fact Ribbentrop was never more than a Keitel in the diplomatic field; he was less a minister than the Führer's private secretary for external affairs.

Of modest origin but provided with a "von" through adoption by a titled relative, he had grown rich by marrying the daughter of the manufacturer of Henckell's champagnes and sparkling wines, a huge concern. A handsome fellow, devoured by vanity and ambition, in about 1920 he found the means of playing a role in the Nazi ranks which had been denied him in Liberal circles. He attached himself to the person of Adolf Hitler, often entertained him at his fine villa at Dahlem, and arranged for him to meet notable Germans and foreigners in interesting and important interviews. Thus Ribbentrop came to be Hitler's confidential agent in matters of foreign policy. Typical of the perfect courtier, he would hurl thunderbolts of flattery at Hitler without turning a hair. His method of keeping in favor was very simple. It consisted in listening religiously to his master's endless monologues and in committing to memory the ideas developed by Hitler. Also, more important, Ribbentrop noted the intentions to be divined behind these ideas. Then, after Hitler had forgotten ever discussing them with Ribbentrop, the courtier passed them off as his own, unfolding them with great warmth. Struck by this concordance, Hitler attributed to his collaborator a sureness of judgment and a trenchant foresight singularly in agreement with his own deepest thought. It must be admitted that sometimes Neurath—timidly, it is true—ventured counsels of moderation. Ribbentrop never did anything of the kind. He not only never contradicted his master or offered the slightest objection, he also systematically piled argument upon argument in agreement. He was more Hitlerian than Hitler. By clearing up the Führer's doubts and by dissipating the Führer's occa-

sional hesitancies Ribbentrop excited the Führer's supreme audacity; he pushed and pulled him into ways toward which
Hitler was all too dangerously inclined.

Hitler was impressed by Ribbentrop's fine presence, by the
charm of the distinguished figure he cut, by his man-of-the-
world manners and by his self-possession. The ease with which
Ribbentrop spoke French and English and the contacts he
boasted in high society in London and Paris won Hitler's regard.

Yet the new Minister for Foreign Affairs was neither prepared nor fitted for his office. Culturally and intellectually
he was mediocre. His ignorance of historical and diplomatic
questions was prodigious. His mission as Ambassador to London proved a resounding failure; his personal spite at this was
to falsify his every judgment of Great Britain's material or
moral resources. In the Wilhelmstrasse administration, which
he claimed to domineer as a subaltern dominates his platoon,
he was cordially detested. He retorted by bullying his subordinates and inflicting upon his department all sorts of preten-
tious and worthless fellow Nazis. In his contacts with chiefs of
diplomatic missions he behaved in arrogant, brutal, and peremptory fashion, fancying that language of this nature was
best calculated to inspire foreigners with a lofty idea of the
new Germany. As he evoked the military might of the Reichswehr he was very prompt to raise his voice and to become
threatening. It was difficult to conduct a genuine conversation with him. Like the Führer he copied, he indulged in
lengthy monologues; he never caught, let alone retained, the
arguments of his interlocutor; he listened only to himself, repeating the lesson he had learned.

This, then, was the man of whom Hitler said, as he wagged
his head, admiring: "He is smarter than Bismarck!" Such an
appalling error proves how blind the Führer was to men and
events at the very moment when he was about to embark upon

the rashest of undertakings. Truly this Ribbentrop whom he lauded to the skies was to exercise upon him the most constantly nefarious influence.

Be that as it may, Blomberg's untimely marriage precipitated a crisis out of which Adolf Hitler's power emerged strengthened and unified, equal to that of the most absolute sovereigns. What was he to accomplish with all these powers he had gathered and concentrated in his own hand? Any possible doubt on that score was promptly dispelled by the fusion of the Ministry of Economy with the agencies of the Four-Year Plan. These agencies were occupied with material preparations for war: the new dispensation signified that, from now on, the Ministry of Economy was to devote itself wholly to the same task. "Henceforth," said the *Lokalanzeiger* lapidarily, "all the forces of the Reich are taut as a bow from which, when the hour has struck, the arrow will fly straight to the mark."

What, if anyone is curious, happened to the luckless Fritsch? The Court of Honor, with Goering as president, acquitted him of the infamous accusation. The witness for the prosecution, having been shown up, confessed that he had been bribed to utter this calumny. He was immediately shot. The General was offered a new command. He refused to accept it until punishment had been visited upon the person responsible for the plot to dishonor him, i.e., Himmler. Fritsch never obtained satisfaction. He was appointed honorary colonel of a regiment of artillery as a public token of his vindication. Nothing further was done for him. His comrades no more took his part than they had taken Schleicher's.

When war broke out against Poland in 1939 it was Fritsch's plan that the German armies used. Reduced to the role of spectator and parasite, he followed the operations in melancholy fashion with the orderly officer assigned to him. One day he was reported killed at the gates of Warsaw. Many believed that the Gestapo had murdered him; it seemed only too plausible. But I have heard another version on good authority. It is said that his orderly officer, advancing on open ground under fire, was hit, and that Fritsch, coming out of his trench to the rescue, fell in his turn.

Hitler ordered him to be given an imposing funeral.

IX. HITLER AND MUSSOLINI

WITHOUT Mussolini's agreement, Hitler would never have dared to carry through his plans for the annexation of Austria and the rape of Czechoslovakia. It was the German-Italian alliance which opened the way to the realization of Hitler's most ambitious plans. In a word, the understanding between the twin dictators gave rise to World War II.

Both men were victims of pride, of the will to power, of hunger for grandeur and thirst for glory, or nervousness and of violent sentiment, of cynicism, of gifts for dissimulation and treachery, and of great eloquence. Both men were possessed by a virtually monstrous passion which led them to believe their nations an instrument created to serve their own ambitions. Yet how different they were!

Hitler's features were flabby; his forehead, his nose, and his mouth were mean, his expression set, dismal, and vulgar. His eyes, globular and dull gray, came to life only in anger or in a trance; he rolled his *rs* so that they rang like rocks in an avalanche. His gait was stiff; he rarely smiled or laughed.

Mussolini was molded with more art. His cast of features was after the pattern of Caesar's: a broad brow, his, a square jaw, an avid and greedy mouth. His face was mobile: in a flash it reflected the most contrary feelings. His swart complexion afforded a fine background for his jet-black, flashing eyes. His voice was sharp, his speech precipitous. His back arched, he stood before his audience, prompt, supple, and agile. His smile was subtle, his laughter truculent.

Hitler's intelligence was intuitive, Mussolini's deductive. Hitler was a dreamer who heard voices; he communicated with the stars. He had no sense of conversation, he read little, worked scarcely at all, and gave his subordinates a free hand. He spoke and understood only German; he knew nothing about foreign countries. His personal needs were slight; he practiced an almost ascetic hygiene. If the company of women pleased him, they played no major part in his existence.

Mussolini was positive and precise; he had a hand in everything and drew everything into his orbit. He would spend long hours at his desk, accumulating and annotating reports, intervening at every moment in the various departments assigned to his collaborators. He devoured newspapers, books, magazines, and pamphlets; he understood French, English, and German; he spoke French well and German fairly well but with a bad accent. He had roamed about outside his own country and possessed a certain experience of foreign lands. He had an itch for writing; a journalist, he at once translated ideas and emotions into a newspaper article, unsigned, to be sure, but easily recognizable as such. His conversation was lively, brilliant, attractive. He loved a generous life. And he loved women, too; as he grew older they occupied him increasingly.

He was attached to his family and, if not a good husband, he was at least a good father.

Certainly Nazism owed a great deal to Fascism. It proceeded directly from Fascism; it was an imitation or transposition of Fascism along German and Prussian lines. It borrowed Fascism's characteristic institutions: its militias, its Brown Shirts, the Roman salute, the organization of its youth movement, its *Dopolavoro* or workers' physical education program, and even the title of Führer which is but a translation of Duce.

It is reported that in its early days Nazism received subsidies from the Fascists. After the Munich putsch failed in 1923, numerous Nazis, Goering among them, found refuge and help in Italy. Hitler never forgot and never repudiated this debt; he always professed great admiration for Mussolini, respecting him as the initiator, the forerunner, the master. In his study at Munich he had a bust of the Duce and he never removed it, even at the time of their worst disagreements.

Mussolini, in his dealings toward Hitler, felt himself the senior, the superior, and he naturally assumed an attitude of patronage. He was flattered that his disciple steered a country like Germany along a course charted by Italy. However from the beginning this junior inspired him with a mistrust which was never to be completely dissipated. As an Italian, Mussolini was attracted by German power, discipline, and method, but he never overcame the basic instinct of aversion that his people entertain for the Teuton.

Contrarily Hitler, as a German, could not resist the Italian charm, vivacity, and warmth. But this did not prevent him from sharing his fellow countrymen's tendency to judge "the mandolin player" as a whimsical child, a braggart, a somewhat ridiculous and not very dependable person. I have been told that during Mussolini's tour of Lybia, Hitler's confidants used to amuse themselves by straddling chairs, thrusting their chins forward, and, with a cane or umbrella for prop, brandishing the "Sword of Islam" as they rolled their eyes fiercely about their sockets. I do not know whether Hitler ever violently detested Mussolini, but certainly Mussolini once loathed Hitler. Their friendship was long, and rough, in the making. Before embracing each other they had almost come to blows.

When Hitler assumed power he immediately manifested the desire to carry out the program set forth in *Mein Kampf*, which called for fellowship with Italy. The privilege of his only visit was granted to the Italian Embassy in Berlin. He piled token upon token of his sympathy for the Italians. Mussolini answered his advances courteously but not without reserve and caution.

The two did not meet until a year and a half later, in June 1934, in Venice. Their first contact was disastrous. Ill-advised, Hitler turned up in civilian dress, wearing a brown plush Homburg, a black suit, a trench coat, and patent-leather shoes that hurt his feet. He looked for all the world like a minor clerk in his Sunday best or a yokel sporting his finest clothes to go to town, infinitely shabby beside a Mussolini plumed, tightly corseted in military uniform, booted, and laden with decorations. The Duce cruelly abused the advantages given him; everywhere he took precedence over his guest, thrusting him into an inferior position. At the Piazza San Marco Mussolini harangued the populace from a balcony, without bothering about Hitler, who stood on a neighboring balcony, listening; all the applause and cheers went to Mussolini, nobody gave Hitler a thought. Later, in the gardens of the Villa Pisani at Stra, Hitler, intimidated and disconcerted, burst into a flow of vehement, confused arguments, scarcely allowing the Duce leisure to give him a few words of advice.

Mussolini, after the interview, roundly declared: "The man is crazy!"

Hitler returned to Germany humiliated, discontented with himself and with his host, and anxious to demonstrate that he was of other mettle than that superficially attributed to him. A fortnight later the massacre of Röhm and his companions confirmed Mussolini in his judgment; the Duce believed that these wholesale shootings were a poor piece of work, an inelegant butchery.

On June 2 the assassination of Dollfuss changed Mussolini's contempt into anger and furious indignation. (Apparently he was oblivious to the death of Matteoti.) He reacted fiercely, as to a personal affront. For a spell he maintained the closest solidarity with France and Britain. Had this united front endured, Hitler's plans would have been cut short and the peace of Europe safeguarded. Fate willed otherwise, Italy's aggression against Abyssinia and civil war in Spain were to start things all over again, to upset the situation and to link these enemy brothers together once more.

It is astonishing that Mussolini should have ventured upon the conquest of Ethiopia. Truth to tell, it was no personal ambition of the Duce's but a national ambition of Italy's. Italy was accustomed to the idea that Ethiopia must naturally and legitimately open up for Italian colonial expansion. Probably she would have been allowed to develop her action in Africa had she proceeded more soberly through the patient ways of peaceful penetration.

How could the Duce have failed to foresee the serious difficulties which his warlike enterprise must needs arouse? Perhaps he believed that Britain, rewarding his collaboration in Europe, would give him carte blanche. Perhaps he believed that the support promised by Laval would help him to triumph over British opposition. More likely Germany's example weighed heavily upon his mind. He could not help being impressed, tormented, and goaded into emulation as he saw how successfully Hitler chalked up coups that appeared rash to the point of insanity. Was not this German, born yesterday and a nonentity but for Mussolini, now eclipsing him? Was the disciple to prove himself stronger than the master? Hitler was no longer the man in the trench coat, the humble visitor in Venice; he was already a forceful figure taking Europe by storm. Mussolini feared lest, compared with Hitler, he appear pusillanimous and lose his prestige. More, he could not but note how feebly the League of Nations, Britain, and France reacted to Hitler's repeated defiance. Hitler had faced the odds and cleared the hurdle. Why should Mussolini not do as much? Arguing thus, Mussolini plunged into his mad adventure.

"A mad adventure!" By a quirk of circumstances, this was exactly the opinion Hitler held in the beginning. On January 1, 1936, he told me so. Attempts at mediation, as framed in the Hoare-Laval plan, had just failed. "I do not understand Mussolini's attitude," Hitler said to me. "He should have accepted these proposals immediately. For him, here was an unhoped-for chance!"

At the moment, the German General Staff was convinced that Italy was headed for defeat. At the close of a diplomatic dinner General von Blomberg explained to me that the use of motorized weapons in a land and country such as Abyssinia was an error. Dust, he said, jammed the motors, and oil filtered through the couplings; asses and camels were alone serviceable. I took the liberty of disagreeing and we argued the matter.

For all that, contacts between Rome and Berlin were resumed. The Duce frequently received Ambassador von Hassell in audience. The Reich announced that it would remain neutral. It would not participate in sanctions against Italy; it would furnish Italy with such resources—coal, steel, chemical products—as its soil provided. Mussolini, forsaken by all, was grateful to Hitler for this help, but his blood boiled and he accumulated a tenacious rancor against the League of Nations, Britain, and France.

Hitler seized the occasion to invade the demilitarized Rhineland zone and to tear up the Treaty of Locarno on March 7, 1936. Italy, a guarantor power, was uninterested; Mussolini was returning favor for favor. All efforts made to replace the violated treaty by a new one left him cold. Was he already

planning to form a closer link with Hitler? Both wished a rapprochement but each wished the other to be the first to
solicit it; both were embarrassed by the past, a very recent
past. Mussolini had not abandoned his distrust; he remained
hesitant. His son-in-law, Ciano, and his daughter, having become violent Germanophiles, openly supported an alliance between Italy and the Third Reich; they kept pressing him.
In June Mussolini determined to send his daughter, Countess
Edda, whose impressions and judgment he welcomed, on a
voyage of discovery to the land of the Nazis. Thoroughly
scandalized by the lady's deportment, the Nazis nevertheless
employed every charm at their disposal in order to please her, to
flatter her tastes and to captivate her. They dragged her from
fête to fête and she returned to her father enthusiastic and delighted. The Germans, learning from experience, and familiar
with the Duce's sudden turns of humor and his impetuous
temperament, proceeded to play a cautious hand. The Italian
victory in Ethiopia increased German interest in the peninsula.
Yet the Germans remained discreet, attentive; they avoided all
alacrity, importunity, insistence; and slowly, they gained
ground.

At the end of June, General Valle visited the German Air
Corps. Early in July a mission of German officers lunched in
Rome. In order to clear the atmosphere of a problem that re-
called dramatic memories, Hitler concluded an agreement with
Schuschnigg on July 11, 1936, which led—quite wrongly, of
course—to the inference that he was resolved never again to
threaten the independence of Austria. In August, at the
Olympic Games in Berlin, the Italian Crown Prince, his sister,
Princess Marie, and the Duce's son were treated as privileged
guests. In September an official Fascist delegation attended the
Congress of Nuremberg. And Germany, by raising its consulate
at Addis-Ababa to the status of legation, was the first state
to recognize the annexation of Abyssinia.

Little by little such successive and persevering steps forged the Axis, and this weird term denoting a union around which the world was to revolve became a part of the vocabulary of politics.

The Spanish Civil War tightened the bonds already formed. It was Mussolini who drew Hitler into this escapade. He was the first to help Franco, as was proved by the Italian military planes that crashed near Nemours and Oran on July 31. It was he, too, who convinced Hitler that the victory of the Spanish republicans, inflaming the USSR and France by contagion, would give Communism such tremendous impetus as to endanger the totalitarian governments. In the light of Spanish events, the dictators gained a clearer consciousness of the fellowship which joined them in defense before it was to unite them in conquest.

This solidarity asserted itself in the heart of the Control Commission in London, where the dictator governments, vying with each other in hypocrisy, appeared as accomplices. Mussolini intervened against the "Reds" more fully and more brutally than his confederate. This time he exceeded Hitler in audacity and impudence; he had once more become the master and trailblazer. While invoking nonintervention and accusing France of failing to keep her pledges, he was sending whole combat divisions into Spain at such a rate as to accomplish the depletion of his stores and arsenals, already seriously tried by war in Ethiopia.

More adroit, Hitler used the battlefields of Spain as a proving ground for his planes, tanks, and other military matériel. In turn, all his pilots flew there to test their ships and to perfect their talents in the Iberian skies. Every week, on a certain day, a huge transport plane landed at the Tempelhof Air Field in Berlin; about thirty men piled out, to disappear into a hut and to emerge, shortly after, in the uniforms of Luftwaffe officers. They constituted the relief of the so-called volunteer pilots returning from Spain. As they played the same game, Hitler gathered strength, Mussolini wore himself out.

From October 20 to October 27, 1936, Ciano, now the Duce's foreign minister, spent a week in Germany. He was received in Berlin with spectacular honors. Against all custom, he failed to leave his card on the foreign ambassadors; there was no ceremony or reception to which the chiefs of missions were invited to meet him. Germans and Italians were locked in a strictly private confabulation. Their intimacy was thus proclaimed to be exclusive. From Berlin, Ciano went to Berchtesgaden for conference with Hitler. A subsequent communiqué stated that the parties interested had concluded no pact or treaty. They had simply drawn up a protocol of decisions arrived at. These decisions embodied a mutual exchange of information and mutual consultation. The two governments were thereafter to consult and to act together in regard to General Franco, to the struggle against Communism, to the question of European pacts, to colonial problems, and to matters concerning access to raw materials. In other words they consolidated the collaboration they had practiced in Spain. From their Spanish experience and Franco's victory they had learned the lesson that, helping each other, they need fear neither the League of Nations nor France nor Britain nor Russia.

At the time, I wrote the following to the Quai d'Orsay: "The arrangement concluded as a result of Count Ciano's visit leaves the impression that Germany and Italy realize how much the power and prestige of France and Britain are diminished; making the most of this, they are eager to take the lead in Europe and to form the nucleus of a new organization of the continent. Apart, neither state would be strong enough to play this role; united, they believe they may attempt to do so. The solidarity of their regime against Bolshevism, their kindred aversion to the League of Nations, the desire of one to be revenged upon Britain and of the other to pay France back, seem to them to constitute sufficient mutual bonds. . . . It is reasonable to fear that the Germano-Italian entente is a decisive step toward the creation of a group of Central Powers stretching from the Baltic to the Adriatic. . . ."

Brilliant as was Ciano's reception, it could not approach the splendor of Mussolini's own visit to the Third Reich one year later, in September 1937. No monarch had ever been received in Germany with such pomp. Preparations amazing in their extent and magnificence were made in Munich and in Berlin. Alighting from his train, Mussolini, marching between twin rows of busts of Roman emperors, appeared as their successor. His monogram, a huge M surrounded by a crown and perched at the top of a high column, dominated the square in which the population acclaimed him.

In Berlin a triumphal route several miles long had been staked out; it ran from the Imperial Castle to the Olympic Stadium, bordered by giant banners that hung from the roof tops to the street. Where the route led into a square or a place, immense pylons displayed alternately the ax and bundle of Fascism and the eagle of the Reich. Along the famous avenue Unter den Linden rose hundreds of columns, each surmounted by a gold eagle with spread wings that shone at night. Standing forward in his automobile, Mussolini beamed at the delirious ovations of the Nazis. Hitler, accompanying him, was careful to lag slightly behind in order not to divert to himself the slightest part of the applause. The press published dithyrambic articles comparing this event, in its importance, to the Battle of Valmy, it spoke of a turning point in history. "Liquidation of the prnciples of 1789 has begun," the journalists thundered.

On September 26 and 27 Mussolini attended the Wehrmacht maneuvers in Mecklenburg. Real shells were fired. He was shown the armored divisions in action, the new artillery, the latest explosives, and the most modern planes; he was taken to Essen, to Krupp's, so that he might be completely edified by the Reich's military power and the value of German friendship. Next day at 7:00 P.M., on the grounds behind the

Olympic Stadium, a monster rally took place, with huge crowds attending. Hitler celebrated his guest as one of those unique beings and rare geniuses who, across the centuries, "are not made by history but make history themselves." He paid honor to the community of the twin empires whose one hundred fifteen million men, struggling shoulder to shoulder against the destructive virus of the democratic and Marxist Internationale, were resolved to resist all efforts made to split them.

Mussolini replied in a strident voice and in a German so halting and so disfigured by his Italian accent that he could barely make himself understood. He too indulged in grandiloquent praise of the two realms, in bitter criticism of the democracies, those fifty-two Genevese states which had pretended to impose their will upon Italy. Germany, he pointed out, was not among them. He pledged eternal friendship to the Reich. "Tomorrow," he went on, "all Europe will be Fascist; one hundred fifteen million men will arise, joined together in an unshakable faith."

A fierce storm broke out in the midst of his oration. Bursts of thunder and flashes of lightning, across a sky overrun by sinister clouds in the half-darkness of dusk, suddenly created a background of tragedy. The very elements warned mankind of what evils the mating of the dictators was to let loose upon it.

After the Duce's visit a remarkable change became evident in the respective attitudes of the twin dictators. Mussolini now offered pledges to the Reich as though anxious to dispel any doubt of his utter loyalty, of his more than verbal faith. On November 6, 1937, he signed the anti-Comintern Pact concluded the year before between Germany and Japan. On December 11, 1937, he quitted the League of Nations. Hitler, for his part, abandoned the precaution and consideration he had displayed hitherto. He had "angled" for his acolyte and led him on to commit himself. Now Mussolini was captivated and captured. From now on Hitler held him. Unable to retreat or to escape, Mussolini was compelled to cling to him like ivy. Britain and France, separated from Central Europe by a solid barrier, were now powerless directly to succor Austria or Czechoslovakia.

On March 12, 1938, Hitler invaded Austria. He did not warn or consult his partner, he faced him with an accomplished fact. He merely dispatched the Prince of Hesse, son-in-law of the King of Italy, with a letter of explanation and apology. Mussolini, undoubtedly shocked, betrayed no sign of his personal feelings. Incoherence, one of the chief characteristics of the Duce's foreign policy, was again apparent. Faced with the rigorous continuity and the ironclad methods that inspired his ally's actions, ignoring the accusing ghost of the wretched Dollfuss, he stood by and accepted the annexation of Austria by Germany. "Once an event is fated," he said, "it is better that it should happen with you than in spite of you, or, worse still, against you!" He certainly hoped that his sacrifice in the cause of German amity would subsequently prove profitable.

Early in May, Hitler repaid the Duce's visit. This time he had no fear of being treated as he had been four years before in Venice. Nor did Mussolini intend to be outdone as host or on any other ground. The King and the Duce met the Führer at dusk at the Ostia station. Gala coaches, flanked by cuirassiers with swords drawn, formed a glittering procession; searchlights played upon it as it slowly moved forward toward the Quirinal through a profusion of swastikas, allegorical motives, banners and flags. A more military note also marked the Führer's visit as fifty thousand members of the Fascist Vanguard and Youth movements paraded for his benefit. He witnessed bombing exercises and infantry maneuvers. On May 5, at Naples, he attended a magnificent naval review, with two hundred five battleships participating; at a given signal, ninety submarines rose simultaneously from the depths of the sea.

It was Hitler's turn to gape as he realized that Italy's power on the seas corresponded to Germany's on land. At least this was being suggested to the visitor from over the Alps, nor is it certain that he too in turn was not intoxicated by the spectacles offered him.

Was Hitler deceived as to the true strength of the Fascists? When he stirred up the Czech crisis that autumn Mussolini did not support him but held him back. It has been alleged that the pair were hand in glove on the issue, but on September 28, at noon, I was with Hitler when he was informed that the Italian Ambassador sought urgently to communicate to him a telephone message from the Duce, and I do not believe that Hitler's surprise was feigned.

The Munich Conference, due at once to certain advisers of the Führer and to Mussolini's intervention under British pressure, accentuated the respect which Mussolini still commanded from his German colleague. But this was probably the last occasion on which Hitler proved docile to the influence of his comrade.

Hitler's sudden entrance in Prague on March 15, 1939, gave Mussolini a jolt; he was angry and worried. He understood that this overt violation of the Munich agreement risked causing a conflagration which he judged premature. Moreover Hitler had once again acted without consulting or warning him, merely dispatching a letter to him after the deed was done. In spite of my efforts no one in Paris or London understood that here was a chance, the last chance, to separate the Duce from his partner. Seeing that Britain and France did not counter immediately Mussolini regained his calm. A new source of worry arose; he realized that so far the Axis had proved profitable, especially to Germany. And he was eager to show that he too was capable of taking measures that served his own interests without bothering to warn his associate. Such was the meaning of the Albanian expedition, decided and executed suddenly in April. In his complex feelings toward Hitler jealousy and rivalry played no uncertain part; besides he was afraid of being duped, of being dragged further than he cared to go, and he wished to assert his personality.

On May 22, 1939, the two governments signed an agreement, the "Steel Pact." The clause Mussolini considered paramount was not one which stated that the contracting parties would intervene side by side in defense of territories vital to them, nor one which guaranteed to each party the other's full political and military support in case of foreign aggression, nor even one whereby the conclusion of a separate armistice or peace was prohibited. It was, on the contrary, the clause stipulating mutual consultation on the general European situation and on measures to be taken in defense of their respective interests. By these means the Duce hoped to protect himself from the Führer's unilateral decisions. He hoped he had assured himself of means whereby he might exercise a timely influence on his ally, preventing him, as he had at Munich, from rushing into a dangerous enterprise at a moment and in circumstances that were embarrassing to Italy.

Unfortunately for Mussolini the letter of a treaty never proved an obstacle at which Hitler balked. Worse, the Germano-Italian Pact contained a clause difficult to reconcile with the pledge of mutual consultation, namely the clause promising the immediate armed intervention of each state in case the other were drawn into complications of war with another power or powers. Which of the two pledges had precedence, that of consultation or that of aid? Would aid be granted only if previous consultation had occurred? This point was not clearly stated.

Mussolini left his acolyte no doubt of the manner in which he envisaged the future of their collaboration. In an interview after the conclusion of the Steel Pact, held, if memory serves, at the Brenner Pass, he explained to Hitler that the decisive war he was bent on should not take place before 1942. The delay was necessary so that Italy might reconstitute her military forces and complete her preparations. In 1942 Italy was to hold an International Exposition at Rome, which was to bemuse the vigilance of her adversaries and to increase the stock of foreign currency that she required. Hitler fell in wholly with this plan; peace, a hypocritical and precarious peace, seemed to be assured for three years. It was not assured for three months!

Driven on by his demon, convinced that he had but scant time to carry out his whole program, the Führer put his irons back into the fire. Renewing the tactics he had so successfully employed against Austria and Czechoslovakia, he invented a conflict with Poland in order to create the pretext which would serve him to settle the question of Danzig and the Corridor. But this time he was wrong; he had overreached himself.

Hitler in this instance consulted Mussolini no more than he had in previous instances; he made his moves as he pleased without asking advice of Rome and without informing Rome of the march of events. Aware that he would have received only counsels of moderation and reminders of agreements made, he was unwilling to let this disturbing element mar his game.

For the Duce, this combination of circumstances was highly dramatic. He was faced with precisely the eventuality he most dreaded and wished most to avoid. War had broken out three years too early and Italy was forced to stand with her back to the wall at a most unfavorable moment. He attempted to resort to the formula which had proved effective at Munich; on August 30 he proposed a meeting of the adversaries. The invasion of Polish territory by the German armies cut his efforts short. Still he persevered, reiterating his offer. But Britain, her indignation and wrath aroused, foiled Mussolini's plan by exacting that the Reich troops first retreat to their point of departure across the frontier, and the war proceeded.

According to the terms of the Steel Pact, Mussolini ought to have sped to Germany's aid. To be sure, by the same terms Germany ought to have informed Italy and acted in concert with her. The spirit of the pact put Italy in the wrong, the letter, Germany. Mussolini based his conduct upon the letter of the pact, he was disloyal to its spirit: Italy stood aloof from the conflict. She did not proclaim her neutrality, she simply declared herself a "nonbelligerent."

Hitler asked nothing of his ally; he exerted no pressure upon him. Nevertheless the dereliction of his friend disappointed him. He pretended to accept as valid the abundant explanations Mussolini supplied; but at bottom he was mortified and hurt. His associates, failing to maintain the same reserve, gave free reign to their anger and contempt. The old anti-Italian prejudice rearose in the German mind. From this point on there was to be an ineffaceable shadow, grievance and resentment in the relations between the leaders of the two countries. Mussolini signified to Hitler that his nonbelligerence was but a temporary measure and that Italy would participate in the war as soon as she had completed her preparations. Meanwhile Ciano was telling me: "Do not wear yourself out making propaganda. Win victories and we will be with you. Otherwise we will go against you." Which of the two, the father-in-law or the son-in-law, spoke sincerely?

Toward the end of 1939 the Duce, ashamed of his shortcomings, retired to sulk in his tent. But it must be admitted that late in January 1940 he reassumed the direction of affairs and thenceforward worked to steer Italy into the war. Informed no doubt of Germany's plan to launch a decisive attack on France the following spring, he judged that this offensive held the most serious chances of success. All the same, his intervention on July 10, when France lay prostrate, bore all the marks of a base and shameful calculation; even the Germans, who had not invited it, considered it as such. German consideration for this ally of the eleventh hour was not increased. There are reasons to believe that when the conditions of the armistice were drawn up Hitler bore heavily upon Mussolini to temper the Italian's appetites.

Against the hopes of the dictators the armistice concluded with France did not put an end to war. This time they were both disappointed, especially Mussolini, who must have felt that his country was not strong enough to endure a long war. Now, doubtless more firmly than he would have wished, Mussolini found himself bound to Germany for the future; they were chained together by his dependence upon her. For all his affectation of a stiff, starched manner, for all his strutting, he was in a position of inferiority that wounded his pride. In order to rise above it he attacked Greece, having decided, again in his turn, to proceed without previously consulting his associate. The result increased his humiliation and made him even more dependent upon Hitler. Forced to call the Reich to his aid in the Balkans, later he would have to summon them to Africa for the same purpose. The master now was wholly at the mercy of his disciple.

Their friendship proved equally fatal to both. Without Mussolini, Hitler could never have carried out his plans for conquest and his ambition for hegemony. Without Hitler, Mussolini, contenting himself with making speeches, would never have yielded to his most dangerous temptations. Separately they might have lived; their union caused their destruction, and in the last analysis each died through the agency of the other.

X. THE MUNICH CONFERENCE

ODAY when people discuss the Munich agreement, they seem to me all too prone to forget the circumstances which preceded and accompanied Munich, the whole long and painful story which I have attempted to sketch broadly. *"Principiis obsta!"* says Ovid. "Resist from the beginning." Yield but once on the question of principles and, one weakness leading to another, you no longer know where or how to stop. The Munich agreement was the logical consequence of the policy practiced by Britain and France—but inspired mainly by Britain—from the time Hitler first began to break treaties and menace the peace. Munich cannot be separated from such episodes since Munich is simply their extension. Nor can it be isolated from the annexation of Austria, which occurred six months before.

I have dealt with certain phases of the duel between the German Goliath, a hypocrite and criminal, and the Austrian David, plucky enough but armed with a poor sling and betrayed by his own compatriots. It lasted for several years, punctuated by the murder of Dollfuss and by the unheard-of treatment meted out to Schuschnigg by Hitler at Berchtesgaden. I have related the first of these events; the second is too well known to bear repeating.

But how to account for the weakness of the great powers when faced with the actual annexation of Austria—a *coup de force* which clearly showed the methods Hitler planned to use in creating the "Greater Reich"? First, the democratic peoples no less than their governments entertained feelings which stand as keystone to the whole period: a basic pacifism, an aversion to permitting Europe to plunge into a general war. They were inclined to believe that peace was worth safeguarding even at the price of sacrifices however painful. They had proved it on many occasions after 1934; in the course of the constantly recurring conflicts arising from the Spanish Civil War they proved it again, with remarkable patience and calm, by circumscribing the area of the fire. But they also had further, more particular worries.

France of course understood that Austrian independence formed the basis of European equilibrium and raised the problems of security and international honor. Her Minister of Foreign Affairs, Yvon Delbos, stated this in excellent terms on February 26. Unfortunately on March 12 France was in the midst of a domestic crisis; the public learned simultaneously of the Germans entering Vienna and of the resignation of the Chautemps cabinet. The task of his successor proved laborious. Leon Blum assumed it: presenting himself before the Chambers he proclaimed the country's passionate attachment to peace and its will to gather all the pacifist forces in the world to achieve collective security. He remained in power barely one month. These were poor conditions for attempting vigorous action.

In Britain, Neville Chamberlain was at the helm. But on February 20 Eden, his foreign secretary, made his exit. His act was interpreted as a sign that within the British Government the "conciliators" had the upper hand. And in effect he was succeeded by Lord Halifax, who, in 1937, had paid Hitler a visit at Berchtesgaden and from his contacts with the leading Nazis never retained the impression that to compromise with them was vain.*

The British Ambassador in Berlin was no longer Sir Eric Phipps, a good observer and perspicacious judge of the swastika government. Nevile Henderson, his successor, also possessed a clear mind and a loyal character but he was less subtle and he harbored more illusions; besides his mission was to spare the susceptibilities of the Third Reich and to seek all means of agreement. Further, Britain began negotiations with Italy in view of an agreement which she hoped might incline the Duce somewhat less toward Berlin and more toward London.

Was the occupation of Austria going to ruin these plans? Many Britons believed that the Anschluss was inevitable and must be effected sooner or later. . . . Who then wished Austria any good? Certainly not Poland or Yugoslavia or Czechoslovakia whose President Beneš said one day that he had rather see the Germans in Vienna than the Hapsburgs.

Hitler's arrival on Austrian soil immediately took on the aspect of a triumph. In the beginning the Führer did not know under what form and within how long a time he would proceed to annex Austria. The demonstrations in his honor scattered all his doubts. On March 13 a new Reich law in-

---

* During the Nuremberg trials Ribbentrop claimed that Lord Halifax had given Hitler to believe, at Berchtesgaden, that Britain would not oppose a possible annexation of Austria.

corporated Austria in the Reich, and one month later, on April 11, a plebiscite approved this measure almost unanimously. Were Austria's protectors to show themselves more Austrian than the Austrians? Faced with the popular attitude, which overshadowed all memory of the cynical violence with which Germany had got rid of men like Dollfuss and Schuschnigg, the powers were doomed to remain inactive. Early in April, France and Britain prepared to transform their legations in Vienna into consulates general. The Third Reich had absorbed Austria as a snake gobbles down his prey.

But by the same token the military defenses of Czechoslovakia had lost part of their efficacy; by occupying Austria the Germans had outflanked them.

At that moment no one took heed, though everyone knew that Nazism was profoundly hostile to Czechoslovakia. Periodically Goebbels' press launched into significant campaigns against the Czechs. Two parallel themes were developed in this propaganda.

The first consisted in denouncing the collusion of the Czechs with Soviet Russia and in asserting that the Prague Government had covered the country with airfields, making of Bohemia a vast platform whence airplanes might take off to bomb Germany. The falsity of these allegations was pointed out times without number; nevertheless the Reich press, far from publishing a correction, persisted in stating that Czechoslovakia was a permanent menace to German security.

The second theme consisted in accusing Prague of systematically mistreating the Germans of Sudetenland, much like the Vienna Government had been accused of mistreating the "German-minded" part of the population. The German press echoed the complaints of their blood brothers and exposed at length and indignantly the injustices and vexations they suffered; it called for a speedy end to this intolerable abuse, which incidentally had never been mentioned before

Hitler's advent to power and the reform of the Reichswehr.

Embroidering upon the whole, the gazettes recalled with suspicious perseverance the atrocities committed of yore by the Hussite ancestors of the Czechs. The entire policy reeked of evil intent which the Nazi chieftains did not even trouble to conceal. One evening at dinner at the French Embassy, when champagne had disposed him to be confidential, Goering tackled the subject squarely. "Consider the shape of Czecho-slovakia on the map," he told me. "Isn't this a challenge to common sense? Czechoslovakia is the vermiform appendix of Europe! We shall have to operate!" And he added: "How will France act if we do so?"

I replied that he must make no mistake: France would respect its pledges and come to the aid of the Czechs.

"Well, so much the worse!" he concluded grimly.

However, Hitler dared not "operate" on Czechoslovakia, annexing Sudeten territory and Austria at one fell swoop. On the contrary, during the night of March 11-12, as his armies marched upon Vienna—this warlike machine, incidentally, did not work perfectly on that road—he charged Goering to calm the apprehensions of Dr. Mastny, Czechoslovak minister in Berlin. Next day Dr. Mastny was further reassured that his country need fear nothing, since the German troops had been ordered not to approach its frontiers and the German-Czechoslovak arbitration treaty was still valid.

Then, as the occupation of Austria was accomplished with-out striking a blow and amid a ringing of bells that celebrated the apotheosis of the Führer, things changed quickly on his return to Berlin. Hitler repented his lack of audacity. He felt that while he was about it he could have absorbed Sudeten-land as cheaply. Thenceforward his sole idea was to make up for his foolish mistake.

All Hitler's personality and the personality of every Ger-man is here reflected. He was a *Nimmersatt*, a man never sated; he lacked all sense of proportion; he set a value only upon what he did not yet possess; he was urged to extremes by a demon.

Everything was ready for the fulfillment of the Führer's will. His machinery was set up; he need but set it in motion by employing the technique that had served him so well in Austria. Konrad Henlein was prepared to direct operations. On April 24 a congress held at Carlsbad unified the political groups into which Sudeten Germans had been split. By a piece of barefaced anticipation, Krebs, a Czechoslovak refugee in Germany, was designated as their "Gauleiter." Deputy Kundt, a lawyer, was appointed to formulate the claims and to conduct the procedure of forthcoming negotiations.

The Prague Government was not to escape the necessity of negotiating. Britain and France invited it to do so and it consented, actually favoring certain important reforms. But it was soon clear that conversations were not likely to succeed. Prime Minister Hodža proposed as many as three plans, all of which were successively rejected. What the public—puppets on wires manipulated by Berlin—wanted was exactly what Czechoslovakia could not and would not grant: the creation of a state within a state. These parleys, alternately raising the hopes of public opinion and awakening its apprehensions, left it unnerved. In the intervals between sessions brawls of all sorts and bloody frays broke out everywhere.

Early in May Hitler returned the visit that Mussolini had paid him the autumn before and witnessed military spectacles destined to convince the world of Axis power and of the intimate solidarity of the twin dictatorships.

Late in April unwonted movements of Reichswehr troops took place on the Czechoslovak frontier. Rumor pointed to an imminent invasion; Britain and France asked for an explanation. Berlin countered with a furious denial, expressing its indignation that certain London and Paris journals dared pretend that this step had intimidated Hitler. Yet the Franco-British attitude was in no wise comminatory. On July 2 Neville

Chamberlain declared that Britain would go to war if its own liberties were endangered and if war were the only means available to defend them; but he added that he would personally bend every effort to avoid a repetition of 1914 and would continue his policy of appeasement. He thus established Britain's position.

Edouard Daladier for his part declared on July 12 that France would not repudiate the obligations which bound her to Czechoslovakia. But he voiced the hope that matters would not go so far as to force her to honor these obligations; he trusted that the Chancellor of the Reich would continue loyal to the peaceful aspirations he had always publicly proclaimed. The French Government, Daladier concluded, would follow the policy that had been agreed upon.

Meanwhile an excellent source from amid Hitler's intimate circle warned me that the Führer had decided to settle matters; if we failed to give him satisfaction by the end of September, he would invade Czechoslovakia. The actual date (September 27 or 28) was indicated.

Neville Chamberlain's chief concern was to be the pacifier of Europe. At this time he made a far-reaching decision which was to weigh heavily upon the subsequent evolution of events. On August 2 he sent Lord Runciman to Prague, commissioning him to investigate on the spot. Despite Chamberlain's protestations that Runciman was but a private investigator, that he would not act as arbiter, and that the government would not be bound by his advice, the fact was that arbitration was to be exercised by an eminent person enjoying the confidence of the British Cabinet. For six weeks Lord Runciman conferred with both parties, Henlein's representatives, and members of the Czech Government; he traveled over the country questioning the local populations; finally he declared himself in favor of the German Sudeten theory. Their claims he considered justified; he recommended a plebiscite, which Prague doggedly opposed.

While he was carrying out his mission there was no sign of conditions easing; on the contrary everything grew increasingly serious. The information I had gathered was being clearly confirmed. On August 12 Hitler mobilized three or four hundred thousand civilian workers to build the Siegfried Line facing France. The Reichswehr conducted maneuvers to which a vast number of reservists were summoned. It decided to retain the class which should normally have been released in September, thus giving it at least one and one half million men under arms. France, in turn, took corresponding measures. Europe was living on a volcano.

On September 5 the annual Nuremberg Congress met; it was like a vigil of arms. Hitler's speeches were incendiary and his lieutenants outdid him in threats leveled at those whom Goering dubbed "the ridiculous dwarfs of Prague."

On September 7 I attended the reception tendered by the Führer in a hotel of the city to the diplomats present. According to custom, the dean of the ambassadors was called upon to deliver a brief address. I made the most of it, stressing each syllable *staccato* as best I could, to offer Hitler a sort of warning and solemn adjuration. "The noblest laurel," I told him, "will ever be that which may be culled without bringing tears to the eyes of a single mother!" The audience knew what I meant; everyone turned toward Hitler. I looked at him steadily. His pale face remained impassive.

On September 12, at the final session of the Congress, he repeated that matters could no longer be put off. The Sudeten Germans must obtain the right to order their own existence without delay; and, he vowed, Germany would never again bow to a foreign will. On September 13 Henlein broke off the current discussions. On the morrow the press announced Neville Chamberlain's proposal to visit the Führer "in order to attempt to find a peaceful solution."

The head of the British Government suffered no considerations of dignity and prestige and no cares for his health or comfort to stop him. Despite his age he took the trouble to go in person to knock at the door of the gangster who reigned over Germany. Chamberlain doubtless thought European peace would be lightly won at the price. But in the British Premier's initiative Hitler saw merely a confession of weakness in the simple, modest bearing of the old man, merely a subject for mockery and the confirmation of Ribbentrop's contemptuous judgment of Britain and the British.

The interview in Hitler's Berchtesgaden chalet lasted three hours. The Führer was calm and courteous as he explained profusely what he wished to obtain and would consider satisfactory. In sum, cession to the Reich of all Sudeten districts incontestably peopled by a German majority and, where doubt prevailed, a referendum. Chamberlain entertained the demand, promising to deliver an answer within a week. This time Hitler went to meet him; the interview took place at Godesberg on the Rhine. The British Premier evidently believed the Reich claim to be not unreasonable. His report from Runciman could but confirm his opinion. But now the point was first to convince his colleagues, next the French Government, and finally, if possible, the Prague Cabinet.

Tackling the task, he managed to convince his colleagues. Then he summoned the French ministers Daladier and Bonnet, who reached London on September 18. The day was Sunday. A meeting held in London on Sunday! Franco-British consultation required no less than three sessions held the same day from 11:00 to 1:00, from 3:00 to 6:00, and from 10:30 to 12:30.

Daladier and Bonnet clung to the thesis the French Government had already defined. If war was necessary, France would fight; but it would hesitate to oppose the British Premier's efforts at conciliation. France admitted the principle of cession to Germany of districts populated by a majority of Germans, but this must be determined and controlled by an international organization. She had reasons to believe that the

Czechoslovak Government was not absolutely opposed to this; she further insisted that if Czechoslovakia was to be deprived of Sudetenland, at least the new frontiers should be covered by efficient guarantees, specifically British and French. At the conclusion of the conference a communiqué recorded the complete agreement of the two governments. The consent of Prague now remained to be won.

The Czechoslovak Cabinet protested at first and resisted. But it was basing its arguments on shaky premises. The liberties and the relative autonomy it was ready to allow the Sudeten Germans in some sort implied the confession that in the past this minority had not been treated as justice or fitness demanded. Czechoslovakia refused a plebiscite which the European public tended to regard as an equitable means of deciding between the two adversaries. The Runciman report stood against the Czechoslovak Government. It had also to count not only on Italy's hostility, whose Duce ceaselessly encouraged the investigating Lord and backed up Hitler, but on that of Poland and of Hungary, who believed the time come to seize Czechoslovak territory that separated them and to establish a common frontier. The Soviet Union would doubtless uphold Czechoslovakia, but only after France and following France's example; and France, needing British support, could not champion the Czechoslovakian cause until she had allowed Britain to exhaust the attempts at conciliation that Neville Chamberlain was making. Otherwise France would be accused of responsibility for starting the war and driving the world to a catastrophe.

Abandoning its objections and reservations, the Prague Government finally bowed to the inevitable. "We are sacrificing ourselves for the salvation of Europe!" its Propaganda Minister cried tragically. Hodža, resigning, was succeeded by General Sirovy.

Chamberlain was now in a position to bring Hitler the awaited reply. On September 20 he flew off to Godesberg, where the Chancellor greeted him. But this was not the same Hitler of a week before. Chamberlain was faced with a stiffened, categorical man, whose tone and whose pretensions had risen several degrees. To have won recognition of the principle that districts German in majority were to be ceded and other districts submitted to a plebiscite was not enough for him. He now exacted, in the form of an ultimatum, that cession be effected by October 1, that Czechoslovakian officials and army units withdraw immediately from the districts concerned to make room for the Wehrmacht, and that the plebiscites decided upon be completed before November 25.

What could have happened from one week to the other? What could have caused this brutal change? Was Hitler merely emboldened by the hesitation and confusion he believed he detected in the enemy camp? Was he carried away by his mania for always calling for more and going to extremes? Perhaps. . . . However, at the time, the Nazi leaders, especially Goering, told me that the German telephone monitoring system had caught conversations exchanged between the Prague Cabinet and its legations in London and Paris. These Czech conversations, couched in the boldest terms, revealed an intent to temporize and to work for the overthrow of the Chamberlain and Daladier cabinets. I must add that the Czechoslovaks have steadfastly denied the truth of this allegation.

At any rate Chamberlain, astounded by the Führer's attitude, declined further converse and prepared to quit Godesberg. During the night of September 23-24 he took leave of his host. Hitler, in the interval, had calmed down slightly; he recast his ultimatum as a memorandum which Chamberlain consented to submit to the parties interested.

War seemed no less unavoidable. Mobilization orders were published. The Sudeten Germans constituted volunteer legions. The Hungarians called three classes to the colors. The Poles reported trouble at the Czech border town of Teschen. France increased her protective army. Daladier and Bonnet returned hurriedly to London; they arrived September 25, once again on a Sunday, for a final Franco-British conference. General Gamelin was summoned to join them the following day, a proof that the possibility of war was being frankly considered.

Neither the General nor the ministers avoided the issue. Yet the study of military prospects was anything but heartening. Everyone knew that the Reich had planned the invasion of Czechoslovakia down to the slightest detail; the operation was to mark the first exposition of *Blitzkrieg*. German airplanes had long ago rehearsed over dummy targets the bombings they might have to make; Germany flattered herself upon her ability to paralyze all of Czechoslovakia within a few hours. Italian hostility would prevent the Allies from bringing immediate aid. Besides Britain was merely beginning to rearm; she had not even resolved to establish conscription and the air force now being set up was not yet superior to the German.

France's war machine left much to be desired. Late in July as I discussed the threatening due date of September with Premier Daladier, he expressed the hope that my forecast would prove false. He needed a delay of six months more in order to match the German 105-gun with equivalent French matériel. In August, General Vuillemin, Commander in Chief of the French Air Force, came to Germany at the invitation of Goering, Commander in Chief of the German Air Force. He was most cordially received. The most recent models were exhibited for his benefit; he was shown over the training camps, workshops, factories, and plants of the anti-aircraft organization; nothing was hidden from him and he was able to confirm the accuracy of information I had been filing in Paris for many months. At the end of his visit and of a farewell luncheon at Karin Hall, Goering asked the fateful question: "If Germany and Czechoslovakia go to war, what will France do?"

"France will honor her signature," the General answered.

But a few minutes later, as we drove back to Berlin, he confessed: "Should war break out as you expect late in September, there won't be a single French plane left within a fortnight!"

Amid such conditions it is conceivable that the representatives of France had grounds for anxiety.

Was it worth anyone's trouble to approach Hitler once more? On December 26 Hitler, in a speech at the Sportspalatz, hurled impassioned invectives upon Dr. Beneš, the Czechoslovak premier; his was a furious personal challenge without precedent in the annals of contemporary history. Was it the signal for war? Everyone thought so. Was the world to stand by, arms akimbo, while Czechoslovakia was invaded? Roosevelt did not think so, for he sent the Führer two messages appealing to his feelings of humanity. Chamberlain did not think so either, for, on September 27, he declared in a broadcast: "*However much we may sympathize with a small nation confronted by a big and powerful neighbor, we cannot in all circumstances undertake to involve the whole British Empire in war simply on her account. If we have to fight, it must be on larger issues than that.*"

Since all appeal to Berlin seemed futile, British diplomacy turned toward Rome where it fondly believed it was on excellent terms with Mussolini.

Daladier and Bonnet were not idle either. During the night of September 27-28 I was instructed to see Hitler at the earliest possible moment, to insist on the seriousness of his stand, to represent to him how unreasonable his attitude, and to attempt to persuade him not to carry out his threatened invasion of Czechoslovakia before October 1, since this act would undoubtedly cause a world war.*

* I should like to point out here that, in relating the memories and thoughts which the Munich Conference aroused and left within me, I offer the testimony of one who was but a purveyor of information, a go-between, an observer and an executant. I was never consulted when the major decisions were made, so I have no special cause to plead.

At 8:00 A.M. on September 28 I asked for an audience with Hitler. I had had a map drawn with the districts admittedly German heavily colored in red. I proposed to use it in order to show him how very much he could gain without a general conflagration. Until 10:00 A.M. my request remained unanswered. Fearing to be fobbed off, I sent the French military attaché, General Renondeau, to the Chief of Staff of the Reichswehr, bidding him to emphasize the responsibility incurred by the military high command in case of war and to inform the Reichswehr of the message I was charged with but as yet unable to deliver.

At 11:00 A.M. Hitler invited me to proceed forthwith to the Chancellery. His aides were in a state of high excitement. Officers of the SS and the Wehrmacht kept coming and going, all agog and obviously worried. In the room leading to the large salon where Hitler received me I saw many tables set up with cloths, napkins, glassware, and couverts. I was informed that at one o'clock the commanders of the invasion units were to meet for lunch. The invasion was scheduled for 3:00 P.M.

The Führer, flanked by Ribbentrop, looked brisk, nervous, and tense. I accosted him at once, flourishing my map before him. I reminded him that once before, at a critical juncture in the Spanish Civil War, we had safeguarded peace.* If he believed that he could localize the conflict today, I told him, he was in error. If he attacked Czechoslovakia, I said, all Eu-

---

* Early in 1937 it was rumored that important German contingents were about to land in Spanish Morocco, where barracks had already been prepared for them. The French and British press and the Paris and London Governments were much exercised. Irremediable incidents were feared.

On January 11 Hitler received the diplomatic corps. After exchanging the traditional congratulations I went up to him and, taking him aside, I begged him to tell me whether it was true that Germany had sent or planned to send any units to Spanish Morocco. Hitler instantly declared that Germany had neither sent troops nor had the slightest intention of doing so. At my request he authorized me to use his statement. I immediately referred to Paris and, in conjunction with Neurath, published a communiqué which restored calm in the capitals of Europe.

rope would be caught in the holocaust. Was he willing to assume the dread responsibility for such horror when already 75 per cent of what he claimed was granted him?

Hitler seemed perplexed, Ribbentrop broke in to attenuate the effect of my remarks. I dealt with him roundly, turning to Hitler to address him alone and continuing to argue most urgently.

Suddenly an SS entered announcing that Attolico, the Italian Ambassador, had just arrived with an urgent message for the Chancellor. Hitler left the room for about a quarter of an hour. When he returned he said: "It was Mussolini; he too asked me not to go ahead!" I summed up my previous arguments, pointing out their unexpected confirmation by the Duce.

The Führer was listening to me less attentively, his thoughts elsewhere. His expression of hesitation was more clearly marked. At last he rose. I asked him whether I was to advise my government that he was inflexible; he replied that he would give me his answer early in the afternoon. He was much disturbed, I felt, as I left. At the door of his reception room I met Goering and Neurath, who beckoned encouragingly. I passed the Wehrmacht generals as they began arriving for luncheon, and returned to my embassy.

At 2:30 Goering telephoned to me on behalf of the Chancellor, who suggested a conference at Munich next day, September 29, and requested me to invite the French Premier to attend. I forwarded the invitation without comment; an hour later it was accepted. I immediately informed Goering. *"Gott sei Dank,* thank God!" he cried. "Bravo!"

Are we to conclude that Hitler had been bluffing and was happy to seize this opportunity to call off his bluff? All the observations I was able to make, and all the information I was able to gather during that so poignant period, point to the contrary. It is true that there were powerful influences around him, dissuading him from carrying out his plan: the General

Staff, for instance, and Goering, all of whom judged that the Reich should further increase its margin of superiority. It is also true that the people displayed no enthusiasm; they had watched without joy, indeed with consternation, the passage of the regiments through the capital. But Hitler was not one —he proved it—to stop before such obstacles. Had we broken off sharply and cut short all discussion, I remain convinced that his pride would have rebelled, that he would have picked up the gauntlet and plunged into the adventure against all comers.

At all events, the mere citing of the circumstances proves that on the eve of the Munich Conference the situation was no longer uncompromised. It was dominated by the efforts of the British Government which was determined, under Neville Chamberlain's leadership, to keep the Empire out of war at any price. It was dominated by Lord Runciman's report which favored the Sudeten Germans and by the decisions made in London and accepted reluctantly in Prague which settled the main points concerning the return to Germany of the contested districts. It was dominated by the false position in which the Czechoslovak Government was unfortunately placed. Finally it was dominated not only by the anxiety to spare Europe the horrors of war but quite as much by the Franco-British desire to gain time and profit thereby in order to complete preparations and armaments which were held to be insufficient or faulty.

Mussolini arrived from Italy by rail on the morning of September 29. Hitler raced to meet him, boarded his coach at Kufstein, through which the former Austrian frontier had passed, and conferred with him during the rest of the journey. Ovations hailed the two dictators as they crossed the Bavarian capital.

Meanwhile Daladier, coming from Paris, alighted at the airport at 11:15, accompanied by Léger, Secretary-General, and

Rochat, Director of Public Affairs at the Quai d'Orsay. I was waiting for them. Broad-backed, sunburned, his head buried deep between his shoulders, his brow deeply furrowed with wrinkles, Daladier appeared gloomy and preoccupied. Léger seemed even more so. A company of Reichswehr presented arms. Ribbentrop and Weizsäcker, Secretary of State at the Wilhelmstrasse, greeted Premier Daladier, who was immediately driven to the Hotel Vier Jahreszeiten, an old establishment of excellent reputation.

At noon Goering called to escort Daladier to the Führerhaus, the scene of the conference. Bedecked with braid and decorations, his face radiant with a cordial smile, his hand outstretched effusively, the Marshal wished to please by his straightforward manners, his air of frankness, his very stoutness. The three of us climbed into an open car. Warm applause and spontaneous cheers rose from the crowds on the sidewalks. Daladier was visibly surprised at this cordial demonstration.

The Führerhaus, where our auto stopped, was one of two recently constructed buildings which closed the rectangle of the Royal Square on the side where the Glypothek stood. A characteristic specimen of Hitlerian architecture, it repudiated detail, ornament, curve, and roundness of form, seeking to impress by the Doric simplicity of its lines and the massive aspect of its proportions. For sole decoration the façade bore a bronze eagle with wings outspread. Within, it was spacious and well-ventilated, boasting a fine stone stairway and resembling some mammoth modern hotel furnished by a professional interior decorator.

The members of the Conference met in a salon where a buffet had been set up. They shook hands courteously but coldly and stared at one another: Mussolini, squat, laced into his uniform, the features of a Caesar, patronizing, completely at ease as though in his own house, flanked by Ciano, a tall, healthy fellow, very solicitous of his master, more the orderly

officer than the minister of foreign affairs; Chamberlain, griz-
zled, bowed, with bushy eyebrows and prominent teeth, his
face blotchy, his hands reddened by rheumatism, standing
between Wilson and Strang, clad in black like him, discreet
and self-effacing; Hitler agreeable despite his heavy rude peasant voice, but worried, excited, very pale, and incapable of
speaking with his guests since he knew no English or French
or Italian and they no German, except Mussolini, to whom
Hitler clung like his shadow.

The meeting began at 12:45 in an adjoining room. The ambassadors were not admitted. Two hours later, as the meeting
adjourned, I was informed that the four participants exposed
their point of view in turn in general terms. Hitler delivered a
diatribe of extreme violence against Czechoslovakia. There-
upon Daladier clearly and vigorously posed the crucial question: Did the Conference wish Czechoslovakia to exist or not?
Was the proposed amputation intended to make her healthier
and to give her better chances for life in the future? Or was
it but a means to weaken her, a mutilation bound to bring
about her death? If the point was to prepare the dismember-
ment and disappearance of Czechoslovakia, then he, Daladier,
had no business in this place. He refused to be associated with
such a crime and would take his leave. If, on the contrary,
the point was to assure Czechoslovakia's future, then he was
prepared to concur with the others in a spirit of reciprocal
concession and collaboration. The French Premier spoke in ac-
cents of a determination and nobility that moved his hearers.

Mussolini declared that Hitler's idea had been misunder-
stood, and, like the Duce, all protested that they wished to
consolidate and to respect the existence of the Czechoslovakian
state.

At three o'clock luncheon was served.

There was a second session at the close of the afternoon.
This time I entered by permission and sat behind Daladier.
The delegates were grouped in a semicircle around a vast fire-

place, the British on the left, the Italians and Germans in the center, the French on the right. Within the British group there was scant conversation; within the German and Italian groups there was much. Mussolini was deeply ensconced in his arm-chair. His extraordinarily mobile features were never at rest for a moment; his mouth would part for a wide smile or contract in a pout; his brows rose in surprise or were knit threateningly; his eyes, generally curious and amused in expression, would suddenly dart lightning.

Standing at his side, Hitler gazed intently upon him, subject to his charm and as though fascinated and hypnotized. Did the Duce laugh, the Führer laughed too; did Mussolini scowl, so scowled Hitler. Here was a study in mimicry. It was to leave me with the lasting and erroneous impression that Mussolini exercised a firmly established ascendancy over the Führer. At any rate that day he did.

No one presided at this session and there was no methodical agenda. For want of directive, the discussion proved difficult, confused, and interminably long. Hampered by the necessity of a double translation, it kept constantly changing its topic and ceased whenever a contradiction arose. The atmosphere grew thicker and heavier. At last toward evening the British produced a typewritten memorandum from their files. It had been drawn up by Horace Wilson with Strang's assistance. The debate, which had wavered, now concentrated upon this proposal for an agreement.

While the delegates recessed we translated it from English into French and German. Then the discussion was resumed. It presented no difficulty save on two counts.

The first concerned Article 6, which the French sought to temper so that the transfer without plebiscite of German majority zones might admit of exceptions in the judgment of the international commission which was to control the whole operation. There was much conflict on this question. Hitler opposed the idea, fought long and hard against it, and finally yielded. The second difficulty arose from Amendment 1, concerning the international guarantee of Czechoslovakia's new borders against all unprovoked aggression. France and Britain offered such a guarantee; Italy and Germany hesitated and made reservations. They were unwilling to be bound until the claims of their friends the Hungarians and Poles were settled. But they promised the guarantee asked for so soon as the problem in question were solved. At 1:30 A.M. the agreement was signed.

It provided for the evacuation, in four stages, of districts "preponderantly" German; this was to begin on October 1 and be completed by October 10. Conditions were to be determined and supervised by an international commission composed of representatives of Britain, Italy, Germany, and Czechoslovakia. The commission was also to rule upon what districts were to hold plebiscites and, until these had been completed, international contingents were to occupy the territory. Previous plebiscites in the Saar were to serve for model and the operation was to be concluded by the end of November at latest. Inhabitants of these transferred districts were to enjoy an interval of six months before opting between inclusion and exclusion. A German-Czechoslovak commission would assure the details governing the right of option and would arrange the exchange of populations.

Compared to the Godesberg ultimatum the Munich agreement marked a considerable withdrawal of German claims. But that fact did not lessen the painful character of the Munich decisions. The French felt it fully. A land which had always been their loyal ally was suffering a large-scale material reduction and horrible moral humiliation. It was being deprived of cities and regions which formed a valuable part of its riches. It had had perforce to yield to the threats of might. It had been sacrificed to the cause of peace.

We were bitterly aware of the cruelty of the event. Daladier shook his head, muttered, and cursed circumstances. He refused to take part in the congratulations exchanged by the other delegates. Worst, the most painful step had not yet been taken; we had now to break the news to the Czechoslovaks who were awaiting the outcome of the Conference at their hotel. Mastny, their minister in Berlin, broke into tears. I consoled him as best I could. "Believe me," I said, "all this is not final. It is but one moment in a story which has just begun and which will soon bring up the issue again."

Returning to our hotel at 2:30 A.M., I called Bonnet by telephone to inform him of what had happened, while Daladier, still cursing and lost in gloomy thought, weighed the difficulties he was likely to meet on his return to Paris. Bonnet swept aside my detailed explanations. "Peace is assured," he said. "That is the main thing. Everybody will be happy."

Next morning at 11:30 Chamberlain visited Hitler without informing his French colleague and obtained from the Führer a written engagement of nonaggression and mutual consultation as well as a promise of friendly relations between the two states. At the same hour a crowd formed before the Hotel Vier Jahreszeiten and obliged Daladier to appear at the balcony. The French Premier left Munich at 1:20 P.M. on the airplane *Poitou*; Ribbentrop saw him off.

The sequel is well known: Daladier's arrival at the Bourget airport, the delirious ovation of the crowd much to the Premier's surprise, the joyful demonstrations that greeted him, the pilgrimage to the tomb of the Unknown Soldier, the vote of approval in the Chamber of Deputies on October 4 carried by 535 votes to 75.

As for me I returned by plane to Berlin on the morning of September 30 to face the most crushing chapter of the whole tragic episode. I was a member of the international commission created by the agreement; I had to witness the surgical operation, the cutting up of the panting victim. Things moved swiftly and in the beginning normally. But when we came to such zones as might qualify for a plebiscite difficulties rose at once. The Czechoslovaks possessed no recently drawn ethnographical map. We were obliged to refer to a linguistic map drawn in 1910 by the Austrian Government.

The zones to be ceded to Germany without plebiscite were those which, according to the text of the agreement, were "preponderantly" German. What did this term "preponderance" actually mean? I held that it meant a "very large majority," say 75 per cent. The Czechoslovaks went further, claiming that it meant a majority of at least 80 per cent. My British and Italian colleagues, Nevile Henderson and Attolico, broke away from me, affirming that "preponderance" meant simply "majority." Despite every kind of pressure I was unwilling to share their opinion, and the conference had to interrupt its labors. I had retired to my embassy when Ribbentrop awakened me in the middle of the night, begging me to meet him at once at the Hotel Kaiserhof where he had established his offices. I found him very excited, pacing up and down the room with giant strides. He informed me that my obstruction threatened to revive the crisis which the Munich Conference was meant to have settled. Hitler was even now a prey to the fiercest anger; he accused me of dishonesty; he was preparing to order the Reichswehr to seize the contested districts if they were not ceded to him willingly, as had been agreed.

I told Ribbentrop that this anger and attempt to intimidate were quite spurious. What was the question at issue? To clarify the sense of the word "preponderance" which figured in the original English text of the Munich agreement. To do so we had but to ask the British and French signatories of this text for a definition. Paris and London were immediately consulted; they confirmed the German interpretation. For "preponderance" we were to read "majority." I could but bow to this decision. All districts with a German population of 51 per cent were automatically to go to Germany. In most zones where plebiscites might have been held, they now became unnecessary. The Czechoslovaks lost more territory than they had foreseen; their distress increased proportionally. In the end they abandoned all idea of plebiscites and decided to deal directly with the Germans.

The aftermath of the agreement proved equally disappointing. The Munich Conference had not relieved the tensity of the European situation. The joy that had greeted the safeguarding of peace was soon followed by a realization of the price it had cost. And this price was deemed excessive.

Hitler too was deeply disappointed. He had thought in his pride to gather laurels and to hear canticles in his praise. Far from it. Here were certain voices in Britain and France heaping reproach upon the authors of the agreement, and these very authors preaching distrust. Hitler was violently irritated. He did not consider that he had carried off a success at Munich; on the contrary he felt that he had abandoned his early plans, faltered and yielded. As on the morrow of Vienna he regretted his pusillanimity. He believed or wished to believe himself deceived and bilked by the artful Britons and frustrated in the true aim of his ambition, which was to seize Prague. He now thought of one thing only: to seize Prague at all costs. His humor found expression in a gloomy, threatening speech made at Saarbrück as early as October 9.

I had been informed at an earlier date of his state of mind. I knew that he planned once again to evade obligations before the ink of his signature was dry upon the documents that bound him. I at once felt the fragility of the Munich agreement. Accordingly I attempted to calm Hitler down, to bring him to bind himself to France by an engagement similar to that he had concluded with Chamberlain. I wished to flash before his eyes the possibility of further arrangements, economic and financial, which might lead to a future organization of Europe; I hoped to direct his mind toward prospects and in directions other than those of violence. And since Goering had opposed war and favored the Munich Conference, I tried to win him over to the consolidation of peace on the basis of the agreement of September and to persuade him of what advantages the Reich might gain if it remained true to its pledged word.

All this proved vain. Hitler, breaking his word, yielded to temptation and to his evil genius and on March 15, 1939, marched into Prague.

That day he sealed his doom.

Britain, finally enlightened by the occupation of Prague, understood what she was up against. She realized that the man observed neither faith nor law, that no treaty could stop him, that he aimed at hegemony, that he constituted a permanent danger for British liberties and for world democracy. From that day forward Britain resolved in her mind to crush this man, cost what it might. Would she have seen this so clearly, would her determination have been as firm, would she have shown such indomitable valor in the trials of war if Neville Chamberlain had not previously reached the extreme limits of conciliation? Would Roosevelt have been able to reverse public opinion in the United States and totally support the cause of the European democracies if he had not realized at the outset that France and Britain had gone to all lengths in order to spare the world the scourge of war? There is reason to doubt this.

Some people believe that if war had broken out in September 1938 it would have followed a different course. Perhaps at that time we might have had the support of the Soviet Union, whereas in 1939 Russia, vexed at being left out of negotiations at Munich, bargained with Berlin and stood aloof from the conflict. This objection carries much weight. And yet who believes that Poland, caught between Russia and Germany in 1938, would have joined the Allies? Have people forgotten that Poland refused Russia permission to send her troops through Polish territory if Russia went to Czechoslovakia's aid? More important still, neither Hitler nor Chamberlain would have consented to invite Russia to participate in the Munich Conference. To do so would have meant the sabotage of the conference before it came to be; it would have meant preventing the meeting and abandoning the conciliation which British policy so ardently desired.

The agreement afforded us a year of respite at a moment when neither France nor Britain judged herself to be sufficiently prepared for war. What advantage did we gain by this delay and did we make full use of it? There perhaps lies the real question, yet it is the question people ask most seldom.

In reality, conditioned by a long series of previous acts and dominated by what should be termed "peace psychosis" just as we speak of "war psychosis," the Munich agreement was a humane work, fraught with both advantages and disadvantages. It necessitated too many and too painful sacrifices for us to congratulate ourselves upon it; it brought too many advantages for us to recall only its grievous aspects. The passage of time should therefore permit one to be neither pro-Munich nor anti-Munich but, in this instance, to rise to the serenity of history.

XI. THE EAGLE'S NEST: MY LAST INTERVIEW WITH HITLER

W HEN the Comte de Chambrun, French Ambassador to Italy, returned home, only a chargé d'affaires was left to serve as link between the two countries, because France could not agree with the Fascist Government upon terms whereby a new ambassador was to be accredited to "the King of Italy, Emperor of Ethiopia." In Paris re-establishment of normal conditions was considered highly desirable. The Munich Conference, which everyone hoped would clear the atmosphere, finally determined the French Government to fill the vacancy in the Farnese Palace.

For my part I did not share the enthusiasm aroused in some quarters by the signing of the treaty on September 29. I believed that nothing must be neglected in order to strengthen the agreement made in Munich and to develop this agreement along lines that might keep the Führer in the paths of peace, but in my heart I doubted the result of such efforts.

I have already mentioned that I had been struck by the reciprocal attitudes of Chancellor and Duce as I observed them with strained attention during the melancholy Munich meeting. Mussolini had so manifestly dominated his partner, Hitler had so solicitously consulted Mussolini at every juncture, the Duce himself had contributed so usefully to make Hitler accept the final solution, that I concluded that Mussolini had been sincerely won over to the cause of peace. The only influence still capable of acting on the Führer, I thought, was that of his Italian ally. "It is useless to try anything more in Berlin," I said to myself. "Mussolini holds the key to the future." Thus I was led to wish I might be sent to Rome.

Besides I was not sorry to be leaving Berlin. I had spent seven long years there, interesting, to be sure, but also filled with disturbances, alarms, tempests, and tragedy. I had not known a moment of quiet or relaxation. I had lived in the insecurity and anxiety of the morrow, forced to exercise a continual vigilance and stress of mind, my eyes fixed upon a flame which, no sooner extinguished, rose again to draw inexorably closer to a barrel of dynamite. I was obsessed by this regime, by its methods and language and mystery and police, by its tyranny and pride and songs and parades, by its clicking of heels and hallucinating thud of boots along the streets. I was weary of trying to hold back a Hitler who always slipped through my fingers.

I realized that the work awaiting me in Italy would be trying. But surely Italian skies would prove more clement and Italian men less inhuman? I harbored no illusions about Hitler, but I did about Mussolini. I never supposed that the Duce

would undertake brutally to destroy them; it never occurred to
me that in Italy I would be subjected to discourtesies the Nazis
would never have dreamed of. Nor did it occur to me that I
was to spend hours even more painful than those I had suffered
in Germany.

When my appointment to Rome was officially announced I
received many protestations of friendship and regret from
residents of Berlin. These messages, accompanied by photo-
graphs, souvenirs, and gifts of various kinds, breathed an
accent of perfect sincerity. Ribbentrop solemnly presented me
with the insignia of the Grand Cross of the Order of the
Eagle of the Reich. This did not prevent him, however, from
anticipating my arrival in Rome with a report which described
me as a dangerous character and my obvious mission as the
sabotage of the Axis.

Hitler himself was bent on giving an unusual form to the
farewell audience granted me on the occasion of the last political conversation I was to have with him. He summoned me
neither to the Chancellery in Berlin nor to his Berghof chalet
at Berchtesgaden, but to his mountain retreat, which his intimates only, and no foreigner, had ever visited. In his mind
this was a rarer favor than I appreciated at the time. Later
he felt particularly offended because he believed that I had
failed to value his gesture and the intent that inspired it.

I was never to see him again, our interview of October 1938
being our last.

Inviting me on the evening of October 17, Hitler placed
one of his personal airplanes at my disposal. I flew next day to
Berchtesgaden, arrived there at about 3:00 P.M. and proceeded
by automobile.

From afar the extraordinary place to which I was summoned
looked like a sort of observatory or hermitage, perched at an
altitude of over six thousand feet, atop the crest of a ridge of
rocks. A hairpin road about ten miles long, cut boldly through
the rocks, wound upward. Its daring layout honored the talents

of the engineer Todt and the dogged labors of the workmen who had accomplished this gigantic task within three years. The road led to the entrance of a long underground passageway dug deep into the soil and commanded by a massive double door of bronze. At the end of this corridor a roomy copper-lined elevator awaited the visitor; its shaft, hewn vertically through the rock, rose over three hundred seventy feet to the level on which the Führer had his dwelling.

I was ushered into a squat, solid building which consisted of a gallery with Roman pillars, an immense glassed-in rotunda (giant logs blazed in a huge fireplace and there was a long table with some thirty chairs around it), and several handsomely appointed rooms on the side. To look out in any direction over the endless panorama of mountains was like looking down from an airplane. In the hollow of the amphitheater lay Salzburg and its neighboring villages, dominated, as far as the eye traveled, by a horizon of chains and peaks with meadows and woods clinging to the slopes. Hitler's house gave the impression of being suspended in space; the whole view, bathed in the chiaroscuro of autumn dusk, loomed grand, savage, hallucinant. Was this the Castle of Monsalvat, peopled by the Knights of the Grail, or a Mount Athos, where the cenobite may meditate, or Antinea's palace amid the heart of the Atlas Mountains? Was it the execution of the fantastic sketches Victor Hugo had penciled in the margins of *Les Burgraves?* Was it a billionaire's folly or the hideout where brigands relaxed and heaped up their swag? Was this edifice the work of a normal mind or of one tormented by megalomania and haunted by visions of domination and solitude? Or had it been built by a man who was simply a prey to his fears? . . .

The Chancellor greeted me amiably and with courtesy. His face was pale and drawn with fatigue. This was not one of his days of excitement; rather, he was in a phase of relaxation. He led me at once to one of the bay windows of the main room, showed me the view, and enjoyed the astonishment and admiration which I did not seek to conceal. Then he expressed his regret at my forthcoming departure. We exchanged a few compliments of courtesy and a few polite phrases. At his order tea was served in one of the adjoining salons, to which Ribbentrop accompanied us while other Nazi familiars remained aloof in neighboring rooms. The servants having retired and the doors closed upon them, we began a three-party conversation, into which Ribbentrop entered rarely but always in order to repeat and to stress the Führer's remarks.

Hitler professed disappointment at conditions following the Munich agreement. He had believed that the meeting of the Big Four, "dispelling the specter of war, might mark the beginning of an era of improved relations between the nations." He observed nothing of the sort. The crisis was not over; unless conditions changed, it would soon break out anew. Britain re-echoed "with threats and calls to arms." This provided the Chancellor with a chance to inveigh against Britain's selfishness and the ingenuous ideas she possessed concerning the superiority of her rights over those of others.

I pointed out that after the joy inspired by the safeguarding of peace, a reaction was inevitable. The spectacle of the sacrifices Czechoslovakia had been forced to make and the harsh treatment inflicted upon her could not fail to move men's hearts and even to disturb their conscience. I added that the Führer's Saarbrück speech, especially, left the impression that these sacrifices had been made in vain; resulting in merely increasing the appetites of the Third Reich, they considerably strengthened the thesis upheld by those opposed to the Munich agreement.

Hitler protested. It was not he who had begun, it was the British. He had not uttered a single word against France. As for Czechoslovakia, it was not true that he had ill-treated her; he had simply asserted the rights of the German people, who had been downtrodden.

I interrupted, saying that we must not dwell upon the past; the future was more important. After joy at the safeguarding of peace and bitterness at the price paid, a third moment was at hand. Statesmen must now decide with greater calm whether the Munich agreement was to be but a short-lived episode or whether, on the contrary, it proved by experience that the democracies and the authoritarian regimes could work together for a general peace. If so, then they should attempt to develop this experience and put it to greater profit in order to bring back normal and lasting conditions of life to Europe.

Hitler declared that for his part he was well disposed toward this; if he had invited me to visit him, it was as much to discuss the subject with me as to allow me to take my leave of him.

The three subjects we now treated successively formed a program which began with purely Franco-German relations and extended to questions concerning all the powers; on each subject the Chancellor argued, objected, and made suggestions like a man who, having pondered matters, was not to be caught off his guard.

As to the possibility of a written recognition by France and Germany of their mutual frontiers and an agreement of reciprocal consultation wherever the relations of the countries were affected, Hitler announced that he was prepared to concur immediately. He said that, at bottom, he found this hypothesis most attractive. He emphasized the difficulties likely to arise from a nonaggression pact unless reservations were made in the matter of the Covenant of the League of Nations or in that of existing agreements made with third parties. He hoped that these difficulties might be removed or sidestepped; and at no moment did he ask that France scrap the pact binding her to Soviet Russia.

In regard to limitation of armaments he outlined the theory whereby Germany, situated centrally in Europe and open to simultaneous attack on several fronts, could boast no true equality unless she enjoyed a superiority over each of the countries capable of attacking her. Also he feared that if he mentioned limitation of armaments the British would pretend that he was retreating before British energy.

On the other hand he was inclined unhesitatingly to tackle the problem of the humanization of war and to go quite far on this ground. In it he saw "a happy preamble, an auspicious preface which might give an atmosphere more favorable to a subsequent study of the armaments question."

As for monetary and economic problems Hitler always relied upon others to handle them. Still he conceived, on this occasion, the advisability of inviting experts to "resume the work already begun and to examine what possibilities the present juncture might offer."

At the end of our discussion he ordered Ribbentrop to put his organization to work, having his experts explore the suggestions furnished by our exchange of views in order to establish concrete formulas. Paris, having examined these rough sketches, could then give its opinion of them. I promised that we would receive them sympathetically and give them a serious study, inspired by the same peaceful preoccupations as those which appeared to move the Führer. Meanwhile Germany would approach Italy. France could, for her part, sound out Britain. No promise was made on either side save that of proceeding in all good faith to investigate. We agreed that public opinion must not be informed until we were certain of a positive result.

I also attempted to induce Hitler to disclose his thoughts on two other subjects: Hungary's claims and the Spanish war.

He frankly acknowledged that the Hungarian claims were excessive. For him, the only criterion was ethnographic—the race. It had been the only one, he said, which he invoked when tracing the new Czech frontiers; the Hungarians and Poles had but to do the same. Obviously the efforts of the Poles to win a common frontier with Hungary were not to his liking.

He boasted that he was responsible for foiling Hungary's request for an appeal to the four powers signatory at Munich. "Such a conference," he remarked, "would have confronted us with two very different theses. Whatever my private opinion, I would have had to support the Hungarians and Poles because of our political bonds and Mussolini would have done likewise. You and the British, for similar reasons, would have defended the Czechs. Thus three weeks after the Munich agreement we would have faced a conflict which this time could not have been settled. By avoiding this I did Europe a service. I preferred to exert pressure upon the Hungarians and the Czechs, persuading them to renew their interrupted negotiations and to be less exacting. Mussolini helped me. But the whole business shows how wrong Britain and France were in guaranteeing the Czech frontiers even before these had been clearly defined. The most vexatious complications may arise from this!"

As for Spain the Chancellor repeated that he had never intended to set up a permanent establishment there. He had won a few economic advantages, which he would have obtained in any case. He declared that he in no wise intended to use Spain as a lasting threat against France. Spain herself needed to maintain good relations with France, as General Franco's attitude during the Munich crisis had clearly demonstrated. Let all the foreign volunteers be removed and the two Spanish parties be left to fight it out. In these circumstances Franco would finally triumph and France would have nothing to complain about.

For two hours Hitler allowed me to question him, answering without the slightest embarrassment, quite simply and apparently quite frankly.

The castle of Antinea was now bathed in the shadows that lay over valley and mountain. I took my leave. The Führer expressed the wish that I might subsequently return to Germany and visit him in a private capacity. Several times he took my hands in his and shook them. Emerging from the lift and from the underground, I found the car awaiting me at the door and returned via Berchtesgaden to the airport whence I flew through the darkness to Berlin.

Throughout our conversation, except for a few violent outbursts when he spoke of Britain, Hitler was calm, moderate, and conciliatory. A witness would have been justified in believing that here was a well-balanced man, filled with experience and wisdom, who desired nothing so much as to see peace reign among the nations. At certain moments he spoke of Europe and of his sentiments as a European, more genuine than those which many men advertised noisily. He spoke of the "white civilization" as of a precious common possession which must be defended. He seemed to be sincerely struck by the persistent antagonism that survived the Munich agreement and clearly revealed to him what was Britain's attitude.

Manifestly the prospect of an early crisis and a general war was on his mind. I labored under no illusions about his character. I knew him to be changeable, dissimulating, contradictory, and uncertain. The same man, good-natured in appearance and sensitive to the beauties of nature, who across a tea table expressed reasonable opinions on European politics, was capable of the wildest frenzies, the most savage exaltation, and the most delirious ambition. There were days when, bending over a map of the world, he upset nations and continents, geography and history, like some demiurge in his madness. At other times he dreamed of being the hero of an eternal peace within whose framework he would raise the loftiest of monuments.

These were the essentials of the report I dispatched to the Ministry of Foreign Affairs immediately upon my return to Berlin. I added:

"The advances Hitler is inclined to make toward France are dictated by feelings which he shares, intermittently at least, with most Germans, namely weariness of an age-old duel and the desire to end it. Today these feelings are accentuated by the memory of the Munich Conference, by the sympathy

Premier Daladier aroused in him, and also by the idea that our country is at present evolving along lines which will enable it to understand the Third Reich better. However we can rest assured that, at the same time, the Führer holds fast to his plan of splitting Franco-British unity and stabilizing peace in the West in order to have his hands free in the East. What projects are running through his head? Is Poland or Russia or the Baltic group destined in his mind to pay the price? Does he yet know?

"Hitler is the sort of man who bears the most constant and diligent watching and who can be trusted only with reservations. Personally I do not conclude that we should elude his suggestions for that reason. In the present circumstances, as in many previous, I judge that the main point is to know how far to go and with whom we are dealing. It does not follow that an attitude of abstention and negation is the right one. Dr. Goebbels recently observed—and rightly—that no one can win in a lottery without at least taking the trouble to buy a ticket. We are bound by the strictest duty to neglect no single path which may lead to peace. If through deceit or calculation Hitler happened to venture far enough in this direction, possibly he could not retreat, even if he wished to.

"Who shall explain the astounding turns of face which this impressionable, restive and diseased dictator can accomplish? Who shall foretell his personal fate or that of Germany tomorrow? The Conference of Munich done, it was normal and necessary that the results, so passionately implored by public opinion, be extended. As things look today, it is Germany who seeks to take the initiative, to indicate formulas of procedure, and to draw up a plan of action.

"Should we turn a deaf ear, we would be the losers by providing Germany with the alibi she may be seeking in order to cover her future undertakings. Further, the engagements she seems prepared to contract can have but a limited scope. If she fails to keep them, she will be deemed guilty of a moral responsibility which will weigh heavily upon her.

"France should therefore consider the proposal without fear. It may not be rash to believe that the experiences she has newly weathered will finally convince her of the necessity of national order and national cohesion, of a certain moral reform, and of a swift and drastic improvement in her military equipment."

XII. HITLER,
A MAN "POSSESSED"

WHAT manner of man was Hitler? How often people have asked me this question! As I conclude this book, I cannot do better than answer this question briefly as a sort of summary of all I have said. A Hitler cannot be confined within a simple formula. For my part I knew three facets of his personality, each corresponding to a like facet in his nature.

His first aspect was one of pallor; his jumbled complexion and vague globular eyes, lost in a dream, lent him an absent, faraway air, the troubled and troubling face of a medium or somnambulist.

The second aspect was animated, colored, swept away by passion. His nostrils would twitch, his eyes dart lightning; he was all violence, impatience of control, lust for domination, abomination of his antagonists, cynical boldness, with a fierce energy ready at no provocation to pull down the universe about his ears. Then his "storm and assault" face was the face of a lunatic.

Hitler's third aspect was that of any naïve, rustic man, dull, vulgar, easily amused, laughing boisterously as he slapped his thigh; a commonplace face without any distinguishing mark, a face like thousands of other faces spread over the face of the earth.

People who spoke with Hitler sometimes saw these three expressions successively. At the beginning of the conversation he seemed not to listen, let alone understand; he remained indifferent, amorphous. His interlocutor had before him a man lost, for hours at a stretch, in some strange contemplation. This was the leader whose lieutenants blamed his indecision, weakness, and vacillation. . . . Then, suddenly, as though a hand had released a lever, he would burst forth into a harangue, uttered in shrill, excited, choleric tones. His arguments, gathering speed and volume, came more abundant and virulent, emphasized by raucous tones, by a rolling of *r*s and by the harsh accent of the Austrian mountaineer, and he roared and thundered as though addressing thousands of listeners. Here was the orator, the tribune full of *pectus,* at once chesty and throaty, the great orator of the Latin tradition who instinctively employed all the figures of rhetoric; here was the virtuoso, playing upon all the chords of eloquence, excelling in caustic irony and in invective. This apparition proved the more striking to native crowds because they were little accustomed to it, political eloquence in Germany being generally colorless and boring.

When Hitler launched into this sort of tirade or diatribe it was useless to seek to interrupt him or to protest. He would

have blasted that luckless imprudent who dared to, exactly
as he blasted Schuschnigg and Hácha, the President of rump-
Czechoslovakia, when they sought to object to his ideas. These
"fits" might last ten minutes or a half hour or even three quarters of an hour. Then, suddenly, the flow stopped; Hitler
would fall silent. He seemed exhausted; it was as though his
batteries had run dry. Sinking into a sort of hebetude, he relapsed into inertia. This offered the proper opportunity to present objections, to contradict him, to drive home an opposing
thesis. When in this state he ceased to grow indignant; he
would hesitate, ask for time to think things over, procrastinate.
If, in this instant, a man found a *mot* to touch him, or a wit-
ticism to break the strain, immediately the deep wrinkles vanished from the Führer's brow and his tenebrous face lit up
in a smile.

These alternate states of excitement and depression, these
fits mentioned by his familiars, ranged from the most devas-
tating fury to the plaintive moanings of a wounded beast. Because of them, psychiatrists have considered him a "cyclo-
thimic"; others see in him the typical paranoiac. This much is
certain: he was no normal being. He was, rather, a morbid personality, a quasi-madman, a character out of the pages of Dos-
toevski, a man "possessed."

Were I, following Taine's doctrine, to designate his *faculté
maîtresse*, the preponderant factor in his character, I would
first think of his pride and his ambition. But it would be more
accurate to resort to the Nietzschean vocabulary for a term
which includes both pride and ambition, a term which Hitler,
incidentally, used frequently to employ—"the will to power."
Did he not baptize the first Nuremberg Congress after his
access to power: "The Triumph of the Will"? This "Will,"
celebrated by an awe-inspiring festival, was the will to power,
conceived by Hitler as that mainspring essential to the supreme
individual and to the pre-eminent race, the sign whereby they
were known to be so. Such the force that moved him! It im-

pregnated and swelled every fiber in him, it emanated from him, it rose from his every pore.

He craved power for himself, but for Germany too. Better, he did not distinguish between himself and Germany, he identified himself with her. His followers repeated: "Hitler is Germany, Germany Hitler!" as a political slogan, but this slogan expressed Hitler's most profound feelings. Austrian by birth, he bore Germany an exclusive and passionate love. From his earliest youth he had been a chauvinist and a pan-Germanist. He suffered in his own flesh the ills and humiliation of a country he regarded as his true fatherland; he vowed to wreak his revenge by avenging Germany. To take his place at the head of Germany was for him the means of raising Germany to her proper rank, at the head of the universe. Could he possibly have preferred to attain his ends without having recourse to warfare? Surely not. From the very outset, war figured in his forecasts and in his plans.

Obviously the will to power can never be sated; it surpasses itself ceaselessly because it finds its sole happiness in the exercise of its activity. Hitler was not content with creating the Third Reich and shaking off the shackles of the Treaty of Versailles; he must go further. He determined to create the "Greater Reich" which, rising above the ruins of Czechoslovakia, Poland, and Russia, was to establish its hegemony throughout Europe. Had he succeeded, he would undoubtedly have intervened later in the Americas; he was already preparing for this. It is to President Roosevelt's undying credit that he understood what Hitler was about.

Hitler's imagination was wildly romantic; he fed it upon elements gathered pretty much everywhere. He was not uncultured, but his culture was the ill-digested culture of one self-taught. Gifted with a faculty for assimilation and simplification which won him the plaudits of his admirers, he had studied the works of Houston Stewart Chamberlain, Gobineau, Möller van den Bruck, Nietzsche, and Spengler. He had gone deeper into the matter in the course of endless conversations with numerous friends like Rosenberg, Haushofer, and Feder. Out of all this he had built up the fanatical vision of a new Germany which was to restore the Holy Roman Empire of the German Nation for the benefit of a purified race, the master race. Based upon the solid foundation of the peasantry, it was to be ruled by a party, a political elite, a sort of knightly hierarchy, an Order of the Templars, around which partner and slave peoples were to revolve. The master race, purging the world forever of the Jewish poison, would destroy the source of all poisons, whether democratic or parliamentary or Marxist or Communist or capitalist or Christian. Practicing a morality and a religion both new and positive, this German Empire would regenerate the Western world. It would operate a revolution the effects of which would be felt for thousands of years; in width and depth, it was to rival the Christian revolution.

These were the delirious visions he indulged in during his nocturnal reveries in the Chancellery at Berlin or when, retiring to his Eagle's Nest, he gazed at the mountains and plains and forests and lakes spread out below. Now, recalling his origin, he was in his own eyes an architect, demolishing and rebuilding, and erecting new continents on a titanic scale. Now he was swathing his dreams in Wagnerian harmony, for he was not simply infatuated with Wagner's music but he also believed Wagner a prophet, the prophet of National Socialism. He "lived" Wagner's work, he believed himself to be a Wagnerian hero; he was Lohengrin, Siegfried, Walther von Stolzing, and especially Parsifal, who cured the bleeding wound in the side of Amfortas and restored its magic virtue to the Holy Grail. There was in Hitler much of King Louis II of Bavaria.

It would be wrong, however, to maintain that this visionary lacked a sense of the reality of life. He was a cold-blooded realist, a profound schemer. Lazy, incapable of applying himself to any regular work, completely the opposite of Mussolini, who loved to annotate reports, Hitler gleaned oral information from others down to the slightest detail. Nothing that happened in the Reich escaped his notice; he allowed his collaborators great freedom but he knew every move they made. He is therefore answerable for everything that was done; he willed or tolerated the direct excesses and the most evil of crimes.

Serving his will to power, he made use of the most formidable intellectual resources: an extraordinary obduracy, an uncontrolled temerity, a sudden and implacable power of decision, an instantaneous and piercing scrutiny, an intuition which warned him of danger, permitting him more than once to sidestep the plots hatched against him.

He was bound to his people as though with antennae which informed him what the crowd desired or feared, approved or blamed, believed or disbelieved. Thus he could direct his propaganda with equal certainty and cynicism and an undisguised contempt for the masses. To violence and brutality he joined an aptitude for ruse, for hypocrisy, and for lying, the whole heightened by the rivalries and discords to which his party was ceaselessly a prey. He was skilled in lulling his adversary to slumber until the opportune moment came to get rid of him; while he was signing treaties he was anticipating how to wriggle out of them.

With such compelling means at his disposal, how was it that he failed in the final analysis?

He perished through the excess and the hypertrophy of a pride swollen out of all proportion by success and flattery. Musing upon his career, from the days when he used to sleep in the Vienna municipal lodginghouse upward to that prodigious ascent which invested him with powers that no emperor had ever possessed, he persuaded himself that Providence protected him and made him invincible. He, the unbeliever and anti-Christian, considered himself as the elect of the Almighty, and invoked Him more and more in his speeches as time went on. He was superstitious; he used to cast his horoscope. He consulted the stars, and they foretold that, after unheard-of good fortune, he was to go down in catastrophe.

He was impelled by the notion that his career was fated to be brief—ten years at most—and by his impatience to accomplish his work ere the time allotted him were consumed. But he was also terrified lest his adversaries manage to arm themselves in time to match the Wehrmacht's superiority. Of this superiority and of the irresistible power of his air force he had no doubt whatever. Nor did he question either the efficacy of his methods or the congenital infirmity of democratic government.

Pride blinded him; it was pride that led him to commit the crime of *Überhebung,* the deadly sin of presumption and excess. Was he to succeed in defiance of the traditional wisdom and morality? Were we to revise the most deep-rooted notions in our minds and in our hearts and bow before the monstrous triumph of cynicism and violence? How often, during a captivity the outcome of which was problematic, I prayed Heaven to let me live long enough to witness what end fate held in store for this destiny!